# Europe and Latin America in the World Economy

*A Publication of the Americas ✕ Society*

# Europe and Latin America in the World Economy

edited by
## Susan Kaufman Purcell & Françoise Simon

foreword by
## Gonzalo de Las Heras

LYNNE
RIENNER
PUBLISHERS

BOULDER
LONDON

Published in the United States of America in 1995 by
Lynne Rienner Publishers, Inc.
1800 30th Street, Boulder, Colorado 80301

and in the United Kingdom by
Lynne Rienner Publishers, Inc.
3 Henrietta Street, Covent Garden, London WC2E 8LU

**Library of Congress Cataloging-in-Publication Data**
Europe and Latin America in the world economy / edited by Susan
  Kaufman Purcell, Françoise Simon : foreword by Gonzalo de Las Heras.
     p. cm.
  "An Americas Society publication"—CIP data sheet.
  Includes bibliographical references and index.
  ISBN 1-55587-498-3 (pbk.)
  1. Latin America—Foreign economic relations—Europe. 2. Europe—
  Foreign economic relations—Latin America. 3. Latin America—
  Foreign economic relations—United States. 4. United States—
  Foreign economic relations—Latin America. 5. Latin America—
  Economic integration. 6. Economic integration.
  I. Purcell, Susan Kaufman. II. Simon, Françoise.
  HF1480.55.E86E865 1994
  337.408—dc20                                                94-14624
                                                                   CIP

**British Cataloguing in Publication Data**
A Cataloguing in Publication record for this book
is available from the British Library.

Printed and bound in the United States of America

The paper used in this publication meets the requirements
∞ of the American National Standard for Permanence of
Paper for Printed Library Materials Z39.48-1984.

5  4  3  2  1

*To our late friend and colleague,*
*A. Blake Friscia*

# Contents

# Tables and Figures

## Tables

## Figures

# Foreword

## Gonzalo de Las Heras

With the collapse of the Soviet Union, the ability of countries to compete economically has replaced the earlier Cold War focus on military competitiveness. Instead of a world divided into two main blocs, each headed by a nuclear superpower, the new structure appears increasingly tripolar, dominated by regional economic groupings in Europe, Asia, and the Americas.

The economic integration of Europe, of course, began long before the collapse of communism. In fact, the process was partially an attempt to make Western Europe less vulnerable to the Soviet threat by strengthening economic relations among the Europeans. Nevertheless, the past few years have seen the acceleration of European integration, paralleled by a growing debate over how wide and how deep such integration should go.

Latin American integration efforts also preceded the collapse of the Soviet Union, but the process that began in the early 1960s was aborted in the 1970s, a victim of intraregional squabbles and national development strategies that proved too costly and inefficient to be sustained. The new push toward economic integration in Latin America, which began after the Soviet collapse, is more promising, since it is more attuned to the exigencies of the new global economy.

Given the very different histories of European and Latin American economic integration, as well as the differences in the levels of development of both regions, it may seem fanciful to attempt a comparison of the two processes and the implications of both for European–Latin American economic relations. The two regions, however, are facing some similar decisions. Both must decide how wide and how deep their respective integration processes should go. European integration is proceeding at multiple speeds, with the core countries moving forward faster than the others. Latin America is also characterized by a multiple speed process, although in its case, there appear to be two core groups, NAFTA in North America and MERCOSUR in South America. One is a free-trade area, while the other seems modeled on the early European Common Market.

Yet the key issue for Latin America in the 1990s—the one that will ultimately determine the extent and success of integration—is no longer the continued dismantling of trade barriers or the adoption of comparable macroeconomic policies. Instead, it involves the political, social, and institutional development of the region. High on the list of what needs to be done is judicial reform and related changes that, for example, will introduce more predictability regarding how property rights and corruption claims are treated. Also crucial is human-capital development, since the region shows a widening income gap and lags behind competing markets such as East Asia in social indicators such as primary education and health care.

The European Union faces many similar problems in integrating the transition economies of Eastern Europe and developing political institutions in these countries. An additional challenge of Eastern European transition economies is that, unlike Latin America, they also require major efforts in financial institution building.

This book examines these issues, as well as the ways in which integration is affecting economic relations between Europe and Latin America. It reminds us that the success of integration ultimately will depend on the existence of individuals, firms, and institutions in both regions with a stake in the survival of open markets and democracy.

# Preface

This book is the result of the combined efforts of many individuals. We are especially grateful to the members of the study group "Europe and Latin America in the World Economy," whose information and ideas regarding European–Latin American–U.S. relations were useful and stimulating. The cooperation of the European Commission in Brussels and New York is also greatly appreciated.

We thank Linda Pakula, assistant to the vice-president of the Americas Society until August 1993, for the fine work she did in organizing and supervising the study group and for serving as its rapporteur. Thanks also to Heather Higginbotham, her successor, for her assistance in preparing the manuscript for publication and for supervising the publication process. Stephanie Crane, secretary to the vice-president of the Americas Society, provided assistance in the final stages of the publication process. Ross Culverwell, intern and later assistant to the vice-president, also greatly contributed to the book's publication.

We are especially grateful to Ambassador Angel Viñas, head of the Delegation of the Commission of the European Communities to the United Nations, and Dr. Francisco Bataller M., principal administrator of the Commission of the European Communities, for their constructive critiques of earlier versions of the manuscript. We also acknowledge Linda Wrigley for her useful contributions to the editorial process and Lynne Rienner for her assistance as publisher.

This book, and the study group on which it is based, were made possible by a generous grant to the Department of Latin American Affairs of the Americas Society by the Andrew W. Mellon Foundation.

*Susan Kaufman Purcell*
*Françoise Simon*

# Introduction

## Susan Kaufman Purcell & Françoise Simon

After the "lost decade" of the 1980s, Latin America is today regarded as one of the world's more exciting emerging markets. In great part, this is the result of economic austerity and restructuring policies that transformed the region's relatively statist, closed, and inward-looking economies into more open and competitive ones with increasingly dynamic and modern private sectors. These structural changes have been paralleled by an impressive transformation in the attitudes of both the governments and people of Latin America regarding foreign investment. In contrast to the hostility that existed in the 1970s, the region now regards foreign capital as necessary for Latin America's further development and has been engaged in a variety of efforts to attract it.

Although the United States remains Latin America's most important trading partner and source of foreign investment capital, Western Europe has not neglected the economic transformation that has been occurring in the region. The Europeans have been especially interested in Latin America's impressive efforts at regional integration over the past few years, believing that their own experience with the creation of the Single European Market (SEM) allows them to make a unique contribution to Latin America's new development strategy. At the same time, however, the end of the Cold War, particularly the collapse of communism in Eastern Europe, has understandably required Western Europe to devote more time, energy, and resources to the newly independent countries on its eastern border. As a result, it remains unclear whether the European–Latin American economic relationship will experience continued growth and, if so, how much priority Western Europe will give to Latin America as an emerging market. Neither is it clear how continued economic integration within Europe and within Latin America will affect European–Latin American economic ties as well as U.S. relations with both regions.

In order to explore these and related issues, the Americas Society invited a number of experts on U.S.–Latin American, U.S.–European, and European–Latin American relations to participate in a study group called "Europe and Latin America in the World Economy." The group included business executives, former and current government officials, media representatives, and academics from the United States, Europe, and Latin America. Papers commissioned for each of the four sessions of the study group were subsequently revised to take into account the ideas and observations

1

of the study group members as well as those of discussion leaders. The final versions of the chapters included in this book nevertheless represent the personal views of each of the authors, not the conclusions of the study group as a whole.

In the first chapter, "The Economic Relationship Between Europe and Latin America," the late A. Blake Friscia of New York University and Françoise Simon of Columbia University present an overview of European–Latin American trade relations, patterns of European direct investment in and lending to Latin America, and the varieties of European economic assistance to the region. They conclude that the consolidation of the Single European Market in Europe and competition from Central Europe may negatively affect some Latin American exports, although primary products may benefit. In the area of foreign direct investment, Europe will want to maintain its competitive position vis-à-vis the United States in Latin America. The outlook for European banking and finance is also strong, but economic development assistance will probably not increase as rapidly as in the past and will become more technical.

In "The Impact of Regional Integration on European–Latin American Relations," Françoise Simon and Susan Kaufman Purcell of the Americas Society examine the possible implications for Latin America of Europe's evolving integration process. They then discuss the current integration process in Latin America and the policies that the European Union (EU) has adopted to assist the process. Finally, they examine how integration is influencing Europe's trade and investment strategy in Latin America and the ways in which regional restructuring is impacting Latin American companies in various industry sectors. They conclude that on both sides of the Atlantic, an initial, centrally planned integration process is giving way to a fuzzier, multitiered, and multipolar set of hybrid groupings, but that, in general, the European model is largely not applicable to Latin America, which may see a "shakeout" of its subregional blocs. From a business standpoint, the economic links between the two regions reflect the worldwide shift from interregional trade to investment.

In "Germany and Latin America" Wolf Grabendorff of the Institute for European–Latin American Relations (IRELA) points out that Germany is Latin America's most important economic partner after the United States. German transnational actors such as parties and trade unions also play an important role in Latin America. Nevertheless, the German commitment to European integration and to the restructuring of a unified Germany imply that Latin America is of limited and declining importance for Germany. Despite this geopolitical reality, Latin America, particularly Brazil, Mexico, and Argentina, is of growing importance for German investment, and Germany continues to be Latin America's most important EU aid donor.

In the fourth chapter, "Spain and Latin America: The Resurgence of a Special Relationship," Edward Schumacher of the *Wall Street Journal* emphasizes the important role that Spain has played since it joined the European Union in shaping the latter's policies toward Latin America. He argues that the historical and cultural links between Spain and Latin America have also encouraged Spanish efforts to forge an Iberoamerican commonwealth of Spanish- and Portuguese-speaking countries. Finally, Schumacher examines Spain's growing involvement in Latin America's privatization projects as well as its evolving trade relations with the region. He concludes that although Spain's trade with and investment in Latin America are growing as Latin America restructures and opens its economies, they are paralleled by an even more rapid and intense integration with Europe.

In the fifth chapter, "Eastern Europe and Latin America," Eusebio Mujal-León of Georgetown University argues that there have not been significant economic relations between Eastern Europe and Latin America during the 1980s and early 1990s. In fact, the two regions can be regarded as competing for investment capital. Since 1989, capital flows to Eastern Europe have been modest while those to Latin America, although more substantial, are still too short term. Mujal-León points out, however, that Eastern Europe is the Mexico of the European Union. He argues that, as a result, capital flows to Eastern Europe will increase, although they will not necessarily divert investment from Latin America because the two regions will continue to offer different opportunities to potential investors.

In the final chapter, "The Trilateral Relationship: Latin America, Europe, and the United States," Riordan Roett of the Paul H. Nitze School of Advanced International Studies (SAIS) of Johns Hopkins University outlines the historical ties between Europe and Latin America, arguing that the conflictual relationship between Europe and the United States over Central America in the 1980s has been replaced by a return to more cooperative relations in the aftermath of the Cold War. He points out that Europe's economic relations with Latin America are second only to those of the United States. The future will probably see a continuation of U.S. leadership in Mexico and Central America, while Europe's emphasis on the southern part of South America will be maintained. Despite a slow but steady increase in European investment, financial operations, and bank lending in Latin America, Roett sees no European plan to challenge U.S. hegemony in the Americas.

# The Economic Relationship Between Europe and Latin America

## A. Blake Friscia & Françoise Simon

Economic integration in Europe[1] presents both challenges and opportunities for Latin America. The implementation of the Single Market initiated in January 1993 may have both a positive and a negative impact on European–Latin American trade. Further, the November 1993 approval of the European Union is bound to influence not only investment, but also foreign assistance to nonmember states, including those in Latin America. Finally, trade, investment, and aid will all be further affected by the widening of the EU; this includes the accession to the EC-12 of three EFTA countries (Austria, Sweden, and Finland) as well as the recent Association and Cooperation Agreements with major Eastern European countries and with Russia and the Ukraine.

Europe is Latin America's second most important export market and source of direct investment. European banking and finance are playing a key role in bringing external capital into the region. Although the Single Market will present growth possibilities for Latin American exports, questions remain about potential trade diversion against Latin American goods. Direct concessionary aid from Europe is of minor importance to the region; nonconcessionary loans, investments, and credits are of greater significance.

For Europe, market liberalization and economic growth in Latin America lead to a better export market, and Latin American privatizations present attractive investment opportunities. There is uncertainty, however, about whether Europe will turn inward with its deepening and widening process, and whether trade, aid, and investment will shift away from Latin America and move toward Eastern Europe and the Mediterranean Basin. A tentative conclusion is that, influenced by Sunbelt members such as Spain and Portugal, Europe will try to strengthen its links with Latin America, but not at the expense of its neighbors to the east and south.

## SCOPE OF FOREIGN TRADE

### Current Situation

Given the differences in development and income between Europe and
Latin America, one may expect an imbalance in their trade patterns and in
the nature of their trade portfolios. Indeed, while Latin America holds a
less than 2 percent share of Europe's trade, Europe is Latin America's second largest trade partner (after the United States) and accounts for 23 percent of Latin America's trade. These asymmetries, however, mask the considerable absolute value of trade flows between the two regions and their
special importance for some products and for some countries.

Total Latin American–Caribbean exports amounted to over $140 billion
in 1991, a 41 percent increase from 1985. Exports to Europe were $32 bil-
lion, and their growth rate—almost 69 percent—considerably surpassed that
of Latin America's exports. (See Table 1.1 for Latin American–Caribbean
trade with Europe and Figure 1.1 for world trade comparisons) On the import side, there has also been a rise in Europe's share of Latin American purchases, from 20 percent in 1985 to 23 to 25 percent in recent years. As with
exports, Latin American buying from Europe has risen faster than the rate of
Latin America's total imports, more than doubling since 1985.

Even though Europe is becoming more important to Latin America,
the United States continues to be Latin America's major trade partner, accounting for 41 percent of Latin America's exports and almost 45 percent
of its imports. (See Table 1.2) Latin America also has a much greater
strength in the United States, accounting for 12.5 percent of U.S. imports,
as against 2 percent of Europe's. This strength is due in part to geographic
linkages (driven by Mexico) but also suggests the difficulties Latin American producers have had in gaining market access in Europe because of restrictive practices or insufficient product competitiveness. Latin America's
concentration in exporting primary goods with slow demand growth has
also contributed to its decline in European markets.

### Recent Evolution

During the debt crisis in Latin America in the 1980s, the region ran large
($4 to 5 billion) annual trade surpluses with Europe. (See Table 1.1) How-
ever, these were driven by the need to generate foreign exchange to pay interest on the large Latin American debt. Only in 1991 did these surpluses
decline, from $27 billion in 1990 to almost $10 billion in 1991, as imports
from Europe began to grow more rapidly. This decline was in line with the
improved 3.5 percent real gross domestic product (GDP) growth of Latin
America in 1991 as the region began to recover.[2] Finally, in 1992 the trade
balance shifted to a deficit of almost $6 billion and the current account

**Table 1.1  Latin American–Caribbean Trade with Europe, 1985–1991 (Millions U.S. $)**

| | Total LAC Exports | Exports to Europe | Europe % Share of LAC Exports | Total LAC Imports | Imports from Europe | Europe Share of LAC Imports % | LAC Trade Balance vs. Europe |
|---|---|---|---|---|---|---|---|
| 1985 | 99,317 | 19,383 | 19.5 | 72,801 | 15,021 | 20.6 | 4,362 |
| 1986 | 82,423 | 20,597 | 25.0 | 72,637 | 18,367 | 25.3 | 2,230 |
| 1987 | 92,428 | 21,914 | 23.7 | 84,179 | 21,993 | 26.1 | –79 |
| 1988 | 106,250 | 26,717 | 25.1 | 92,116 | 23,327 | 25.3 | 3,390 |
| 1989 | 113,585 | 28,916 | 25.5 | 99,632 | 23,280 | 23.4 | 5,636 |
| 1990 | 127,913 | 32,631 | 25.5 | 110,825 | 27,666 | 25.0 | 4,965 |
| 1991 | 140,444 | 32,732 | 23.3 | 142,395 | 32,570 | 22.8 | 162 |
| % Change 1985–91 | 41.4 | 68.9 | | 95.6 | 116.8 | | |
| Growth Rates % per Year | | | | | | | |
| 1985–91 | 5.9 | 9.1 | | 11.8 | 13.8 | | |
| 1986 | –17.0 | 6.3 | | –0.2 | 22.3 | | |
| 1987 | 12.1 | 6.4 | | 15.9 | 19.7 | | |
| 1988 | 15.0 | 21.9 | | 9.4 | 6.1 | | |
| 1989 | 6.9 | 8.2 | | 8.2 | –0.2 | | |
| 1990 | 12.6 | 12.8 | | 11.2 | 18.8 | | |
| 1991 | 9.8 | 0.3 | | 28.5 | 17.7 | | |

*Source:* International Monetary Fund, *Direction of Trade Yearbook*, 1992.
*Note:* Latin America–Caribbean (LAC) consists of forty-one countries or territories listed in the IMF *Yearbook*; Europe consists of the twelve members of the European Community and the seven members of the European Free Trade Association.

Table 1.2    Latin American–Caribbean Trade with Major Areas, 1991
             (Millions U.S. $)

|  | Exports | Export Share % | Imports | Import Share % | LAC Balance vs. Area |
|---|---|---|---|---|---|
| United States | 57,365 | 41.0 | 63,536 | 44.6 | –6,171 |
| Europe | 32,732 | 23.3 | 32,570 | 22.8 | 162 |
| European Community | 30,300 | 21.6 | 28,715 | 20.2 | 1,585 |
| Japan | 8,204 | 5.8 | 8,767 | 6.2 | –563 |
| Eastern Europe and Former USSR | 2,369 | 1.7 | 906 | 0.6 | 1,463 |

*Source:* International Monetary Fund, *Direction of Trade Yearbook,* 1992.
*Note:* Europe consists of the European Community plus the European Free Trade Association.
LAC = Latin American–Caribbean.

deficit widened to $32.7 billion. In 1992–1994, Latin America's improved economic climate attracted sufficient external funds to offset these deficits.[3] However, the December 1994 devaluation of the Mexican peso, triggered in part by a large current-account deficit financed by speculative, suggests caution about the region. In particular, Latin America must now be more concerned with its longer-term competititve position in European trade.

## Latin America's Export Portfolio

As might be expected, given development variances, Latin America's exports to Europe are still dominated by commodities. (See Figure 1.2) Although only 17 percent of these exports were manufactured goods in 1980, they had increased by 30 percent ten years later.[4] However, only 2 to 3 percent of these exports are high-technology goods, such as chemicals, pharmaceutical products, transport equipment, and scientific instruments.[5]

Another characteristic of the Latin American export portfolio to Europe is that it is dominated by certain product categories. Of the $32.6 billion in EC imports from Latin America in 1990, about 33 percent were food, beverage, and tobacco products and almost 20 percent were agricultural raw materials and metals.

Among developing regions, Latin America is the nearly exclusive supplier to the EC of fresh and prepared meat as well as soybeans. About half of the EC's imports of bananas and green coffee come from Latin America. In metals, Latin America supplied 70 percent and 50 percent, respectively, of the EC's imports of iron ore and pig iron. About 33 percent of EC copper imports come from Latin America. Crude petroleum from Latin

**Figure 1.1  World Trade Comparisons, 1991**

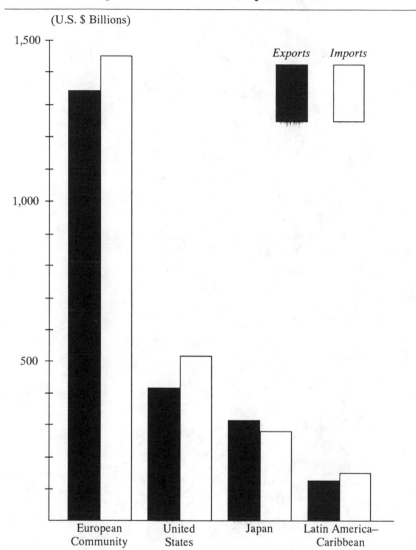

*Source:* International Monetary Fund.

America is also a major export to the EU, although it is declining due to falling prices and competition from Russia and other regions.[6] Latin American industrial exports include chemicals, automobile engines and parts, and clothing.[7]

A. Blake Friscia & Françoise Simon

Figure 1.2  Latin America's Export Portfolio to Europe, 1980–1990

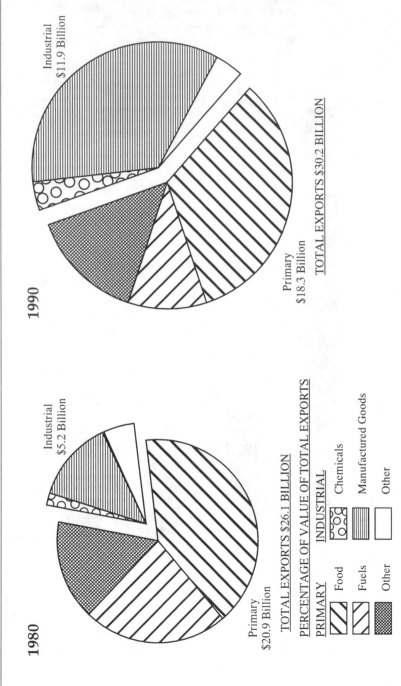

*Source:* United Nations.

## Latin America's Import Portfolio

As could be expected, European exports to Latin America consist largely of industrial goods. Machinery and transport equipment dominate, with about half of total exports in 1990[8]—about the same as a decade earlier, which may reflect an intervening increase in local production. However, the Latin American balance of trade with Europe still shows large deficits in industrial goods (from $9.5 billion in 1980 to $4.3 billion in 1990).[9]

## Trade Concentration

Latin American trade with Europe is highly concentrated. Six countries (Brazil, Argentina, Mexico, Chile, Colombia, and Venezuela) account for 85 percent of all Latin American exports to the EU. Brazil is by far the largest exporter, with over $10 billion or almost 37 percent of the region's exports to the EU. Leading Brazilian exports to the EU are manufactured goods, coffee, soybeans, iron ore, and orange juice. Three other significant exporters are Argentina, Mexico, and Chile, each representing over 10 percent of all regional exports to the EU. However, although Europe buys over 30 percent of Argentine and Chilean exports, it is relatively less important to Mexico. The same pattern prevails for Colombia and Venezuela, the other major exporters with over $1 billion in annual sales to the EU.

On the import side, trade is even more concentrated. Brazil and Mexico alone buy half of all Latin American exports from Europe. Mexico leads with over $6 billion, or almost 28 percent of total imports from the EC in 1991; 80 percent were in industrial goods, including a significant share of high-technology products (20 percent). For Brazil, manufactures also dominate, with high-technology products accounting for 28 percent of a $5 billion total in 1991.[10] Venezuela, Argentina, Chile, and Colombia are also significant importers with $1 to 2 billion annually from the EU. (See Tables 1.3 and 1.4, and Figure 1.3)

Trade concentration also prevails in Europe, where the six largest markets (Germany, Italy, France, Britain, Holland, and Spain) buy 87 percent of all EU imports from Latin America. (See Table 1.5) Germany leads both in the share of total trade and in the total value of its imports.

## EU Import Trends

Overall EC imports from Latin America doubled in the 1970s, representing a 12 percent annual growth rate, which then fell back to only 2.5 percent in the 1980s; this change parallels economic growth in the EC, which reached 4 to 5 percent annually in the 1970s, but was less than 2 percent in the 1980s.[11]

Similarly, Latin America's share of extra-EC imports has declined sharply. For instance, Germany's share has dropped by almost 67 percent,

Table 1.3    Relative Importance of the European Community
             for Latin American–Caribbean Exporting Countries, 1991

|  | Exports to the EC (Millions U.S. $) | EC Share of Each Country's Exports (%) |
|---|---|---|
| Brazil | 10,746 | 32.3 |
| Argentina | 4,227 | 31.9 |
| Mexico | 3,332 | 8.5 |
| Chile | 2,884 | 31.9 |
| Colombia | 1,878 | 28.2 |
| Venezuela | 1,615 | 10.2 |
| Peru | 841 | 24.5 |
| Ecuador | 609 | 17.0 |
| Costa Rica | 440 | 27.2 |
| Jamaica | 389 | 27.6 |
| Uruguay | 384 | 24.3 |
| Paraguay | 221 | 30.0 |
| El Salvador | 193 | 26.6 |
| Trinidad & Tobago | 183 | 9.2 |
| Bolivia | 179 | 27.5 |
| Honduras | 174 | 22.3 |
| Dominican Republic | 146 | 15.8 |
| Guatemala | 129 | 10.7 |
| Nicaragua | 111 | 30.5 |
| Panama | 92 | 26.9 |
| Total, Twenty Countries | 28,503 | |

Source: International Monetary Fund, Direction of Trade Yearbook, 1992.

and Britain's by 62 percent, since 1960. This decline reflects a diversion of EC buying from Latin America to Asia and the Mediterranean basin and also greater intra-Community trade. (See Table 1.6)

## European Export Trends

EC exports to Latin America peaked in 1981 but then declined until 1989, when the Latin American economies began to revive. It was not until 1991 that total EC exports to Latin America finally surpassed their 1981 peak. Germany holds the largest share of Latin American exports with about 35 percent. This position has held constant since 1960. The next two countries are Italy and France, with about 16 percent each, thanks to substantial rises in the same period. But Britain has been a big loser in market share, dropping from almost 22 percent in 1960 to a little over 10 percent in 1991.

Table 1.4    Relative Importance of the European Community
             for Latin American–Caribbean Importing Countries, 1991

|  | Imports from the EC (Millions U.S. $) | Share of Country Imports from EC % |
|---|---|---|
| Mexico | 6,214 | 12.6 |
| Brazil | 5,128 | 21.9 |
| Venezuela | 2,505 | 23.8 |
| Argentina | 2,304 | 28.8 |
| Chile | 1,405 | 18.3 |
| Colombia | 1,193 | 21.0 |
| Ecuador | 654 | 23.7 |
| Peru | 530 | 17.8 |
| Uruguay | 336 | 20.6 |
| Dominican Republic | 326 | 14.2 |
| Jamaica | 264 | 13.1 |
| Trinidad & Tobago | 247 | 15.0 |
| El Salvador | 235 | 15.7 |
| Guatemala | 229 | 12.4 |
| Costa Rica | 199 | 10.8 |
| Paraguay | 199 | 13.0 |
| Bolivia | 172 | 19.6 |
| Honduras | 133 | 15.1 |
| Panama | 124 | 7.3 |
| Nicaragua | 106 | 14.0 |
| Total, Twenty Countries | 22,503 | |

*Source:* International Monetary Fund, *Direction of Trade Yearbook,* 1992.

The big gainer, meanwhile, has been Spain, whose share of the market has risen from 2 percent in 1960 to over 10 percent in 1990. These trends highlight the shifting positions of Britain and Spain in Latin America, not only in trade but also in commercial bank lending. Indeed, Spain leads all of the EU countries, with over 9 percent of its non-Community exports going to Latin America, although this still represents a decline from a high of 22 percent in 1970. (See Table 1.7) Spain is now the EU country with the largest share of its imports coming from Latin America.[12]

## The Outlook for Latin American Trade with Europe

With the moderate growth expected for Europe, the immediate prospects for Latin American exports to the region may be subdued. However, within a longer term (four- to-five-year) horizon, consolidation of the

Figure 1.3   Leading Latin American Countries in Trade with the European Community, 1991

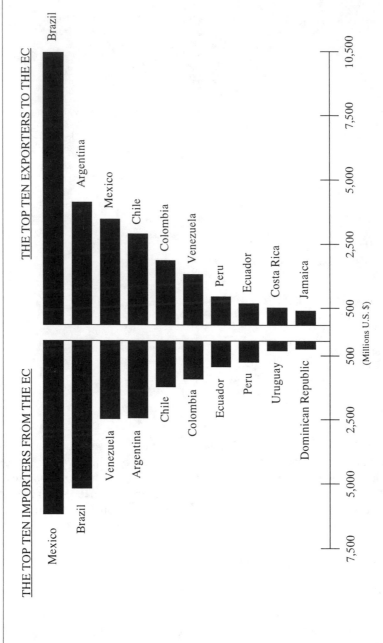

*Source:* International Monetary Fund.

**Table 1.5**    Performance of European Community Countries in Imports from Latin America, 1960–1991

| | Total EC-12 | Germany | Italy | France | Britain | Neth. | Spain |
|---|---|---|---|---|---|---|---|
| **I. EC Imports from Latin America** | | | | | | | |
| **A. % change from prev. year** | | | | | | | |
| 1989 | 13.0 | 8.3 | 23.9 | 12.0 | 5.0 | 13.9 | 14.5 |
| 1990 | -2.7 | -3.2 | -9.7 | -2.0 | -11.8 | 9.0 | 1.9 |
| 1991 | 2.2 | 6.5 | 0.2 | 0.2 | -5.3 | 0.6 | 8.3 |
| **B. Average annual % change** | | | | | | | |
| 1960–1970 | 5.9 | 5.1 | 10.9 | 7.5 | -1.0 | 6.2 | -1.0 |
| 1970–1980 | 12.8 | 10.7 | 13.0 | 15.7 | 8.5 | 14.6 | 8.5 |
| 1981–1991 | 2.5 | 4.6 | -0.9 | 0.5 | 3.4 | 6.8 | 3.4 |
| **C. Share in % of LA imports** | | | | | | | |
| 1960 | 100.0 | 30.8 | 10.4 | 8.8 | 30.5 | 7.8 | 1.8 |
| 1970 | 100.0 | 28.6 | 16.6 | 10.3 | 15.7 | 8.0 | 8.4 |
| 1980 | 100.0 | 23.6 | 16.9 | 13.2 | 10.6 | 9.4 | 14.5 |
| 1991 | 100.0 | 25.1 | 13.4 | 12.5 | 10.8 | 13.5 | 11.5 |
| **D. % change in share 1960–91** | | -18.5 | 27.6 | 42.0 | -64.6 | 73.1 | 535.8 |
| **E. % share of extra–EC imports** | | | | | | | |
| 1960 | 9.6 | 14.0 | 9.7 | 6.0 | 8.6 | 10.4 | 11.0 |
| 1970 | 7.9 | 9.8 | 10.3 | 6.1 | 5.0 | 8.0 | 14.8 |
| 1980 | 5.8 | 5.7 | 7.2 | 4.7 | 3.4 | 6.2 | 14.1 |
| 1991 | 5.2 | 4.6 | 5.6 | 4.6 | 3.3 | 7.7 | 10.2 |
| **F. % change in extra–EC imports** | -45.8 | -67.1 | -42.3 | -23.3 | -61.6 | -25.9 | -7.3 |

*Source:* EUROSTAT, *External Trade and Balance of Payments, Statistical Yearbook* 1992.
*Note:* LA = Latin America.
EC = European Community.

Table 1.6    Relative Importance of Latin America to the
             European Community Trade, 1960–1991

|  | 1960 | 1989 | 1990 | 1991 |
|---|---|---|---|---|
| **Imports** | | | | |
| LA as % of Total EC Imports | | 2.33 | 2.24 | 2.16 |
| LA as % of Extra–EC Imports[a] | 9.6 | 5.83 | 5.48 | 5.24 |
| | | | | |
| **Exports** | | | | |
| LA as % of Total EC Exports | | 1.44 | 1.39 | 1.57 |
| LA as % of Extra–EC Exports[a] | 8.3 | 2.41 | 3.59 | 4.13 |
| | | | | |
| Leading LA Countries in EC Imports[b] | | | | |
| (As % of total extra–EC imports | | | | |
| from the top 50 EC trade partners) | | | | |
| Brazil—Rank No. 13[c] | | 2.3 | 2.0 | 1.9 |
| Argentina—Rank No. 30 | | 0.6 | 0.8 | 0.8 |
| Mexico—Rank No. 35 | | 0.6 | 0.6 | 0.6 |
| Chile—Rank No. 36 | | 0.6 | 0.6 | 0.6 |
| Colombia—Rank No. 40 | | 0.3 | 0.3 | 0.3 |
| Venezuela—Rank No. 41 | | 0.3 | 0.4 | 0.3 |
| | | | | |
| Leading LA Countries in EC Exports | | | | |
| (As % of total extra–EC exports | | | | |
| to top 50 EC trade partners) | | | | |
| Mexico—Rank No. 24 | | 0.9 | 0.9 | 1.1 |
| Brazil—Rank No. 28 | | 0.9 | 0.9 | 1.1 |
| Venezuela—Rank No. 38 | | 0.4 | 0.4 | 0.4 |
| Argentina—Rank No. 50 | | 0.3 | 0.3 | 0.4 |

*Sources:* EUROSTAT, *External Trade and Balance of Payments Manual,* No. 7, 1992, and
*External Trade and Balance of Payments Statistical Yearbook,* 1992.
*Notes:*
a. Extra–EC refers to the trade of the European Community excluding trade between the EC
member states.
b. The top 50 countries account for 95% of extra–EC imports and 92% of extra–EC exports.
c. Refers to the rank of the country among the top 50 in relation to the leading sources of EC
imports and destinations of EC exports.
LA = Latin America.
EC = European Community.

Single Market will stimulate European growth and the prospects for Latin
American exports. World Bank analyses have shown that, on the basis of
the income elasticity of import demand, with European real growth of 3
to 5 percent per annum, the volume of all imports in Europe should increase by 6 to 10 percent per year on average,[13] provided there is no increase in EU restrictions or protectionism against imports from Latin
America.[14]

**Table 1.7  Performance of European Community Countries in Exports to Latin America, 1960–1991**

| | Total EC-12 | Germany | Italy | France | Britain | Neth. | Spain |
|---|---|---|---|---|---|---|---|
| **II. EC Exports to Latin America** | | | | | | | |
| A. % change from prev. year | | | | | | | |
| 1989 | 14.2 | 11.7 | 24.7 | 6.9 | 1.0 | 24.1 | 1.0 |
| 1990 | -0.3 | 4.7 | -3.0 | -6.8 | 8.7 | -11.2 | 8.7 |
| 1991 | 16.2 | 15.9 | 21.2 | 24.5 | 3.6 | 15.7 | 3.6 |
| B. Average annual % change | | | | | | | |
| 1960–1970 | 5.6 | 5.9 | 6.5 | 5.8 | 3.1 | 4.6 | 19.4 |
| 1970–1980 | 13.7 | 12.9 | 14.9 | 16.2 | 10.5 | 11.9 | 18.0 |
| 1981–1991 | 0.7 | 1.6 | 0.2 | 0.8 | 0.2 | 1.0 | -1.3 |
| C. Share in % of LA exports | | | | | | | |
| 1960 | 100.0 | 34.6 | 12.3 | 12.1 | 21.8 | 6.5 | 2.2 |
| 1970 | 100.0 | 35.6 | 13.5 | 12.4 | 17.3 | 5.9 | 7.4 |
| 1980 | 100.0 | 33.1 | 15.0 | 15.5 | 13.0 | 5.0 | 10.7 |
| 1991 | 100.0 | 34.8 | 16.7 | 16.6 | 10.4 | 5.2 | 8.7 |
| D. % change in share 1960–91 | | 0.6 | 35.7 | 37.2 | -52.3 | -20.0 | 295.5 |
| E. % share of extra–EC exports | | | | | | | |
| 1960 | 8.3 | 10.8 | 12.0 | 6.1 | 5.8 | 8.8 | 16.3 |
| 1970 | 6.7 | 7.6 | 7.7 | 6.1 | 4.9 | 6.7 | 22.5 |
| 1980 | 6.1 | 6.5 | 7.5 | 5.7 | 3.8 | 5.1 | 20.2 |
| 1991 | 4.1 | 4.1 | 5.3 | 4.3 | 2.9 | 3.7 | 9.1 |
| F. % change in extra–EC exports | -50.6 | -62.0 | -55.8 | -29.5 | -50.0 | -57.9 | -44.2 |

*Source:* EUROSTAT, *External Trade and Balance of Payments, Statistical Yearbook* 1992.

Opinions are still divided, however, as to whether the Single Market will be beneficial or detrimental to Latin America, in the sense that it will be trade-creating (increased imports from outside the EU area) versus trade-diverting (shift of imports from lower-cost producers outside the EU to higher-cost suppliers within the EU). Taking into account both higher EU incomes and possible nontariff barriers (technical standards, health requirements, and so on), an IRELA analysis holds that over half of Latin American exports will experience positive effects (mainly primary products such as coffee, bananas, meat, and similar items), but some processed exports (metals, minerals, oil products, some manufactures) could be affected adversely.[15] On the other hand, analysts at the Economic Commission for Latin America and the Caribbean (ECLA) are more concerned about possible new EU restrictions on "sensitive" products such as textiles, clothing, footwear, steel, and certain services. They are cautious about the future of Latin American exports to the EU since Latin America has a low preferential trade position in EU import policy and it could be adversely affected by competition from Central and Eastern Europe.[16]

According to the World Bank, two scenarios are possible. An "optimistic" scenario would produce 1.5 percent additional real GDP growth in the EU as a result of the gains from the Single Market and a successful Uruguay Round of the GATT talks. For Latin America, such an outcome would produce an incremental growth of exports to the EU of 1.8 percent per year.

A "pessimistic" World Bank scenario would show an EU growth increase of 0.5 percent per year that would produce a 0.5 percent gain in Latin American annual exports. Despite these varying estimates, it is likely that, at least in some product categories, there will be a strong boost in demand. Liberalization of the EU's Common Agricultural Policy may boost Latin American meat and cereal exports, in particular.[17]

The issue of European exports to Latin America is less ambiguous. Higher incomes, trade liberalization, and modernization in Latin America all point to an increased import demand. This potential for Europe and Latin America, however, assumes that the North American Free Trade Agreement (NAFTA) and other pacts do not erect tariff or nontariff barriers against nonmembers.

## FOREIGN DIRECT INVESTMENT

### Europe as Challenger

In terms of both annual flow of net foreign direct investment (FDI) and total FDI stock, Europe is second to the United States for most Latin

American countries. In Brazil and Argentina, however, Europe's foreign investment stock is greater than that of the United States. This also applies to the smaller countries of Paraguay and Uruguay. In terms of investment flows, Europe surpasses the United States in Brazil and is a close second in Argentina and Ecuador. Japan ranks as a distant third in most countries, in terms of both stocks and investment flows.

For the six largest economies of Latin America—Brazil, Mexico, Argentina, Venezuela, Colombia, Chile—total net investments from Europe were almost $10 billion in the 1985 to 1990 period, and those from the United States were $17.2 billion. Among individual countries, European net flows were larger than those of the United States only in Brazil. (See Table 1.8)

In addition to investment flows, the motivation for investment is an important factor in assessing possible long-term trends. From 1985 to 1990, the largest European investment flows were to Mexico, which attracted $4.4 billion, and the second largest were to Brazil, which received $3.7 billion. But although 50 to 60 percent of Brazil's investments have been in the form of debt-to-equity conversions, the bulk of Mexican inflows has been "fresh" investments based on the attractiveness of new projects. Most Mexican investments have come from Britain ($1.5 billion) and Germany ($831 million). Britain was also the largest investor in Brazil with almost $1 billion during the 1985 to 1990 period. Except for Spain and Sweden, Germany was the smallest European investor in Brazil during this period.[18] In Argentina, European investments were small in the 1985 to 1990 period, but data problems understate their true magnitude.[19] Venezuela and Chile are also major sites for European investments. Switzerland was the largest investor in Venezuela and Colombia during this period. French, Swiss, and Dutch investments went predominantly to Brazil and Mexico. Italian investments went largely to Argentina, and German and Spanish investments mostly to Mexico.

### Foreign Investment Stocks: Distribution and Trends

The total accumulated stocks in Latin America held by the United States, Europe, Japan, and the developing countries were estimated to total almost $76 billion as of 1988/89. Again, Europe is the challenger, with 37 percent of the foreign investment position, versus 47 percent for the United States and 7 percent for Japan. (See Table 1.9) This investment stock is distributed among three major regional groupings—Mexico and Central America, the Andean Group, and Mercado Común del Sur (Southern Cone Common Market, or MERCOSUR). As might be expected, the United States is the primary investor in Mexico, Central America, and the Andean Group; Europe is the major investor in the Southern Cone, with two-thirds of its

**Table 1.8  Net Foreign Direct Investment Flows from Major European Countries to the Six Major Latin American Countries, 1985–1990**
**(Millions U.S. $)**

| Destination | Total | Countries of Origin[a] | | | | | | | | |
|---|---|---|---|---|---|---|---|---|---|---|
| | | GE | BR | FR | BE | NE | IT | SP | SWED | SWITZ |
| Brazil | 3,691 | 207 | 998 | 731 | 255 | 458 | 490 | 28 | 159 | 365 |
| Mexico | 4,444 | 831 | 1,518 | 709 | b | 253 | 19 | 295 | 120 | 699 |
| Argentina[c] | 121 | 26 | 0 | 5 | 30 | 12 | 4 | 12 | 2 | 30 |
| Venezuela | 794 | 67 | 154 | 133 | 23 | 88 | 73 | 29 | 48 | 179 |
| Colombia | 132 | 24 | -32 | 14 | 16 | 24 | -1 | 10 | 15 | 62 |
| Chile | 474 | 19 | 201 | 36 | 56 | 101 | 3 | 42 | 11 | 5 |
| Total | 9,656 | 1,174 | 2,839 | 1,628 | 380 | 936 | 588 | 416 | 355 | 1,340 |

*Source:* United Nations, Economic Commission for Latin America and the Caribbean.
*Notes:*
a. Country legends are: GE-Germany, BR-Britain, FR-France, BE-Belgium-Luxembourg, NE-Netherlands, IT-Italy, SP-Spain, SWED-Sweden, SWITZ-Switzerland. Other European Community countries are included in the total column.
b. Included in Netherlands.
c. Argentina data available in the 1985–1990 period includes only the years 1985, 1986, and 1989.

investments located in the MERCOSUR countries. Mexico and Central America, with about 24 percent of the total, are the other sites for European investment. The Andean countries receive a relatively small portion of all European investments. (See Figure 1.4 and Table 1.10)

In parallel with trade patterns, European investments as a whole are larger than those of the United States in Brazil and Argentina. Some European countries have particularly strong positions. German investments in Brazil, for example, are over $5 billion, about half of the U.S. investment in the country. Swiss and British investments in Brazil are also large, at over $3 billion each, while Japan also has a sizable $3.5 billion investment in Brazil. In Mexico, where U.S. investments total $19 billion, Britain and Germany each have positions of almost $2 billion. Switzerland and Japan are two other significant investors in Mexico with over $1 billion each.

These different positions of the United States, Europe, and Japan follow what has been described as a "Triad" pattern, in which one among the Triad members is the dominant investor or stockholder in a host country or region. Except for Brazil and Argentina, in which the EU is the dominant Triad investor, the United States is the leader in the Latin American and Caribbean economies. The EU is dominant in Central and Eastern Europe, and Japan leads in most of Asia.[20] Although the United States is the dominant investor in Latin America, it is likely that Europe and Japan will remain actively involved in the region to protect their competitive positions vis-à-vis the United States.[21] In Table 1.11, Triad clusters are shown for the six major countries of Latin America.

Indeed, from 1985 to 1990, the share of European investment rose in Brazil, Ecuador, Mexico, Peru, Uruguay, Venezuela, El Salvador, Guatemala, and Panama. The U.S. position, although still large, declined over the same period. While the U.S. position rose only in Argentina, Chile, and Colombia among major countries, Japan's share grew in eight countries.[22]

### The Outlook for European Investment

There are two views with respect to future European investment in Latin America. One scenario is that the Single Market will present significant new opportunities in Europe itself and will thus divert investments from abroad toward domestic markets. German investments, in particular, are expected to have a sustained focus on Central Europe. The logic of this focus on the home or adjoining markets could thus lead to a possible downturn in flows to Latin America.

An alternate scenario points to the renewed confidence in Latin American economies and the added appeal provided by the creation of NAFTA. In this environment, European and Japanese companies would have to

**Table 1.9**   Stock of Foreign Direct Investment in Latin American Regional Groups by Countries of Origin of Investments, 1988/89

(Billions and percentage shares U.S. $)

| Origin of Investments: | Mexico and Central America $ | % | Andean Group $ | % | MERCOSUR $ | % | Total[a] $ | Share of Total Below |
|---|---|---|---|---|---|---|---|---|
| United States | $16.8 | 46.7 | $5.1 | 14.2 | $12.3 | 34.3 | $35.9 | 47.4 |
| European Comm. | 5.2 | 24.4 | 1.1 | 5.2 | 14.2 | 66.6 | 21.3 | |
| Other Europe[b] | 1.5 | 21.4 | 0.6 | 8.6 | 4.6 | 65.7 | 7.0 | |
| Total Europe | 6.7 | 23.6 | 1.7 | 6.0 | 18.8 | 66.4 | 28.3 | 37.3 |
| Japan | 1.3 | 16.0 | 0.3 | 6.0 | 3.1 | 62.0 | 5.0 | 6.6 |
| Developing Countries[c] | 1.4 | 21.2 | 1.0 | 15.1 | 3.2 | 48.4 | 6.6 | 8.7 |
| Total | $26.2 | 34.5 | $8.1 | 10.7 | $37.5 | 49.5 | $75.8 | 100.0 |

*Source: El Vínculo Ibero-América-Comunidad Europea: Planes, Políticas Y Estrategias de Desarrollo,* Conferencia de Ministros De Planificación de América Latina y El Caribe, Ministerio de Economía y Hacienda, Santiago Chile, 1992, p. 112; and data from United Nations, Economic Commission for Latin America and the Caribbean.

*Notes:* a. Total includes Chile, which is not shown separately.
b. Other Europe includes the EFTA countries.
c. Asia, Middle East, and Latin America. Other developed countries are not included in this table.

**Figure 1.4  Foreign Direct Investment Stock in Six Major Latin American Economies, 1990 (by Countries of Origin, Millions U.S. $)**

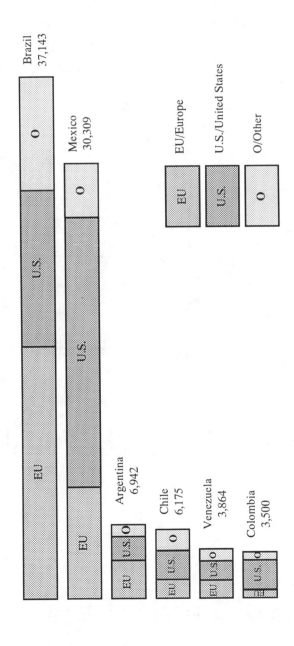

*Source:* Economic Commission for Latin America and the Caribbean.
*Note:* All data 1990, except Argentina for 1989.

**Table 1.10　Stock of Foreign Direct Investment in Six Major Countries in Latin America by Areas of Investor Origin, 1990 (Millions U.S. $)**

| Origin of Investments | Brazil | Mexico | Argentina | Chile | Venezuela | Colombia |
|---|---|---|---|---|---|---|
| Europe | 18,441 | 7,649 | 3,331 | 1,180 | 1,102 | 597 |
| (%) | (49.6) | (25.2) | (48.0) | (19.1) | (28.5) | (17.1) |
| European Comm. | 14,107 | 5,925 | 2,553 | 1,045 | 767 | 372 |
| (%) | (38.0) | (19.5) | (36.8) | (16.9) | (19.8) | (10.6) |
| Belgium-Lux. | 1,133 | b | 204 | 80 | 45 | 35 |
| Britain | 2,708 | 1,913 | 290 | 377 | 228 | 132 |
| Denmark | 50 | c | 4 | 3 | 14 | 3 |
| France | 1,927 | 946 | 482 | 101 | 157 | 52 |
| Germany | 5,614 | 1,956 | 487 | 63 | 79 | 69 |
| Greece | — | c | d | d | d | d |
| Ireland | 1 | c | d | d | d | d |
| Italy | 1,303 | 53 | 587 | 6 | 87 | 3 |
| Netherlands | 1,178 | 392 | 367 | 214 | 111 | 57 |
| Portugal | 68 | c | 5 | d | d | d |
| Spain | 122 | 692 | 126 | 200 | 46 | 21 |
| Austria | 43 | c | 4 | 3 | 4 | 1 |
| Finland | 63 | c | 1 | 1 | d | d |
| Norway | 75 | c | d | 2 | d | d |
| Sweden | 659 | 350 | 129 | 17 | 66 | 36 |
| Switzerland | 3,222 | 1,346 | 577 | 57 | 259 | 173 |
| Other Europe[a] | 271 | c | 48 | 56 | 6 | 15 |
| United States | 10,488 | 19,080 | 2,906 | 2,795 | 1,759 | 2,743 |
| (%) | (28.2) | (63.0) | (41.8) | (45.3) | (45.5) | (70.6) |
| Canada | 1,978 | 417 | 221 | 111 | 72 | 56 |
| (%) | (5.3) | (1.4) | (3.2) | (1.8) | (1.8) | (1.6) |
| Japan | 3,439 | 1,455 | 83 | 196 | 165 | 41 |
| (%) | (9.2) | (4.8) | (1.2) | (3.2) | (4.3) | (1.2) |
| Other Countries | 2,797 | 1,708 | 401 | 1,893 | 767 | 333 |
| (%) | (7.7) | (5.6) | (5.8) | (30.6) | (19.9) | (9.5) |
| Total | 37,143 | 30,309 | 6,942[e] | 6,175 | 3,865 | 3,500 |
| (%) | (100.0) | (100.0) | (100.0) | (100.0) | (100.0) | (100.0) |

Sources: United Nations, Economic Commission for Latin America and Caribbean.
Notes: a. Excluding E. Europe; b. Included in Netherlands; c. Included in other countries; d. Included in other Europe; e. Data for 1989.

continue to invest in order to retain or enhance their market position in the Latin American region, regardless of developments in Europe. Attractive opportunities in the form of privatized state enterprises further support this scenario.

Table 1.11  The Triad Investment Clusters, 1988/89
          (Percent of Stock Held by Each Triad Member)

| Brazil | Mexico | Argentina | Chile | Venezuela | Colombia |
| --- | --- | --- | --- | --- | --- |
| Europe | U.S. | Europe | U.S. | U.S. | U.S. |
| 49.6 | 63.0 | 48.0 | 45.3 | 45.5 | 70.6 |
| U.S. | Europe | U.S. | Europe | Europe | Europe |
| 28.2 | 25.2 | 41.8 | 19.1 | 28.5 | 17.1 |
| Japan | Japan | Japan | Japan | Japan | Japan |
| 9.2 | 4.8 | 1.2 | 3.2 | 4.3 | 1.2 |

*Source:* Table 1.9.

An analysis by the Università Bocconi found that European growth negatively affects European direct investments in Latin America, but GDP growth in Latin America exerts a positive influence. The study concluded that direct investment flows to Latin America "should not be affected in any major way by the European Community's integration process or by recent developments in Eastern Europe."[23] Some recent evidence with respect to the key Latin American countries seems to confirm this finding. In Brazil, for example, 1991 net foreign direct investment flows from Europe were $396 million, and U.S. net flows were $445 million. But, in the first quarter of 1992 alone, European net flows were $482 million and U.S. flows were $541 million. In both periods, Britain was the largest European investor. At the end of March 1992, the European investment position in Brazil was $17.7 billion, versus $11.3 billion for the United States and $5.6 billion for Japan.[24]

In Argentina, 35 percent of the $10 billion in privatizations carried out through December 1992 have been made by Spanish and French companies, versus only 15 percent from the United States. In Mexico, German companies are planning large projects in the petrochemical, automobile, and tourism sectors. Access to the North American market through NAFTA is a major motivation behind these German investments, as it is also likely to be for other European companies.[25] For Mexico, European direct investment flows rose by over 2 percent to $908 million from 1990 to 1991, while flows from the United States declined by over 3 percent.[26] In Chile, authorized foreign investment in the first three quarters of 1992 totaled $1.8 billion; however, $1.1 billion of this was in Canadian mining ventures.[27] Finally, for Venezuela in the first eleven months of 1992, new investments from Europe were $268 million, but investments from the United States were only $224 million. Meanwhile, Venezuelan firms have also made some investments in Europe, as have some Mexican and Brazilian companies. Further investments in Europe are likely.[28]

## EUROPEAN BANKING AND FINANCE IN LATIN AMERICA

### Historical Evolution

European, and especially British, loans and investment funds were an important part of Latin America's early economic development. British finance was supplemented by French and German bank lending and fund raising in the European capital markets during the first two decades of the twentieth century. U.S. commercial banks became more important in the 1920s in Latin American finance, but the groundwork had been laid earlier by the European financial institutions.[29]

After the depression of the 1930s and the defaults of many Latin American governments on their bonds, commercial banks retreated from the region. Renewed lending in the 1970s led to the great buildup of Latin American debt that finally resulted in the crisis of 1982 with Mexico's stoppage of payments on its loans.[30]

### The Debt Crisis and Rescheduling

European banks participated (along with U.S., Japanese, and Canadian banks) first in the rapid rise of Latin American debt and then in its rescheduling and reduction in the mid-1980s. At the height of the debt crisis in 1985, European banks held about one-third of the commercial bank claims on the major Latin American countries. U.S. and Canadian banks accounted for about 40 percent, and banks from Japan and other countries held the balance.[31]

From 1985 to 1987, commercial banks intensified the process of rescheduling or reducing their debt to Latin America through sales, write-offs, or swaps of loans for equity. By 1987, the exit of smaller U.S. banks from Latin America had so reduced U.S. loans in the region that European banks actually led in outstanding claims, with $95 billion of Latin American debt, compared to the almost $75 billion held by U.S. banks. (See Figure 1.5 and Table 1.12) Japanese banks were third with almost $41 billion.

From 1987 to 1991–1992, the reduction of U.S. bank claims on Latin America intensified under the Brady Plan. Thus, from 1987 to 1990, European

**Figure 1.5   Commercial Bank Lending to Latin America, 1987–1992**

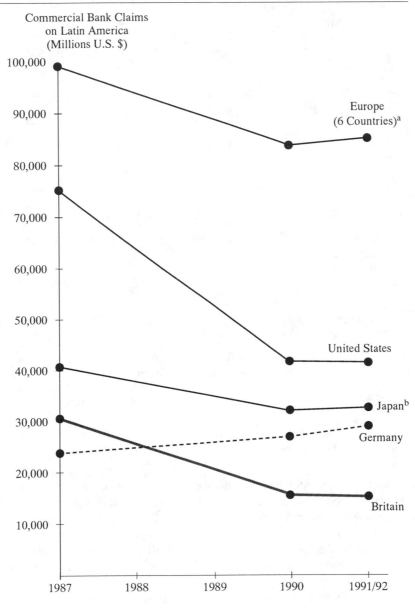

Commercial Bank Claims
on Latin America
(Millions U.S. $)

*Source:* World Bank.
*Notes:* a. The six European countries are Germany, France, Britain, Switzerland, Netherlands, Italy.
b. Japan does not include short-term loans.

Table 1.12   Commercial Bank Claims on Latin American–Caribbean
             Countries, 1987–1992
             (Millions U.S. $)

| Bank Lenders by Country | 1987 | 1990 | 1991 | 1992 | 1987–1991/92 % Change |
|---|---|---|---|---|---|
| Germany | 23,500 | 27,707 | 29,082 | 30,344[a] | 29.1 |
| France | 23,463 | 18,559 | 17,353 | | −26.0 |
| Britain | 30,714 | 16,856 | 16,271 | | −47.0 |
| Switzerland | 7,442 | 7,901 | 8,212 | | 10.3 |
| Netherlands | 4,739 | 6,823 | 7,176 | | 51.4 |
| Italy | 5,666 | 7,396 | 7,117 | | 25.6 |
| Total, Europe of Six | 95,524 | 85,242 | 85,931 | | −10.0 |
| Europe—Percent | (36.8) | (40.5) | (40.3) | | |
| United States | 74,670 | 44,292 | 41,112 | 42,893[a] | −42.6 |
| U.S.—Percent | (28.8) | (21.1) | (19.3) | | |
| Japan[b] | 40,900 | 31,200 | 31,600 | | −22.7 |
| Japan—Percent | (15.7) | (14.8) | (14.8) | | |
| Other Countries | 47,976 | 52,344 | 53,652 | | 11.8 |
| Percent | (18.7) | (23.6) | (25.6) | | |
| World | 259,070 | 210,298 | 212,895 | 213,413[a] | −17.6 |
| Percent | (100.0) | (100.0) | (100.0) | | |

Source: World Bank, Financial Flows to Developing Countries, September 1992; and Japan
Center for International Finance.
Notes: a. First quarter.
b. Medium- and long-term only.

bank claims on Latin America declined by 10 percent, while U.S. bank
claims dropped by 40 percent. As of 1990, European banks held 40 percent
of Latin American debt and U.S. banks only 21 percent, almost a reversal
of their positions in the early 1980s. Except for the British banks, most
European banks had either made only small reductions in their Latin
American debt or had maintained their exposure to Latin America. (See
Table 1.13)

By 1991/1992, clear patterns of change among European banks became
evident. British banks, faced with strong needs to restore profits and reserves
and operating under tight creditworthiness criteria for developing country
loans established by the Bank of England, had reduced their exposure in
Latin America by 47 percent from 1987 to 1991. In sharp contrast, German

**Table 1.13  European Official Development Assistance to Latin America and the Caribbean (LAC), 1980/81, 1990/91**

| Donor Countries: | 1980/81 | | 1990/91 | |
|---|---|---|---|---|
| | Amount Millions U.S.$ | % of ODA to LAC | Amount Millions U.S.$ | % of ODA to LAC |
| Austria | 9 | 3.9 | 24 | 5.6 |
| Belgium | 29 | 5.2 | 55 | 9.7 |
| Britain | 122 | 6.9 | 172 | 8.5 |
| Denmark | 23 | 5.9 | 63 | 7.6 |
| Finland | 7 | 6.1 | 60 | 8.6 |
| France | 195 | 7.1 | 354 | 5.8 |
| Germany | 387 | 12.4 | 652 | 12.7 |
| Ireland | — | — | 1 | 3.2 |
| Italy | 40 | 6.6 | 461 | 18.7 |
| Netherlands | 317 | 22.0 | 362 | 19.1 |
| Norway | 23 | 5.5 | 96 | 10.4 |
| Portugal | — | — | 1 | 0.7 |
| Spain | — | — | 212 | 29.6 |
| Sweden | 48 | 6.0 | 180 | 11.5 |
| Switzerland | 28 | 14.9 | 92 | 14.8 |
| Total Europe | 1,228 | 9.9 | 2,785 | 11.6 |
| United States | 682 | 12.5 | 1,506 | 16.2 |
| Japan | 208 | 6.7 | 637 | 8.3 |
| Canada | 108 | 11.8 | 227 | 13.4 |
| Australia | 6 | 0.9 | 14 | 1.5 |
| Total, Group of Donors | 2,231 | 9.9 | 5,169 | 11.8 |

*Source: Development Co-Operation, 1992, Tables 41–42.*

banks, bolstered by stronger capital positions and taking a longer-term view of Latin American finance, actually increased their exposure in the region by 29 percent from 1987 to 1992. Swiss, Dutch, and Italian banks have also increased their loan exposure to Latin America since 1987, but French banks have reduced theirs. European banks, partly due to the British decline, show a 10 percent reduction in Latin American bank claims. But this is far less than the almost 43 percent reduction in U.S. bank claims and the 22 percent decline of Japanese loans since 1987. (See Table 1.12) As of early 1992, German banks have become the leader by far among European lenders, with over $30 billion in Latin American loans. British banks have lost a considerable position in Latin America,

dropping from $30 billion of loans in 1987 to $16 billion by 1991. The retreat of the British banks in Latin America parallels to some extent the
withdrawal of small and medium-size U.S. banks from the region. Despite
the still cautious attitude of most banks on sovereign lending to governments in Latin America, there has been an overall rise in total bank lending to the region of about 2 percent from 1990 to 1992. These are primarily loans for trade finance and collateralized credits to private sector or
state companies in Latin America. Thus, U.S. banks increased their exposure by $1.7 billion and German banks increased their loans by $1.2 billion from 1991 to 1992.

## European Lending Leadership

In 1985, European lenders held just under 33 percent of the debt of the
largest Latin American economies, whereas North American banks held
almost 40 percent of the loans. But because of the differing practices of
banks with respect to debt write-offs or conversions, by 1991 European
banks held almost 44 percent of Latin American bank claims and North
American banks were down to 28 percent. The relative shift from North
American to European bank loans has been true for all countries except
Mexico. But even for Mexico, the proportion of debt with European banks
rose to almost 33 percent, while the North American portion fell from 40
percent to 35 percent from 1985 to 1991. For Argentina, Brazil, Peru, and
Uruguay, the position of European banks is especially strong vis-à-vis the
North American banks.

## Borrowing Patterns

Among Latin American countries, Brazil is the largest borrower of European bank loans. As of 1991/92, European bank claims against Brazil were
over $26 billion, compared to $17 billion with respect to Mexico, the second-largest borrower. The larger European lending to Brazil is a function
of the closer direct investment and trade ties and the size of its economy.
There has also been less bank debt reduction in Brazil than in Mexico. Argentina is the third-largest borrower, with $15 billion, and Venezuela fol-
lows with $7.6 billion.

  French, German, and Swiss banks have their greatest exposure to
Brazil; British, Dutch, and Italian banks have most of their loans to Mexico. In some cases, the concentration of lending is sizable. Of total French
loans to Latin America, almost 45 percent are located in Brazil, and for
German and Swiss banks this proportion is about 33 percent. Similarly,
about 33 percent of Britain's and Italy's loans are to Mexico.

  In absolute terms, German banks are the largest lenders to Latin America with $30 billion of the $85 billion total among the six major European

countries. French and British banks show a little over half of the German lending to Latin America. As a region, Latin America represents the largest proportion (39.5 percent) of British bank lending to developing countries. This proportion is undoubtedly a legacy of past British financial relations with Latin America. Italian, Dutch, and Swiss banks also have granted about 33 percent of their developing country loans to Latin America, versus about 20 percent for French and German banks.

## Europe's Importance in the Financial Markets

In addition to bank lending, Europe is of crucial importance to Latin American finance because of the Euromarket borrowings. Europe has played a key role in the development of the Eurodollar market and its associated Eurocurrency lending in the form of notes, Eurobonds, and private placements. Borrowings in the form of Euronotes and international bonds issued in Europe has been a major aspect of the Latin American financial revival from the 1982 debt crisis. These market borrowings, however, have been concentrated among the more creditworthy Latin American countries—Mexico, Brazil, Argentina, Venezuela, Colombia, and Chile. Their rapid increase is shown in the more than doubling of international bond issues, from $7 billion in 1990 to over $18 billion in 1992.[32] Also, Euronotes have almost doubled, from $1.5 billion to almost $3 billion, during the same period. In addition to these market borrowings, flows from Europe have been important in the form of purchases of Latin American stocks as well as offerings of European country funds. European investment banks are playing a valuable catalytic role in enlarging the access of Latin America to the international credit and capital markets. Mexico, for example, has raised funds in the deutsche mark, Spanish peseta, and sterling markets. Brazil led all developing countries with international bond issues of $1.5 billion in the second quarter of 1992, and in September Argentine borrowers raised $500 million in Eurobond issues.[33]

## Outlook for Banking and Finance

In recent years, Latin America has become a leader in "emerging markets" investments, offering high yields for floating-rate debt bonds ("Brady bonds") as well as new offerings of Eurobonds and notes. The floating-rate bonds of Brazil, Argentina, and Venezuela, for example, ranged from 16 percent to 18 percent in yields to maturity in December 1992.[34] However, most international banks, including the European banks, are treading cautiously in extending new direct credits to Latin American borrowers, selecting only the most creditworthy and focusing on private-sector firms. Concern for the capital positions of international banks, along with borrower creditworthiness, should mean that nonbank lending through the international markets—especially in Europe—will be the strongest growth element in Latin American finance in the future. Either through investment or commercial banks, European firms should remain of key importance to Latin America. The greater freedom of movement of financial services in the new Single Market of the European Community and a more integrated international securities market should bolster the impact of Europe on Latin American finance. However, recent events in Mexico are likely to exert a negative influence—at least in the short term—on capital inflows in the entire region.

## ECONOMIC ASSISTANCE

### Regional Trends

Official development assistance (ODA) to Latin America from Europe is quite small compared to aid given to other regions. European ODA for Latin America was less than 10 percent of total European ODA in 1980/81. Even so, the absolute amount of ODA of $1.2 billion was larger than the $682 million provided by the United States.

Although ODA for Latin America from Europe, the United States, and Japan more than doubled from 1980/81 to 1990/91, the region still received the lowest amount of assistance among developing countries. Sub-Saharan Africa remains Europe's largest ODA recipient, and the focus of U.S. aid efforts is in the Middle East and North Africa, particularly Egypt. Japan has maintained its traditional assistance primarily to Asia. Yet, in the aggregate, Europe continues to provide more aid to Latin America ($2.7 billion) than does the United States ($1.5 billion). (See Figure 1.16)

Of the twenty-five major country recipients of U.S. ODA, nine are in Latin America. France, on the other hand, does not show any Latin American country among its top twenty-five, with eighteen on its list being African nations. British aid is distributed to twenty-one African and Asian countries among its top twenty-five. The EC Commission, which provides multilateral, as distinct from bilateral, aid, shows no Latin American countries among its top twenty-five recipients.

### Country-Specific Patterns

Distinct changes among donor countries appear if we compare the allocation of ODA from 1980/81 to 1990/91. In 1980–81, the Netherlands directed the largest percentage of its ODA to Latin America, largely because of the Netherland Antilles. Germany had the lead, with $387 million in ODA for Latin America. Significantly, no Spanish assistance to Latin

**Figure 1.6   Official Development Assistance to Latin America by Europe, United States, and Japan, 1980/81, 1990/91 (Millions U.S. $)**

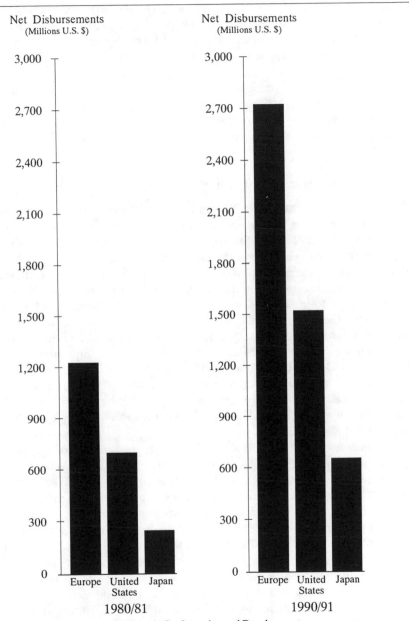

*Source:* Organization for Economic Co-Operation and Development.

America was provided in this earlier period. By 1990/91, Spain had become the leader, with the largest share (almost 30 percent) of its ODA going to Latin America. Italy also raised its assistance to the region, with strong support being given to Argentina and Peru. The Netherlands continues to provide a large share of its ODA to Latin America, particularly to its former Caribbean territories. In terms of total ODA, however, Germany remains the largest European provider to Latin America, with $652 million in 1990/91.

This collective commitment of the European countries to Latin American assistance is impressive, especially considering Europe's closer ties to the Mediterranean region and Africa and in view of the rising demand for multilateral assistance to the countries of Central and Eastern Europe and to Russia.

## Outlook for European Assistance

European ODA to Latin America has grown 8.5 percent annually in nominal terms during the last decade, versus 6.9 percent in its ODA to all regions. It is unlikely that the European pace of assistance to Latin America or to the world can continue at the same rate over the medium term. Most donor countries are reexamining assistance programs. Fiscal constraints may lead to slower growth, and assistance may increasingly take the form of technical help in such areas as the environment, narcotics, and migration. As for Germany, a key country, future large increases in aid volumes to Latin America appear doubtful. The cost of unification and the nation's commitments to Central and Eastern Europe could well limit the extent of Germany's ODA for Latin America. French aid is likely to be increasingly directed to Africa, as will Italian aid. The budget for British ODA to all areas has been increased by 6 percent for 1992/93, but Latin America is not a priority region. Spanish aid to Latin America is unlikely to continue at its recent high rates.[35]

In broader terms, there is a possibility that the creation of the Single Market may lead to diversion of assistance away from Latin America. According to the Overseas Development Institute, the Single Market may result in a loss of trade preferences for some of the African, Caribbean, or Mediterranean Basin countries. If so, compensation could be given in the form of economic assistance, which could help some of the small Caribbean economies. But if the EC uses aid to soften the transition for countries with which it has had special relations, this does not include the major countries of Latin America. If it increases its aid to Africa, the Mediterranean Basin, or Eastern Europe, it may be at the expense of Latin America.[36] However, these possibilities are difficult to quantify. It remains a speculative matter to assess how the greater integration of Europe may affect the level of European assistance to Latin America.

## CONCLUSION

Of the four major economic linkages examined here—trade, foreign direct investment, banking and finance, and economic development assistance—the first shows the most problematic prospects. The consolidation of the Single Market and competition from central Europe may lead to some trade diversion, although the actual impacts of these developments will tend to be category-specific. "Sensitive" products such as clothing and steel may be negatively affected, and primary products may experience a positive effect.

With respect to foreign direct investment, some diversion may also occur but with a more country-specific pattern. Germany's probable continued focus on Central Europe is a case in point. On the other hand, powerful incentives, such as privatization opportunities and the creation of NAFTA, will ensure that Europe and Japan will try to maintain their competitive position vis-à-vis the United States in Latin America.

The outlook for banking and finance is also strong, given the growth of creditworthy private-sector borrowers, the key role played by the EU in Eurocurrency lending, and the strong position in the region of European investment banks.

Economic development assistance will probably experience the most change in the coming years, due to a number of factors. Although European assistance to Latin America was strong in recent years, it is unlikely that its rate of growth can be sustained in the medium term, both because of the rapid development of major Latin American markets and because of other demands on European funds as the Single Market consolidates and expands. Assistance is likely to shift gradually to technical help in such areas as the environment, narcotics, and migration.

Finally, although in terms of trade and investment there has been a clear pattern of strong linkages between Europe and the Southern Cone, financial and ODA flows have been more broadly distributed. As NAFTA proceeds, scenarios for Europe are likely to include a consolidation of its Southern Cone links, but also an increase in its northern investment (particularly in Mexico) to ensure access to a large and dynamic North American market.

## NOTES

After Blake Friscia's untimely death, Françoise Simon built from an early draft of this chapter, updating, restructuring, and entirely rewriting the material in order to achieve this version.

1. Europe as referred to here consists of the twelve members of the European Union (EU) plus the seven members of the European Free Trade Association (EFTA). Central and Eastern Europe are, for the purposes of this chapter, considered to be a separate area. The EU's three new members as of January 1, 1995 (Austria, Finland, and Sweden) are not included in our EU data.

2. Sources on GDP and population: United Nations, *World Economic Survey, 1992;* European Community, *Facts and Figures on the European Community and the United States,* March 1992; Joint U.S. Economic Committee, *Economic Indicators,* July 1982; World Bank, *World Economic Development Report,* 1992.

3. Comisión Económica para América Latina y el Caribe, *Balance Preliminar de la Economía de América Latina y el Caribe,* 1992.

4. EUROSTAT, *EC–Latin American Trade 1979–1987,* Brussels, 1989.

5. A full analysis on the composition of trade can be found in *EC–Latin American Trade 1979–1987,* and a special report on Latin American manufactured exports is included in the 1992 report of the Inter-American Development Bank, *Economic and Social Progress in Latin America,* "Special Section: Manufacturing Exports."

6. *EC–Latin American Trade 1979–1987.*

7. Ibid.

8. Ibid.

9. Ibid.

10. *EC–Latin American Trade 1979–1987,* and International Monetary Fund (IMF), *Direction of Trade Yearbook,* 1992.

11. The EUROSTAT data differ from IMF and UN statistics used in other tables because of the coverage of trade items, country classifications, and timing differences. Consequently, EU trade reported by EUROSTAT is not completely comparable with IMF-reported trade for the EC.

12. See also Table 1.5.

13. The most important determinant of import demand of a country or region is generally considered to be domestic economic growth. This growth is expressed as the income elasticity of import demand, or the change in imports associated with the change in GDP. For the European Community, the income elasticity of imports has been estimated at about 2.0 for the 1980 to 1990 period. See Gerhard Pohl and Piritta Sorsa, *European Economic Integration and Trade with the Developing World* (World Bank, 1992).

14. For further data on the expected relationship of Latin American exports to European growth, plus changes in import volumes and prices, see the IMF, *World Economic Outlook,* October 1992.

15. The gains and losses of Latin American products from the Single Market are in Instituto de Relaciones Europeo-Latinoamericanas (IRELA), *Dossier No. 40, Latin America and Europe: Towards the Year 2000,* September 1992. Another assessment is provided by Christopher Stevens, "The Single Market, All-European Integration and the Developing Countries: The Potential for Aid Diversion," *Journal of Development Planning* 22, 1992.

16. Nontariff barriers against Latin American exports to the EC are discussed in Comisión Económica para América Latina y el Caribe (CEPAL), *Las Barreras No Arancelarias a las Exportaciones Latinoamericanas en la Comunidad Económica Europea,* Santiago, Chile, March 22, 1991, and in a similar CEPAL document, *La Política Comercial de la Comunidad Económica Europea después de 1992: Implicaciones para América Latina,* April 28, 1992.

17. Pohl and Sorsa, *European Economic Integration.*

18. CEPAL, *Inversión Extranjera Directa en América Latina y el Caribe 1970–90, Volumen I: Panorama Regional,* Santiago, Chile, September 14, 1992, p. 42. It should be noted that these are net investments and such flows reflect capital repatriations in a number of instances.

19. Part of this uncertainty results from data-gathering problems for Argentine investments. The Argentine data in Table 1.8 are based on information supplied to

CEPAL by the national authorities in Argentina. Data are missing for three years (1987, 1988, 1990) of the 1985–1990 period. For the period from 1985 to 1990, the total net inflows are only $228 million. However, IMF statistics also reported by CEPAL show total direct investment inflows of $5.7 billion for Argentina during the period, over a third from debt-to-equity conversions. Reported in CEPAL, *Inversión Extranjera*. This report (p. 42) shows a foreign investment inflow into Argentina of $2 billion in 1990 alone.

20. These estimates are based on the report, *El Vínculo Iberoamérica-Comunidad Europea: Planes, Políticas y Estrategias de Desarrollo*, Ministerio de Economía y Hacienda, Santiago de Chile, January 1992, p. 112, with data additions for Chile and Venezuela taken from CEPAL, *Inversión Extranjera*. Note that Canadian foreign investments are not included in data.

21. Presentations of the Triad are found in: United Nations, *World Investment Report 1991, Transnational Corporations as Engines of Growth*, and United Nations, *World Investment Report 1991, The Triad in Foreign Direct Investment*.

22. CEPAL, *Inversion Extranjera*, pp. 55–56.

23. Alessandro Pio, "The Impact of the 1993 Single European Market on Investment Flows between the European Community and Developing Countries: The Case of Latin America," *European Journal of Development Research*, December 1990.

24. Communication from the Central Bank of Brazil.

25. Argentine information from Carlos E. Sánchez, vice minister of economy, Republic of Argentina, in a talk given at the Council of the Americas, New York, December 2, 1992. Other information from *World Investment Report, 1992*, pp. 43–44.

26. Data from Mexico, Secretráai de Comercio y Fomento Industrial (SEC-OFI), Dirección General de Inversión Extranjera, provided by Manuel Suárez-Mier, minister for economic affairs, Embassy of Mexico, Washington, D.C.

27. *Chile Economic Report*, November 1992.

28. Communication from Minister Ricardo Hausmann, Coordinación de Planificación de la Presidencia de la República (CORDIPLAN), Caracas, Venezuela.

29. Carlos Marichal, *A Century of Debt Crisis in Latin America: From Independence to the Great Depression 1820–1930* (Princeton, N.J.: Princeton University Press, 1989).

30. A survey of the Latin American debt crisis is found in the section titled "External Debt," by August Blake Friscia, in *Cambridge Encyclopedia of Latin America and the Caribbean* (Cambridge University Press, 1992).

31. Bank for International Settlements, *International Banking and Financial Market Developments*, Basel, November 1992.

32. It should be noted that some of the international bonds may have a U.S. participation in issuance. Some of the lead managers may also include U.S. firms for securities floated in Europe.

33. World Bank, *Financial Flows to Developing Countries*, September 1992.

34. Reported in Morgan Grenfell, *Developing Country Research*, December 15, 1992.

35. Organization for Economic Co-Operation and Development, *Development Co-Operation 1992 Report*, Introduction and Tables 9, 15, 20.

36. Stevens, "The Single Market: All-European Integration and the Developing Countries: The Potential for Aid Diversion," *Journal of Development Planning*, 22, 1992.

# 2

# The Impact of Regional Integration on European–Latin American Relations

*Françoise Simon & Susan Kaufman Purcell*

The 1980s marked the beginning of a revived Latin American economic integration effort that was influenced by progress in European unification and driven by the requirements of international competitiveness. The formation of major North Atlantic trade blocs—the European Community (EC) and the North American Free Trade Area (NAFTA)—and the erosion of Latin American competitiveness have led to a sense of urgency regarding the restructuring of Latin American economies.

These economies are now faced with a number of possible scenarios, ranging from tighter regional integration to fragmentation. Two key issues are the extent of the integration that is feasible, given wide economic asymmetries within the region, and the tension between "vertical" and "horizontal" relationships, that is, linkages with NAFTA versus connections with the EC and Asia. The pull of NAFTA is clear for the northern groupings of Latin American states: Group of Three, Andean Pact, Central American Common Market (CACM), and the Caribbean Community and Common Market (Caricom). It is less so for the Mercado Común del Sur (or Southern Cone Common Market) (MERCOSUR) countries, which have strong trade and investment connections to Europe as well as to the United States. One alternative to a rigid integration is the Chilean model of globalization, now evolving into a network of multiple linkages: Chile was admitted to the Asia-Pacific Economic Cooperation Forum (APEC), was invited to apply to NAFTA, and in addition is increasing its trade and investment with its MERCOSUR neighbors.

An alternative is suggested by Kenichi Ohmae, who argued that the nation-state is an increasingly dysfunctional unit for managing trade and investment, and that on the global economic map the lines that now matter are those defining "region-states": natural economic zones within states, such as northern Italy, or overlapping national boundaries, such as Singapore's "growth triangle," which includes the neighboring Indonesian islands. Unlike trade blocs, these groupings are manageable in size (5 to 20 million people) but are large enough to achieve economies of scale in terms of consumption and infrastructure.[1]

In contrast to the success and manageability of such region-states as Singapore, the European model of vast, politically driven regional integration has recently met with unexpected challenges. Over the past thirty-five years, Europe did create a single market of 350 million people who have increased their trade with each other at the rate of 9 percent per year; however, Europe's initial ambition to turn this free-trade zone into a full economic and political union has now come into question. Although economic asymmetries in the two regions are vastly different, there are lessons to be learned for emerging Latin American trade blocs from the European model. There are also short- and long-term implications for European and Latin American business in the current trend on both sides of the Atlantic toward economic integration.

We begin, therefore, with overviews of both the European and Latin American experiences with integration, examining the possible implications for Latin America of the European evolution. We also outline the ways in which the current integration processes in Latin America are trying to correct and build upon the region's earlier efforts. We then look at the European response to Latin American integration and the policies that the European Community has adopted to assist the process.

In the second section, we assess the business response to regional integration. In particular, we examine how integration is influencing European trade and investment strategies in Latin America. Finally, we explore what impact regional restructuring is having on Latin American companies in various industry sectors.

Despite the relatively few years that have passed since Latin America began its latest push toward economic integration, there are already signs that the process is having a growing impact on both EU (European Union) policies and European and Latin American business strategies within the region. At the same time, much remains to be done in Latin America to ensure the viability and successful implementation of its restructuring scenarios.

## EUROPEAN AND LATIN AMERICAN INTEGRATION

### European Integration

The European integration model, initially defined as "an ever closer union," now faces an identity crisis thirty-five years later. Through the 1980s, harmonization was viewed as a progressive *deepening* of the economic links among the EC's twelve members, from the 1993 Common Market (stipulating free movement of goods, services, people, and capital) to Economic and Monetary Union (EMU) and, finally, to full political union—all to be accomplished within a twenty- to thirty-year time frame. In the 1990s, however, this model has been challenged both internally and externally. Internally, the EMU goal collided with the reality of economic recession, which led Europeans to focus on immediate national problems. Externally, the liberalization of Eastern Europe has opened the way to a further expansion of the European Union. Within this fluid context, the main debate concerns the "deepening" versus the "widening" of Europe, and the key integration issues can be summarized as a three-tiered dilemma:

- Will the European Union become a "variable-geometry" Europe?
- How will the EEA itself evolve, since Switzerland opted out of it in December 1992 and three EFTA members (Austria, Finland, and Sweden) joined the EU in January 1995?
- Will "Greater Europe" expand eastward or southward? To what extent could a greatly expanded Europe (from fifteen to as many as forty countries at various development levels) be manageable?

In order to explore these issues, we will review the objectives and current status of each "integration tier."

### EC-12

*Chronology and objectives.* Initiated in 1952 with the European Coal and Steel Community (ECSC), then fully implemented as a Common Market by the 1958 Rome Treaties, EC integration came to have in recent years two fundamental objectives: improved competitiveness of the EC vis-à-vis the United States and Asia, and greater cooperation among European firms. (See Table 2.1, chronology) Both objectives were seen as being attainable within the framework of a "deepening" process moving from a common market to a full economic and political union. Much progress has been made toward creating the Single Market, which officially came into being in January 1993, but it is still far from complete. Full economic union, as defined under the Maastricht Treaty, remains even more problematic.

*Single-market/implementation status.* The completion of the single market depends on member states' implementation effectiveness, that is, on their transposition of the 1992 EU directives into national law.

By mid-1994, the overall transposition rate was nearly 89 percent, but it varied greatly by country. Denmark was the most efficient state with a 96 percent rate; Germany had only reached 81 percent, and Greece and Ireland brought up the rear at 78 percent.[2]

**Table 2.1    EC-12 Chronology**

| | |
|---|---|
| 1952 | ECSC (European Coal and Steel Community) initiated with 6 members: West Germany, France, Italy, Benelux. |
| 1958 | Rome Treaties create EEC (European Economic Community) aiming to extend a common market to all economic sectors. |
| 1973 | UK, Ireland, and Denmark join. |
| 1979 | EMS established (zone of European monetary stability linking member currencies). |
| 1981 | Greece joins EC. |
| 1985 | Schengen Accord (5 members, now 8) ensures free movement of people between member states. |
| 1986 | Spain and Portugal join, thus forming the current EC-12. |
| 1989–91 | Plan for EMU (Economic and Monetary Union) launched, then finalized in December 1991 in the Maastricht Treaty. |
| 1993 | EMU ratified by member states. EC becomes the European Union (EU). |
| 1995 | 3 EFTA members (Austria, Finland, Sweden) join the EU. |

Integration also varies within and between sectors. In financial services, the free movement of capital has now been implemented, but insurance has the worst transposition rate at 64.8 percent. Other sectors, such as pharmaceuticals and automobiles, have abandoned or slowed their initial timetables. (See Table 2.2) In air transportation, deregulation plans are now threatened by national subsidies to support loss-making flag carriers such as Air France.

Even though economic asymmetries are far less severe in the EC than they are in Latin America, significant variances remain. Per capita income is the clearest indicator of economic variance; with an EU average indexed at 100, income ranges from 53 in Greece to 129 in Luxembourg. Production costs also vary widely. Total hourly manufacturing labor costs in 1991 ranged from over \$22 in West Germany to \$13 in Britain. (See Figure 2.1) Rates were as low as \$5 in the poorer Sunbelt countries. Among many other indicators of the current lack of economic cohesion, consumer prices tracked in January 1993 still varied by as much as 122 percent, even within the more developed countries in the north. (See Table 2.3)

**Table 2.2     Common Market Implementation by Sector and Area**

| Sector | Goal | Progress |
|---|---|---|
| Airlines | Open skies: Free pricing, new entries, cabotage. | Cabotage to be phased in (1993–97) by all member states. Plans to fully deregulate by 2000 are threatened by national subsidies to flag carriers. |
| Banking/Insurance | Freedom to provide financial services and sell insurance. | Insurance lags (only 65% transposition rate). |
| Pharmaceuticals | Deregulate pricing and standardize testing in EC. | EMEA (European Medicines Evaluation Agency) formed in 1993. No progress on price deregulation. |
| Automobiles | Remove all quotas and tariffs by mid-1990s. | Initial goal dropped in 1991 (EC carmakers requested barriers against the Japanese until 1999). |
| Television | Satellite broadcasts allowed throughout EC. | Goal adopted by EC but not by any individual country. No agreement on standards and advertising regulations. |
| Area | | |
| Capital Movement | Drop all restrictions on capital movement in EC. | Transposition of directives into law completed for free movement of capital. |
| Technical Standards | Harmonize product standards in EC. | Implementation well under way in most sectors. |
| Public Procurement | Open all bidding for public projects. | Overall implementation rate of 75%, but some sectors (services) and countries (Greece, Spain, and Italy) are lagging. |

*Sources:* Eurocom, July/August 1994; Simon Associates.

Figure 2.1 EC Labor Cost Variance, 1991

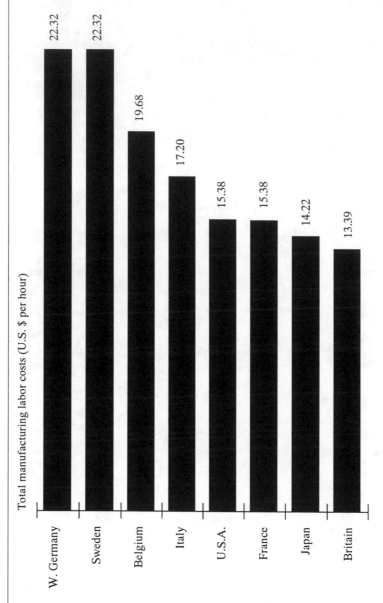

Total manufacturing labor costs (U.S. $ per hour)

| | |
|---|---|
| W. Germany | 22.32 |
| Sweden | 22.32 |
| Belgium | 19.68 |
| Italy | 17.20 |
| U.S.A. | 15.38 |
| France | 15.38 |
| Japan | 14.22 |
| Britain | 13.39 |

*Source: The Economist*, May 16, 1992. ©The Economist Newspaper Group, Inc. Reprinted with permission.

Table 2.3    EC Consumer Prices Variance, 1992

Random Sample, Supermarket Prices, U.S.$

|  | Holland | Belgium | Luxembourg | Germany | France |
|---|---|---|---|---|---|
| Gasoline, lead-free, 1 liter | 1.00 | 0.90 | 0.70 | 0.88 | 0.90 |
| Cigarettes, 200 | 25.85 | 28.20 | 21.81 | 28.94 | 21.15 |
| Rice, 1 kg | 3.66 | 3.24 | 3.81 | 3.72 | 3.36 |
| Tomatoes, 1 kg | 1.39 | 1.96 | 1.93 | 3.09 | 1.45 |
| Color film (36 photos) | 8.20 | 5.72 | 7.03 | 4.94 | 6.24 |
| Compact disk | 22.12 | 21.18 | 20.48 | 21.75 | 18.24 |

*Source: The Economist,* January 9, 1993. © The Economist Newspaper Group, Inc. Reprinted with permission.

*Economic union and status prospects.* Beyond the 1993 Single Market, economic union plans, as defined by the Maastricht Treaty, came into force on November 1, 1993, after the treaty was finally ratified by the last member state, Germany. However, the German Constitutional Court stated that Parliament would have to be consulted before Germany could proceed with a currency union. Such caution is reflected in public opinion. In a March 1993 Eurobarometer poll, 60 percent of Germans polled were against EMU; throughout Europe, only two out of five people surveyed favored the treaty. Economic integration objectives are fading in the leading states, given the current economic context. Unemployment averages 10 percent, from a low of 3 percent in Luxembourg to over 21 percent in Spain. European competitiveness continues to slip, with the EC's share of world exports falling by a fifth since 1980, and with a widening deficit in high-technology trade: From 1982 to 1990, the volume of EC high-tech exports to the rest of the world grew by only 2 percent per year, while high-tech imports rose by 7.7 percent per year. Member states that formerly worried about coping with a united Germany's strength are now concerned about its weakness: From being a major exporter of capital, Germany turned into a net importer, with transfer payments to the former East Germany amounting to DM 130 billion ($80 billion) in 1992.[3]

In this context, the timetable set for European economic and monetary union appears highly unrealistic: By 1996, governments would decide on EMU members according to Maastricht guidelines on inflation, public debt, and budget deficits. If a majority of countries did not meet these guidelines in 1996, EMU would start at the latest in 1999, on the assumption that more than one country would be ready by then. As of 1993, none of the twelve had met all of these guidelines, and Germany had met only one. (See Figure 2.2)

Figure 2.2   Guidelines for Economic and Monetary Union, 1993

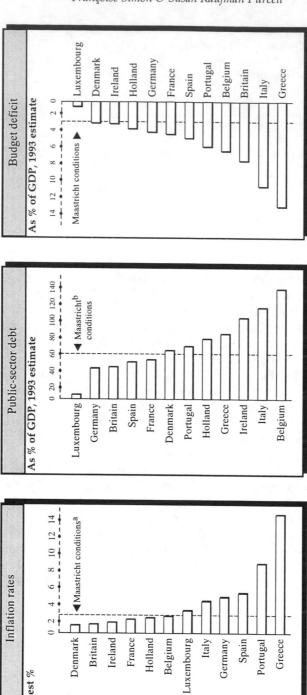

*Source:* National Statistics; OECD; European Commission; Swiss Bank Corporation.
*Notes:* a. Applying the treaty arithmetic to current figures.
        b. Levels laid down in the treaty.

The EMU guidelines are also in clear conflict with the recent evolution of the ERM (exchange rate mechanism). Created in 1979 to control inflation and exchange rate volatility, the ERM collapsed in 1992 when the U.K. and Italy, which were under pressure to lower their interest rates, withdrew and when Spain was later forced to devalue the peseta. By August 1993, the ERM was widened from a narrow band allowing a fluctuation of only plus or minus 2.25 percent to a wide band of plus or minus 15 percent (leaving intact only a bilateral agreement between Holland and Germany). In order for a country to meet the EMU guidelines, its currency must not have been devalued for two years; this is hard to reconcile with the wide band ERM. So far, the Bundesbank has opposed softening the EMU convergence guidelines.[4] The best scenario one might consider under these circumstances is a "building-block" approach, under which an "inner core" EMU comprising Germany, France, the Benelux countries, and possibly Austria, would first be established.

It is clear at this point that the top-down, politically driven lockstep integration model planned for Europe in the 1980s has run up against economic problems and voter resistance. Although economic difficulties may be due in part to an exceptional event (the unification of Germany), grassroots enthusiasm for European integration is consistently lacking. France joined the EMU with a razor-thin margin, Denmark first declined, then joined, as the U.K. did, only with "opt-out" clauses, and the German public is not convinced. The concept of Europe itself is still debated, with federalist Germany favoring a stronger European Parliament, while France and the U.K. would like more power for elected governments, acting through the Council of Ministers.

### European Economic Area

In the same way as European integration is becoming a "variable geometry" process, the European Economic Area (EEA), scheduled to link the twelve EC countries with the seven Nordic and Alpine EFTA countries by 1993, is now a multiple-speed phenomenon.

The EEA Agreement, signed in Oporto in May 1992, provided for the establishment of "four freedoms" (free movement of goods, persons, services, and capital) within the EC and EFTA regions. By extending the current EU, Europe would have the largest economic area worldwide, integrating nineteen countries and their 380 million inhabitants. Trade flows justified this expansion: In 1991, a quarter of the EC's exports went to EFTA, which was thus the Community's primary market. Conversely, EC imports from EFTA jumped from 10 percent to 22 percent of total imports in the 1985–1991 period. Denmark, in particular, imported almost half of its goods from EFTA.[5]

Switzerland's "no" vote in December 1992 on joining the EEA slowed down—although it has not halted—the integration process. The Swiss-German cantons were worried that they would be dominated by the new Germany (the largest contributor to the EC budget, with over $11 billion a year), but Swiss voter resistance may also have been related to significant wealth disparities. All EFTA countries have a per capita GDP higher than the EC average: while the latter stood at $18,000 in 1990, the former averaged $26,000, with Switzerland topping the list at $34,000. Under the EEA Agreement, EFTA was expected to contribute $2.4 billion in 1993–1995 to a cohesion fund designed to help poorer EU countries, of which Switzerland was to pay nearly 30 percent.[6] Its share has now been redistributed. In addition, four EFTA countries (Austria, Sweden, Finland, and Norway) were admitted in 1994 to join the EU, and all ratified by local vote except Norway. It is clear that the EEA will be superseded by a "multiple-speed" expansion of the EU itself, where different countries approve linkages in different time frames.

### Greater Europe

If the EU widening process, once clear-cut, is now fraught with uncertainty, the picture is even murkier for expansion of the European bloc to the east or the south.

Since 1991, several "association agreements" have been signed by the EU and such countries as Hungary, Poland, and the Czech and Slovak Republics, but these agreements retained significant trade barriers on agricultural products and "sensitive" imports such as steel, chemicals, and clothing. In this context, Hungary's hope to join the EU by 1996 appears overoptimistic, and the prospect of the EU expanding eastward to include these three countries, the three Baltic states, and Slovenia, until recently envisaged for year 2000, may in fact take considerably longer.

Although the main argument against the EU's eastward expansion is the disparity in wealth between Eastern and Western Europe, the facts do not support it. Ireland's GDP per capita in 1990 (on the basis of purchasing-power parities) was 63 percent of the EU average, Greece's was 58 percent, and Portugal's 53 percent. In comparison, Czechoslovakia's was 66 percent and Hungary's 53 percent.[7] Although the EU's trade with Eastern Europe remains at a relatively low level, investment may play a key role in narrowing the economic gap. In 1992, foreign investment in Eastern Europe totaled almost $30 billion, with the United States leading and Germany (by the number of deals) and Italy (by the value of its deals) second. While the United States invested $8.7 billion, Italy contributed $7.6 billion (versus only $8 million invested in the region by Japan).[8] Nonetheless, expanding from fifteen to a possible twenty-five states would change the balance of poor and rich countries within the EU and strain its budget (four poor countries out of fifteen would become eleven out of twenty-five). An expanded EU would be unmanageable unless specific measures were taken (reducing official languages from nine to three, cutting the ratio of commissioners to countries, keeping the Parliament's size at the current level, and reallocating Council votes). Given these difficulties, the concept of a "Continental Common Market," as proposed by the European Bank for Reconstruction and Development (EBRD), which would include some forty countries from Iceland to the Newly Independent States, does not appear to be implementable unless the current model is radically modified.

Even as Europe's borders are blurring in the east, they may expand toward the south. Turkey, Cyprus, and Malta are candidates to join the EU, and Morocco and other Maghreb states may have their own agreements. In the latter case, however, the wealth differences already noted in the East would be exacerbated by the nature of the trade portfolio (largely agricultural goods from Morocco, for instance).

At all levels of the three-tier European bloc formation process, there are clear indicators that a shift is now taking place from a rigid, lockstep expansion to a flexible hybrid with both federal and intergovernmental features and with multiple time frames and levels of economic integration. There may be lessons in this evolution for Latin America—such as the need for flexibility and for "multiple-speed" linkages allowing for a gradual harmonization of current economic disparities.

## Latin American Integration

The early 1990s in Latin America saw an explosion of free-trade agreements, prompted by new developments both within the region and external to it. Internally, the onset of the debt crisis in 1982 had forced Latin America to abandon its costly, inward-oriented, and protectionist economic development strategy based on import substitution. Instead, the region began to open its economies to international competition to increase their efficiency.

Economic integration with neighboring countries became feasible as a result of the new liberal economic policies. The fact that by the early 1990s most of Latin America's authoritarian governments had been replaced by democratic ones made the region more politically homogeneous, thereby also facilitating integration.

Internationally, the end of the Cold War greatly improved relations between Latin America and the United States by giving them congruent policy objectives. During the Cold War, Latin America wanted the United States to help the region develop economically, but Washington's emphasis was on security issues, particularly the communist threat to the region. With the collapse of the Soviet Union, the United States could turn its focus toward economic issues. The Bush administration, motivated in part by the imminent creation of the Single Market in Europe and Japan's growing trade with Southeast Asia, proposed a Western Hemisphere free trade area in its Enterprise for the Americas Initiative of June 1990.

The fact that Latin America had tried and failed to create a Latin American free trade area in the 1960s did not discourage either the Latins or Washington from their new vision of an integrated hemisphere. All attributed the failure of the earlier effort to Latin America's inward, protectionist orientation and the Cold War tensions between Latin America and the United States, which had caused the former to try to build a "fortress Latin America" that excluded the richest and most lucrative market in the hemisphere. On the other hand, the new integration effort shares some characteristics of the earlier failed effort. Latin America still suffers from relatively low levels of intraregional trade, and its countries differ greatly in size, level of development, and macroeconomic fundamentals.

Despite these factors, several of the key integration issues of concern to Latin America are precisely those on Europe's agenda. Like Europe, Latin America seems to be dividing into different tiers, whose pace of integration varies. In contrast to Europe, however, the Latin American integration process is not expanding in the orderly, progressive fashion that characterized the European process until recently. Instead, within Latin America several "integration clusters" are being created more or less simultaneously. Furthermore, individual countries within each "cluster" are also signing free-trade agreements with outsiders. The result is a somewhat confusing overlap of agreements that has not yet been sorted out.

The situation is made even more complicated by the fact that integration objectives vary. Most ambitious are the common markets that the MERCOSUR, Andean Group, and Central American countries each have as their goal. The North American free-trade agreement is less ambitious because it does not provide for a common external tariff, the free flow of labor, or common political and economic policies and institutions. The same is true of the proposed Western Hemisphere free-trade area. Several Latin American countries, particularly Mexico and Chile, would like to enter into free-trade agreements with Asia, and U.S. government officials have begun to explore the viability of eventually expanding the North American Free Trade Area to include Asian countries as well.

The key issues for Latin American integration—as with European integration—therefore involve a "deepening" and "widening" process. Yet, Latin America's formation of subregional trading blocs raises certain questions: Will Latin America, excluding Mexico, integrate as a region before seeking integration with North America? Will individual Latin American countries, such as Chile, or subregional groupings such as MERCO-SUR, the Group of Three, or the Andean Group, integrate with North America prior to the creation of an integrated Latin American market? If

Latin America integrates as a region and, ultimately, with North America, will the process proceed at multiple speeds? Will Latin America, or the Western Hemisphere, eventually expand its free trade relationships toward Europe or toward Asia?

In order to answer these questions, we will examine the objectives and current status of the various hemispheric groupings, including the North American free trade area. (See Table 2.4 for a summary of these groupings)

Latin America's support for increased regional integration has produced some results since the early 1990s. Intraregional trade has grown, although admittedly from a very low base. Between 1986 and 1992, intraregional trade increased by 135 percent, compared with an 89 percent increase in Latin America's exports to the United States. By the end of 1993, intraregional exports accounted for 19.2 percent of Latin America's total exports.[9]

Subregional integration is also dynamic but uneven. In most cases, what on paper looks like a subregional grouping is in reality a bilateral free-trade agreement between the two strongest economies involved. This is the case with MERCOSUR and the Andean Group. The success of these subregional groupings therefore depends on the commitment of these "anchor countries." It also depends on the ability of these lead countries to implement responsible economic policies at home. By these criteria, the viability of both MERCOSUR and the Andean Group is far from assured, while NAFTA offers the most solid prospects, since it is based on economic realities. Even before NAFTA, the de facto integration of the Mexican economy with the U.S. economy was clear. In 1992, the United States supplied 70 percent of Mexico's imports and received 76 percent of its exports.

## NAFTA

Given the wide disparities between the levels of development of Mexico and the United States, the idea of creating a free trade area that included these two countries plus Canada, with which the United States already had such an agreement, was initially greeted with skepticism. In part, this attitude reflected a bias in favor of the European integration pattern, which initially joined First World countries and only extended membership to their less developed neighbors three decades later.

Despite the acceleration of the integration timetable in the North American case, the prognosis for NAFTA is good, in large part because of the high level of bilateral trade that already existed between Mexico and the United States at the time of the agreement. The fact that Mexico and Canada are, respectively, third and first most important trading partners means that NAFTA initially will be a de facto "hub and spokes" arrangement, with the United States as the hub and Mexico and Canada as "spokes." As neither

**Table 2.4  Latin American Free Trade Agreements—Current Status**

| Trade Bloc | Countries | Status |
|---|---|---|
| NAFTA | Mexico, U.S., Canada | Tariff elimination effective 1/1/94 over 15-year period<br>Tariffs for cars, financial services, textiles eliminated over 10-year period<br>Tariffs for agriculture eliminated over 15-year period |
| ANDEAN PACT | Bolivia, Colombia, Ecuador, Venezuela, Peru | Free Trade Zone (Colombia/Venezuela) 1/1/92<br>Peru suspended in 1992, reinstated in 1994<br>Intraregional tariff elimination and multitiered CET effective 1/1/95 |
| MERCOSUR | Argentina, Brazil, Paraguay, Uruguay | Common external tariffs of 12% effective 1/1/95<br>Exceptions for capital goods, high tech, and petrochemicals (common tariffs by 2001) |
| GROUP OF THREE (G-3) | Mexico, Colombia, Venezuela | Tariff elimination effective 1/1/95 (over 10-year period)<br>Exception=autos (13-year period) |
| CACM | El Salvador, Nicaragua, Guatemala, Honduras (Costa Rica and Panama) | CET—20% (1993)<br>Costa Rica: Delays in regional tariff and free movement of labor<br>Panama (partial member since 1991) |
| Caricom | Caribbean countries and Guyana | Customs union (1994) with CET of 45%, projected to fall to 20% in 1998 |
| | Chile | Membership in APEC, 10/94<br>Free trade agreement with Mexico (1991)<br>Requested association with MERCOSUR for duty-free trade exempt from MERCOSUR's CET (late 1994)<br>NAFTA members request Chile to join NAFTA, 12/94. |

Mexico nor Canada is comfortable with this situation, both can be expected to make a concerted effort to increase their trade with each other over the coming years.

In addition, Mexico is trying to increase its trade with other Latin American countries in order to reduce its heavy dependence on the U.S. market. In 1991 it signed a free trade agreement with Chile, followed in 1992 by a similar agreement with Venezuela, and in 1993 with Colombia. The accords with the latter two eventually were converted into the Group of Three subregional pact. Free trade agreements with Costa Rica and Bolivia both took effect on January 1, 1995. Mexico is also moving toward a free trade area with Central America and in 1994 joined the Association of Caribbean States, which aims to lower trade barriers among its twenty-five members.

NAFTA's promising future is also related to the limited integration goals of the three countries involved. For now, all that is involved is a free trade agreement, which provides for the elimination of tariffs over fifteen years, beginning January 1, 1994. Most tariffs are lifted immediately. Those involving cars, financial services, and textiles are to be eliminated over a ten-year period. Certain agricultural tariffs are to be eliminated over a fifteen-year period. Each of the three countries can set its own external tariff, in contrast to the situation in a common market where all member countries must adjust to the same external tariff. Although there are no commitments to transform the free trade area into a customs union or a common market, some harmonization along these lines is likely to occur.

Prospects for expanding NAFTA to other Latin American countries will depend mainly on the United States. Despite the commitments on the part of President George Bush and later, President Bill Clinton, to this objective, the expiration of fast-track authority providing for a yes or no vote (with no amendments) by Congress on trade agreements will make congressional approval of additional agreements problematic. On the other hand, if the United States, Mexico, and Canada agree to a more automatic accession procedure, whereby additional countries desiring to join NAFTA would be automatically admitted once they met certain economic requirements, prospects for widening NAFTA to other Latin American countries that meet such criteria will improve.

A more automatic approach would make the widening of NAFTA less dependent on the ultimate success or failure of such Latin American subregional efforts as MERCOSUR or the Andean Group. It would reward countries that have gone farthest in opening their economies, such as Argentina, and encourage laggards to fall into line. Prospects for expanding NAFTA beyond the Western Hemisphere are dimmer, given Europe's absorption with its own integration problems and Asia's reluctance to date to create any formal regional free trade area, even within Asia.

## MERCOSUR

What began as a bilateral agreement between Brazil and Argentina to move toward free trade on a sectorial basis led to the decision, in March 1991, by Argentina, Brazil, Uruguay, and Paraguay to establish a common market by 1995. The progressive decrease in protectionism caused trade among the four MERCOSUR countries to more than double between 1990 and 1993, from $4.1 billion to $10 billion. Looked at from another perspective, intraregional trade among the four countries increased from 9 percent to 17 percent of their total trade during the same period.[10]

With a total population of 196 million people and a combined GDP of $759 billion, MERCOSUR constitutes the largest Latin American trade alliance, yet considerable skepticism existed regarding its viability and prospects until late 1994.[11] The main problem was the vast disparity between the macroeconomic policies of the two anchor countries, Brazil and Argentina. By 1993, Brazil's inflation rate exceeded 2,500 percent annually, while Argentina had moved from a situation of hyperinflation in 1989 to single-digit inflation in 1993. Argentina also opened its economy faster than did Brazil, which helped produce an alarming trade imbalance between the two countries.

The situation changed dramatically after July 1994, when Brazil introduced an economic stabilization program that reduced inflation to single digits by late 1994. One month later, the four MERCOSUR countries settled on a common external tariff of 12 percent, effective January 1, 1995. They agreed to disagree on capital goods, advanced electronics, and petrochemicals, which would not be subject to a common external tariff until 2001. Within MERCOSUR, nearly 90 percent of the products traded could be exported duty-free to member countries from January 1, 1995, onward.

Doubts about the political stability and, by extension, the continuity of the economic opening and stabilization policies in the two key countries also had largely disappeared by late 1994. Argentina's constitutional reform of that year strengthened the reelection prospects of President Carlos Saúl Menem in 1995. In Brazil, the initial success of the economic stabilization plan removed the threat that a leftist labor leader would be elected president and led instead to the victory of the plan's author, Fernando Henrique Cardoso.

As MERCOSUR moved ever closer to becoming a free trade area, investment in the region also increased dramatically. A survey of 550 Brazilian companies in April 1992 showed that 36 percent were planning to increase their links with their MERCOSUR partners, versus 25 percent in 1991.[12] By late 1994, almost 400 cross-border joint ventures had already been formed in sectors such as autos and autoparts, beverages, furniture, metals and telecommunications. Multinational corporations such as Chrysler and General Motors, which had left the region in the late 1970s and early 1980s, respectively, both announced plans to return.[13]

The growing attractiveness of the MERCOSUR market has reduced some of the ambivalence that Argentina, in particular, had regarding membership. When MERCOSUR's future seemed unclear, Argentina seemed more eager to join NAFTA over the Southern Cone market, if forced to choose. With the prospects for a rapid expansion of NAFTA diminished, and the outlook for a successful MERCOSUR enhanced, Argentina decided to concentrate more on its promising nearby markets.

Chile, which had opted to remain outside of MERCOSUR because its external tariff of 11 percent had been significantly lower than those of the four MERCOSUR countries, had favored NAFTA over MERCOSUR even more than had Argentina. Between 1990 and 1993, however, Chile's trade with MERCOSUR increased 67 percent. By the end of 1993, it accounted for 12 percent of Chile's total trade, with Argentina and Brazil constituting Chile's third- and fourth-biggest trading partners, respectively.[14] The new economic realities, combined with diminished prospects for Chile's rapid accession to NAFTA, caused Chile in June 1994 to ask for a special arrangement with MERCOSUR that would allow it to have free trade with MERCOSUR while maintaining its own external tariff for trade with non-MERCOSUR countries. Such an arrangement would allow Chile to pursue its goal of becoming a member of NAFTA. Bolivia, which is a member of the Andean Group, would like to have the same arrangement with MERCOSUR that Chile is seeking.

Whether MERCOSUR lives up to its promise will ultimately depend on the prospects for continued political and economic stability in Brazil and Argentina. Much will depend on what happens over the next several years. If the commitment in both countries to economic stabilization, open economies and political democracy grows stronger, MERCOSUR's future looks bright. By contrast, the viability of the northern blocs is much shakier and highly uneven.

### Andean Group

Like MERCOSUR, the Andean Group, which comprises Colombia, Venezuela, Peru, Ecuador, and Bolivia, is aiming to establish a common market. The original 1996 deadline was accelerated to 1993 but had to be postponed. The two "anchor" countries, Venezuela and Colombia, however, adopted zero tariffs for their bilateral trade, beginning in 1992. By 1993, trade between them had tripled from the 1991 figure. Trade among all members of the Andean Group reached $3 billion by the end of 1993, a threefold increase over the 1990 figure.[15] In mid-1994, the five countries agreed to eliminate tariffs on their intraregional trade, as of January 1, 1995. They also agreed to a flexible common external tariff of several levels, which will give the less developed members of the pact more time to adjust to foreign competition.

Although the five Andean countries have a potential market of 100 million, they show the clearest pattern of external trade dominance. In 1993, Bolivia's trade with the Andean Group accounted for only 5 percent of its total trade. The comparable figures for Peru and Ecuador were 11 percent and 8 percent, respectively. The figures for Colombia and Venezuela were more significant, at 41 percent and 34 percent, respectively, but the bulk of this trade was between themselves.[16]

Although Peru, Ecuador, and Bolivia are all committed to the further liberalization of their economies, the disparities between the two lead countries and their partners raise questions about the pact's viability. Movement away from liberal market policies in Venezuela under President Caldera in 1994 also were problematic. Furthermore, Venezuela and Colombia have joined the Group of Three with Mexico and hope to join an expanded NAFTA. Bolivia itself has stronger links to MERCOSUR than to its own bloc, which helps explain its desire to formalize a relationship with MERCOSUR. In 1992, for example, it earned $76 million on gas sales to Argentina and Brazil alone, whereas its total annual sales to Andean partners were only about $87 million.[17] These forces on the northern and southern perimeter could prove an obstacle to deeper subregional integration and possibly lead eventually to the disintegration of the subregional grouping.

## Group of Three

Colombia, Mexico, and Venezuela are Latin America's main oil producers. Their creation of a trilateral free trade agreement, effective on January 1, 1995, could therefore lead to greater coordination of energy policy in the hemisphere. It is doubtful, however, that the Group of Three, despite its market of 150 million people and its total of $400 billion in economic activity, will become a major trading bloc. Two-thirds of Mexico's trade is with the United States, while the United States is the main market for Colombian and Venezuelan exports. It is more likely that the relationship between Colombia and Venezuela will continue to deepen, which could eventually lead to greater harmonization of economic policies, the free flow of labor, and perhaps a customs union.

## CACM

Similarly, the significant economic disparity in the CACM bloc between Costa Rica and its partners leaves serious doubt as to the group's future. Guatemala, El Salvador, Honduras, and Nicaragua, as well as Panama, which signed in 1993, have begun to dismantle labor and trade barriers. Trade within Central America has nearly doubled from its 1986 low point, but it was still only valued at $1.8 billion in 1992. The region has a common external tariff of 20 percent and is moving toward greater harmonization of economic policies. Plans for moving beyond trade liberalization, however, which included eventually allowing the free flow of labor and the creation of regional political institutions, have now been made voluntary, because of Costa Rica's objections. This country, which has an unemployment rate of 4 percent, compared with Nicaragua's rate of at least 60 percent, is cautious about joining its neighbors' single market plan for fear of a labor invasion. It is clearly looking toward NAFTA instead, as it seeks bilateral trade deals with Mexico and the United States.[18] The future of the entire region ultimately will depend on its integration with Mexico and the United States. Mexico began negotiating a free trade agreement with Central America in 1994, and Venezuela and Colombia announced their intention to do the same. The United States, under the Caribbean Basin Initiative, allows many of Central America's exports (as well as those of the Caribbean countries) to enter the United States duty-free.

## Caricom

Caricom, which represents thirteen Caribbean countries, formed a common market in 1994. Its relatively high common external tariff is projected to fall to 25 percent in 1998. Like Central America, its future depends more on trade links with countries external to the region. Toward this end, it has already signed trade agreements with Venezuela and with Colombia that allow the community's members preferential entry to both markets. It plans to do the same with Mexico. In 1994, Caricom joined with Mexico, Colombia, and Venezuela, and seven Central American countries plus Cuba in forming the Association of Caribbean States. It has a combined market of 200 million people and a total GNP of $500 billion. The new association intends to expand trade and cooperation among its members.

Despite differences in progress toward economic reform, the restructuring process will most likely continue through the decade, primarily because most Latin American countries see it as a prerequisite to their ultimate goal—eventual incorporation into NAFTA or a Western Hemisphere bloc. The subregional blocs are therefore means to an end rather than ends in themselves. This observation is particularly true of the Andean Group, the Central American Common Market, and Caricom. The latter two, whose members are mainly small and poor, need access to larger, more developed markets if they are to prosper economically. The Andean Group's two anchor countries, Venezuela and Colombia, have much more interest in exporting to North America than to their relatively less developed Andean partners.

MERCOSUR is a partial exception to this pattern, principally because Brazil, whose economy is the largest in Latin America, still sees itself as competing with the United States. Brazil is therefore less interested in joining NAFTA than it is in strengthening MERCOSUR so that it can be a counterweight to NAFTA in the hemisphere. It also supports broader trade integration in Latin America, but under its own, rather than Washington's leadership. In October 1993, Brazil therefore called for the creation of a South American Free Trade Area (SAFTA), whose aim is free trade for at least 80 percent of the goods traded within South America by the year 2005. The concept was broadened in August 1994, when the presidents of nineteen Latin American countries pledged to fuse all of Latin America's intraregional free trade pacts into one free trade zone by the end of the decade. The new continental bloc would seek freer trade with the United States as well as with other nations.

## European Community Policies Affecting Latin America

Until fairly recently, European Community policies focused mainly on the former European colonies in Asia and Africa and paid relatively little attention to Latin America. Although Latin American countries are also former European colonies, their "mother countries," Spain and Portugal, were not originally EC members. Only in 1986, when Spain and Portugal joined the Community, did Latin America begin to receive attention on a regional basis.

Compared with other former colonies of Europe, a large number of those in Latin America are relatively wealthy countries. The Community's policies toward former colonies, however, tended to focus on the alleviation of poverty. Little attention was paid to newly industrializing countries (NICs) such as Brazil, Argentina, Chile, and Mexico. Without designing specific policies for these middle-income countries, the Community could not hope to intensify its relationship with Latin America. Furthermore, Europe needed and wanted to expand its trade and investment with these large and fast-growing markets.

As a result of these two factors—the entry of Spain and Portugal and the desire to forge closer relations with the most dynamic economies of the region—the EC after 1986 began to develop policies better geared to Latin American (and Asian) NICs. These policies, which emphasized trade, investment, and the development of ties with the private sectors as well as the governments of these countries, are still evolving.

Prior to 1986, the EC's policies for developing countries emphasized rural development and food aid. Central America and the Andean countries—the poorest of the poor within Latin America—were the main beneficiaries. Interestingly, approximately 40 percent of the technical and financial assistance to Latin America between 1976 and 1991 targeted regional projects and supported regional cooperation and integration. This focus reflected the Community's belief that Central American and Andean integration would enhance economic growth and democracy in both areas.

The European Community also gave some Latin American (and Asian) exports preferential treatment under the Generalized System of Preferences (GSP) well before Spain and Portugal became members. Nevertheless, the far more preferential treatment later accorded to the exports of the Lomé countries—the former French, Belgian, and British colonies in Africa, the Caribbean, and the Pacific—put Latin America's exports to the Community at a competitive disadvantage. After Spain's entry into the Community in 1986, the Spanish became the big promoters of increased European attention to Latin America. Given Spain's historic and cultural links with Latin America, it would gain more influence within the EC if it were seen to be speaking for Latin America.

Spain wanted Latin America to receive the same preferential treatment from the European Community that the signatories to the Lomé Convention of 1975 received. Despite Spain's efforts, however, the best it could get was a joint declaration of intent in which the Community promised to extend and strengthen its ties with the region. The first concrete manifestation of this intention was the Community's decision, in 1987, to admit the Dominican Republic and Haiti, two non-English-speaking Caribbean countries, into the Lomé convention.

Real change only occurred in 1989, however, when the developing areas portfolio, which included relations with Latin America, was given to Abel Matutes, a Spaniard. Helped by Manuel Marín, the Spanish commissioner whose portfolio included relations with the ACP (African, Caribbean, Pacific) countries, the Community began redefining and expanding its relationship with Latin America. Delegations were doubled from four to eight, and EC ambassadors were sent to all Latin American countries. Most important, the new approach produced changes in the treatment of Latin exports to the Community. In November 1990, the EC exempted the Andean countries, except Venezuela, from customs duties for four years, as part of an effort to help them in their struggle against illegal drug trafficking. The following year, in December 1991, Central America and Panama were granted similar terms for three years, to avoid putting them at a competitive disadvantage because of the Andean preferences. Banana exports were conspicuously excluded from these concessions within the EC's GSP, in deference to the interests of the Lomé countries. In February 1993, the EC adopted a single tariff on bananas from Latin America, whereas those from the ACP countries will continue to enter the Community duty-free.

By 1989, the network of EC nonpreferential agreements with Latin America was incomplete and obsolete.[19] Many of Latin America's new democracies were not included, and the agreements did not reflect their new emphasis on private sector–led development. By 1992 new agreements had been concluded with Chile and Paraguay, and existing agreements with

Argentina and Uruguay were renewed. Shortly thereafter, agreements with Brazil, Central America, and the Andean Pact were also modernized.

These so-called third generation agreements continue to provide for traditional development projects, but they also give considerably more emphasis to private sector development, including support for joint ventures between European and Latin American companies, trade promotion, scientific cooperation, technology transfer, energy development, and environmental programs. There are also programs to help Latin America meet the challenge of European harmonization.

These new cooperation agreements (which apply to Asia as well as to Latin America) are multiyear accords, under which the funding for Latin America was increased considerably. Between 1991 and 1995, Latin America is to receive about one billion ECUs for financial and technical help and economic cooperation. This amount represents a 100 percent increase over the previous five-year allocation.[20]

Unlike the EU's cooperation agreements with other regions, those involving Latin America allocate a greater proportion of funds for the strengthening of regional integration. The EU provides major funding to the administration in charge of Andean integration, for example. It has also been deeply involved in the restructuring of the CACM and, in response to Latin American requests, created a "MERCOSUR desk" within the European Commission to coordinate relations.

In mid-1994, EU officials, encouraged by a 33 percent jump in European exports to Latin America since 1992, had preliminary discussions in Brazil about granting preferential tariff treatment to MERCOSUR. The European Parliament also raised the possibility of creating an Atlantic common market and asked the European Commission to explore prospects for negotiating a free trade agreement with the subregional trade groupings of Latin America.[21]

All cooperation accords between the EC and Latin America since 1990 include references to human rights and all, except for those with Mexico, condition cooperation on the continuation of democracy. (A new EC budget line to sustain Latin American democratization was, until 1992, restricted to Central America and Chile, but it is now open to other Latin American countries.) Such conditions were written into the agreements in response to Latin American leaders' requests, and are specific to the region. Attempts by the EC to include similar conditions in their cooperation agreements with Asia were rebuffed.

Latin American leaders, with Spanish help, also succeeded in getting the EC to open the European Investment Bank to Latin America. In 1992, the bank was allowed to start loan operations in countries where the EC had concluded cooperation agreements. The positive impact of this decision, which also benefits Asia, was offset somewhat by the limited funding that will be available during the initial three-year period.

Another breakthrough for Latin America is the recently negotiated fishing agreement between the European Union and Argentina, which will allow the Europeans to fish in Argentine territorial waters. In return, Argentina will benefit from preferential tariffs for the export of its fish to the European Union. It will also receive funds from the EU for research and technological innovation and will end up with an ultramodern fleet as a result of a European-Argentine joint venture.

Despite the new EU approach toward Latin America, it remains unclear whether the EU's efforts will offset the potentially negative impact on Latin America of the creation of a Single European Market. On the one hand, European harmonization will make it easier for Latin America to export to Europe by streamlining regulations. On the other hand, harmonization has, in many cases, led to higher rather than lower standards, which makes it more difficult for Latin America to export to Europe.[22]

In the end, whether Latin America benefits or loses may depend less on Europe's actions than on its own. Much of the decline of Latin America's relative share of the European market over the past decade, for example, can be attributed to the region's near economic collapse in the aftermath of the debt crisis of the early 1980s and to the fact that Latin America's European exports have been concentrated primarily in raw materials and agriculture during a period when commodity prices have been declining. Only if Latin America succeeds, through productivity improvement and technology transfer, in upgrading its export portfolio, will it become more competitive, not only vis-à-vis the EU, but globally as well.

## Implications of the Differences
## Between European and Latin American Integration

The fact that Latin America is following a very different path toward economic integration from that followed by Europe has produced considerable skepticism on the part of many observers regarding the attainability of Latin America's integration goals. The main problems are the following:

- *The Pace of Integration.* Latin America is trying to accomplish in a decade or less what it took Europe thirty-five years to achieve.
- *Overlapping Agreements.* Countries within the various subregional blocs are signing overlapping bilateral or trilateral free trade agreements with both insiders and outsiders.
- *Macroeconomic Variance.* Each subregional group includes countries with vast economic asymmetries. MERCOSUR, for example, includes Brazil, which has the biggest economy in Latin America, and Paraguay, which has one of the smallest and most rural. Within the Andean Pact, Colombia's economy is far more developed than Ecuador's.

- *The Absence of Social Cohesion Funds*. The Latin American integration agreements do not provide for "social cohesion" funds, whereby the richer countries agree to transfer resources to the poorer ones in order to compensate them for loss of control over their economies and to minimize the political fallout from the social dislocation that will inevitably ensue as a result of the process of integrating their economies with more industrialized ones.
- *The Low Level of Intraregional trade*. The more developed countries in each of the subregional blocs have much higher levels of external than internal trade.
- *The Absence of an "Anchor" Country*. Within Latin America, the lead country in terms of the size of its economy should be Brazil. Until recently, its political and economic problems made it unable to play such a role, although this situation may be changing. Mexico's ability to play this role has been hampered by its membership in NAFTA, where the United States is the anchor. There are two lead countries within the Andean Group, and no real leaders in Central America or in Caricom.

These issues, while clearly separating the Latin American situation from the European model, are not intractable. Although it started from a low baseline, intraregional trade has grown rapidly in recent years as Latin America's economies have opened up. The absence of "social cohesion funds" may be offset by the recent establishment, by the United States and Mexico, of a North American Development Bank to fund infrastructure and community development projects. Finally, the potential for fragmentation due to economic disparities and the lack of "anchor countries" can be offset by strong U.S. leadership. A driving force behind Latin America's race to integrate is the hope of eventual linkage to NAFTA. If Washington abdicates its leadership role in forging a Western Hemisphere free trade area, however, and Brazil and/or Mexico do not fill the leadership vacuum, the various subregional trade blocs could splinter or become progressively less relevant to the trade and investment of the major Latin American countries.

## BUSINESS RESPONSE TO REGIONAL INTEGRATION

Although in the 1980s multinational business extended to most of Latin America the familiar dictum about Brazil: "It is the country of the future and always will be," business perceptions from the North and across the Atlantic have recently started to change. However, attitude shifts have been slow to drive actual behavior, particularly in Europe. For the European business community, current trends are still too mixed to fully support

Latin America's hope for a successful transition from the "lost decade" of the 1980s to a "growth decade" in the 1990s.

## The New Business Climate

### Market Liberalization

The macroeconomic stabilization plans adopted by many Latin American countries have clearly begun to pay off, although unevenly.

There has been a trend of declining inflation for most countries. The average weighted increase for the region's Consumer Price Index (CPI), which was as high as 1200 percent in 1989–1990, fell to 320 percent in 1992, and actually dropped to 23 percent if Brazil is excluded.[23] The performance drivers were Chile and Mexico. However, in the wake of the December 1994 peso devaluation, Mexico's inflation is expected to rise from its 1994 low of 7 percent to at least 16 percent by government estimates. Through a strict monetary policy centered on its Convertibility Law (stipulating dollar/peso parity and 100 percent dollar backing for all pesos), Argentina, which had a CPI inflation rate of 1,345 percent in 1990, brought this down to 7 percent in 1993, with an estimated decrease to 4 percent in 1994.[24]

Economic growth, although explosive in 1990–1992 (10 percent in Chile and 9 percent in Argentina for 1992), had slowed by 1993 (6 percent for both Chile and Argentina, and only .4 percent in Mexico).[25] One worrisome factor is the growing current-account deficit in several countries.

Argentina's current account swung from a surplus in 1990 to a deficit of 3.5 percent of GDP two years later. By 1994, Mexico's current-account deficit had reached 8 percent of GDP; the fact that it was partly financed by speculative capital, combined with renewed unrest, triggered investor flight and a sharp devaluation. Although Argentina's peso is, by most measures, far more overvalued that was its Mexican counterpart, this may be partly offset by positive factors: A strict budgetary policy, an increase in longer-term foreign direct investment, and a convertibility system thought to be more solid than Mexico's crawling peg. Nevertheless, there are some expectations that Argentina's currency may come under stronger pressure in the future.

As noted above, Brazil remains a major concern. Its 160 million people account for more than half the population of Latin America, and its $500 billion economy is twice the size of Eastern Europe's. Growth is uneven (negative in 1992, 5 percent in 1993, expected to slow in 1994), but it is running a significant trade surplus. Although it joined the MERCOSUR customs union on January 1, 1995, it will still keep a 20 percent levy on capital goods and another high tariff on high-tech products. It also still has significant restrictions on foreign investment and a seemingly intractable external debt ($119.5 billion in 1992, versus $114 billion in 1993, and an estimated $118 billion in 1994).[26] Finally, a key concern is the outcome of the *unidade real de valor* (URV) plan enacted in 1994 to control an inflation that had averaged 30 percent a month in 1993.

### Barriers to Trade and Investment

Although Latin America is making evident progress, the region still presents significant barriers to trade and investment, particularly in the three major areas of infrastructure, quality competitiveness, and income distribution.

*Infrastructure.* Unlike many Pacific Rim locations, Latin American production sourcing sites can be located near major natural resource stockpiles (energy, metals, and agricultural raw materials). Transportation difficulties seriously erode this advantage. One recent study showed that a typical cargo shipment by road from Cartagena, Colombia, to nearby Maracaibo, Venezuela, took sixteen days: five and a half for transportation and ten and a half for delays and paperwork—despite the fact that trade between the two countries is free of almost all duties and nontariff restrictions.[27] Physical links such as paved roads from Mexico to Chile or railways joining the MERCOSUR, Andean, and CACM countries are largely nonexistent. Within MERCOSUR, the Hidrovía project linking the hinterland to the Atlantic will take ten years to complete at a cost of $980 million.[28] Although air travel is improving thanks to privatization and the expansion of U.S. airlines, cargo is still not cost effective in Latin America. A U.S. greeting card manufacturer, for instance, found that it was cheaper, safer and faster to route all Latin American shipments through a Miami hub than through a Brazilian one.

Telecommunications are no less problematic. In Mexico, privatized Telmex has a backlog of about 1.1 million lines to be installed. In Argentina, Entel (privatized and split into Telefónica and Telecom), despite a 1992 combined investment of $1.4 billion, still had an average repair time of eleven days (down from thirty-four days under state ownership).[29] Distribution networks also vary widely by country, making a single regional strategy impossible. Trade concentration is significant in Brazil, with three major supermarket chains, but small outlets still dominate consumer goods sales in such countries as Bolivia.

Media patterns are somewhat more harmonized because most major markets show a high penetration rate for television. Households with television, as a percentage of total households, range from 90–98 percent in Mexico, Chile, Argentina, and Venezuela to 74 percent in Brazil, and 73 percent in Colombia.[30] A fully panregional advertising strategy is still not feasible, however, because of diverging regulations and localized media. In Mexico, all television advertising is sold through a government agency, and Peru requires local production of all commercials. Furthermore, CPMs (cost per thousand advertising impressions) are high when adjusted for much of the audience's minimal purchasing power.[31]

*Quality and productivity competitiveness.* Although they are top competitive requirements in the Organization for Economic Cooperation and Development (OECD) countries, quality and customer satisfaction have too often been nonissues in Latin America. Trade barriers ensured captive markets, and this factor was compounded by a lack of consumer protection regulation. Competitive imports have now forced plant upgrades, but quality leaders still tend to be foreign. A 1992 study found a significant gap between Brazilian firms and foreign subsidiaries. For instance, 60 percent of local firms had quality control training versus 100 percent of the foreign subsidiaries; only 48 percent of the local firms had reduced production costs versus 80 percent of the foreigners; and only 28 percent of locals had more integration with suppliers versus 71 percent of the subsidiaries.[32] This quality lag is a major factor in the limited scope of Latin America's export portfolio (which still consists mostly of commodities to developed countries, with the exception of Chile).

Similarly, a 1994 McKinsey Global Institute study of Latin American productivity in four sectors (banking, food processing, steel, and communications) found that, in the first three industries, productivity averaged 30 to 40 percent of U.S. levels; in telecommunications, it reached a 60 percent rate. However, privatized sectors are showing significant improvement: From 1989 to 1993 Mexican steel producers closed the gap with the U.S. by 16 points and the Brazilians by 11 points—even though U.S. steel productivity itself rose by 27 percent. By contrast, retail banking (heavily regulated) and food processing (fragmented and undercapitalized) show little or no improvement in the same period.[33]

*Income distribution.* Rhetorical outbursts hailing the creation of MERCOSUR as a huge trading zone of approximately 190 million people and an average per capita gross national product (GNP) close to South Korea's—are highly misleading because they do not factor in Latin America's income distribution, which has become even more highly skewed over the past decade. Companies that depend on the existence of significant middle-class consumer markets are still not likely to find them on the required scale in Latin America. In Brazil the top 10 percent of the population receives 48 percent of the income, and in Argentina 35 percent. Throughout MERCOSUR, the top 10 percent of the income ladder enjoy a GNP per capita of $11,400—close to the $12,500 OECD average, but this represents only 18 million people (comparable to the Czech/Slovak population). By contrast, the middle 70 percent of the income ladder (about 128 million) have a per capita GNP of $1,800, a third of South Korea's and half of Portugal's. The bottom 20 percent (36 million), with a per capita GNP of $332, less than half the average for all developing countries, are virtually outside the market altogether.[34]

Besides presenting a problem at the regional level (lack of midmarket critical mass), income structure and other economic disparities are threatening the ultimate success of current trade blocs. Instead of looking at the trade map to classify countries, for instance, Citibank uses two groupings:

"convergent" countries with effective solutions, such as Chile, Uruguay, Colombia, and Mexico, and "nonperforming countries," such as Brazil and Peru. (See Table 2.5 for economic variance within the region)

## European Trade and Investment Strategies

Despite this mixed economic picture, the recent progress made in some Latin American countries has prompted new European investment (although concentrated in a few sectors) and some reorganization reflecting the emerging subregional blocs. There has been no progress in trade, however, even with Spain and Portugal.

### Trade Patterns

As noted above, EC trade patterns over the last decade reveal two main trends: a sharp increase in intra-EC trade, resulting from the easing of trade restrictions, and an increase of external trade with other developed nations (the OECD share of EC trade rose from 48 percent in 1980 to 60 percent in 1990). EC exports to Latin America as a percentage of total exports decreased from 2.2 percent in 1985 to 1.8 percent in 1990, reflecting the weaker demand in Latin America throughout the 1980s. Although EC imports from Latin America have stagnated, their composition has changed. In 1980, only 11 percent of the import portfolio was in manufactured goods, versus 24 percent by 1990.[35]

Both exports and imports from the EC to MERCOSUR increased from 1988 to 1990, but this was offset by a significant decrease in trade with the Andean Group and by a 30 percent decline in imports from CACM (the primary CACM export is bananas). As noted above, the EU chose in 1993 to give preferential (duty-free) treatment to banana imports from the Lomé Convention (ACP) countries.

From 1980–1989, Spain's exports to Latin America declined both in dollar terms and as a percentage share of Spain's total exports, from 11 percent to 4 percent. Latin America's share of Spain's imports showed a similar decline, from 11 percent to 5 percent. In the same period, Spain's exports to the EC rose from 50 percent to 67 percent of its total exports, and its imports from the EC climbed from 31 percent to 57 percent (see Table 2.6).

### Investment Flows

By contrast with trade, FDI flows to Latin America from Europe, which had declined during the peak of the debt crisis (1983 to 1986), recovered in the late 1980s. In the 1987 to 1990 period, FDI into Latin America from Europe (excluding Switzerland) was $6.3 billion, versus $8.4 billion from the United States, and $1.4 billion from Japan. (See Table 2.7) If Switzerland is included, Europe was the lead investor in the region. In 1991, con-

**Table 2.5  Economic Variance—Latin America**

| | GDP per Capita | | Population | | GDP Growth | | Population Growth Rate | Inflation | | Exports 12 Months | | Total External Debt | | Literacy Rate |
|---|---|---|---|---|---|---|---|---|---|---|---|---|---|---|
| | 1993 | 1994E | 1993 | 1994 | 1993 | 1994E | | 1993 | 1994E | 1993 | 1994E | 1993 | 1994E | |
| Mexico | 3,821 | 4,003 | 91.0 | 93.0 | 0.4% | 2.7% | 2.0% | 8.0% | 7.2% | 51.9 | 60.6 | 127.8 | 136.8 | 89% |
| Mercosur | | | | | | | | | | | | | | |
| Argentina | 7,552 | 8,121 | 33.5 | 33.9 | 6.0% | 5.6% | 1.2% | 7.4% | 3.9% | 13.1 | 14.6 | 71.7 | 76.0 | 96% |
| Brazil | 2,863 | 2,989 | 159.3 | 162.4 | 5.0% | 3.6% | 2.0% | 2,709% | 940% | 38.8 | 42.2 | 114.3 | 116.9 | 82% |
| Paraguay | 1,307 | 1,364 | 4.6 | 4.7 | 2.5% | 2.5% | 2.7% | 15.0% | 15.0% | 1.4 | 1.5 | 2.2 | 2.6 | 91% |
| Uruguay | 4,565 | 4,738 | 3.1 | 3.2 | 5.0% | 3.0% | 0.6% | 14.2% | 15.2% | 1.7 | 1.9 | 5.4 | 5.7 | 96% |
| Andean Pact | | | | | | | | | | | | | | |
| Bolivia | 726 | 750 | 8.1 | 8.3 | 3.0% | 3.2% | 2.9% | 8.5% | 9.0% | 0.6 | 0.7 | 4.7 | 5.1 | 79% |
| Colombia | 1,399 | 1,589 | 34.0 | 34.7 | 5.3% | 4.5% | 2.1% | 22.6% | 24.0% | 7.4 | 8.7 | 18.2 | 20.1 | 87% |
| Ecuador | 1,303 | 1,353 | 11.0 | 11.2 | 2.0% | 3.4% | 2.4% | 31.0% | 25.0% | 2.9 | 3.0 | 13.1 | 13.8 | 87% |
| Peru | 2,198 | 2,412 | 22.9 | 23.4 | 7.0% | 9.0% | 2.1% | 33.5% | 22.0% | 3.5 | 3.8 | 22.1 | 24.3 | 86% |
| Venezuela | 2,977 | 2,729 | 21.0 | 21.0 | -1.0% | -3.0% | 2.3% | 45.9% | 65.6% | 14.1 | 14.5 | 37.2 | 37.5 | 89% |
| CACM | | | | | | | | | | | | | | |
| Costa Rica | 2,364 | 2,481 | 3.1 | 3.2 | 6.5% | 4.5% | 2.2% | 7.3% | 7.9% | 2.0 | 2.3 | 4.1 | 3.9 | 93% |
| El Salvador | 1,350 | 1,482 | 5.5 | 5.6 | 5.0% | 4.7% | 1.4% | 7.4% | 8.3% | 0.6 | 0.6 | 2.3 | 2.6 | 75% |
| Guatemala | 1,121 | 1,205 | 10.0 | 10.3 | 4.0% | 3.8% | 2.9% | 11.2% | 12.4% | 1.3 | 1.4 | 3.4 | 4.0 | 56% |
| Honduras | 591 | 614 | 5.6 | 5.8 | 3.7% | 3.5% | 3.2% | 3.3% | 3.6% | 0.9 | 0.9 | 3.8 | 4.0 | 75% |
| Nicaragua | 442 | 448 | 4.3 | 4.4 | -0.9% | -0.4% | 3.3% | 20.0% | 20.0% | 0.3 | 0.3 | 11.6 | 12.0 | 57% |
| Chile | 3,288 | 3,518 | 13.8 | 14.0 | 6.0% | 4.5% | 1.7% | 12.2% | 10.0% | 9.2 | 10.4 | 21.3 | 22.3 | 94% |

*Source:* International Financial Statistics CD-ROM, World Bank; United Nations Human Development Report; and Salomon Brothers, Inc. Estimates.

*Note:* Population growth rates are calculated as an average of the last five years' growth rates.

**Table 2.6**    **Foreign Trade Among Spain, Portugal, and Latin America, 1975–1989**
**(Percentage Shares)**

|       | SPAIN Exports to: | | PORTUGAL Exports to: | |
| --- | --- | --- | --- | --- |
| Year  | EC | LA | EC | LA |
| 1975  | 44.6% | 10.1% | 50.2% | 2.6% |
| 1980  | 49.5% | 10.5% | 54.9% | 2.6% |
| 1985  | 49.9% | 5.9%  | 58.4% | 1.6% |
| 1989  | 66.8% | 4.1%  | 71.8% | 0.7% |

|       | SPAIN Imports from: | | PORTUGAL Imports from: | |
| --- | --- | --- | --- | --- |
| Year  | EC | LA | EC | LA |
| 1975  | 35.3% | 8.6%  | 44.5% | 5.9% |
| 1980  | 31.3% | 10.5% | 45.2% | 5.0% |
| 1985  | 36.7% | 11.5% | 45.7% | 6.1% |
| 1989  | 57.1% | 4.9%  | 68.1% | 3.7% |

*Source: United Nations, Handbook of International Trade and Development Statistics, 1990.*

**Table 2.7**    **FDI Flows to Latin America and the Caribbean from Europe, the United States, and Japan, 1979–1990**
**(Excluding Flows to Offshore Centers; US millions)**

|                  | 1979–82 | 1983–86 | 1987–90 | Total |
| --- | --- | --- | --- | --- |
| Europe[a]        | 5,097  | 3,506 | 6,314  | 14,917 |
| United States    | 8,524  | –415  | 8,412  | 16,521 |
| Japan            | 2,058  | 555   | 1,364  | 3,977  |
| Total (of above) | 15,679 | 3,646 | 16,090 | 35,415 |

*Source: Foreign Direct Investment in Latin America, Institute for European–Latin American Relations and Inter-American Development Bank, Madrid/Paris, 1993, p. 3.*
*Note:* a. Excluding Switzerland.

tributions from Spain, Italy, Germany, and the Netherlands continued their upward trend. Spanish FDI in Latin America, in particular, rose from $193 million in 1980 to $580 million by 1991, and Spain is increasingly concentrating these investments in Argentina, Chile, Brazil, and Mexico. (These four markets accounted for 84 percent of Spanish FDI to Latin America in 1990.) Overall, there is a clear pattern of European FDI flows to Southern Cone countries, while U.S. flows dominate in Mexico. In

1991, 75 percent of German investment went to Argentina and Brazil, and about 80 percent of Dutch investment also targeted Brazil; similarly, Italy's flows went mainly to Argentina and Brazil as well as to Chile.

Within the Southern Cone, each major market shows a distinct investment pattern. In Argentina, Spain and France were the lead investors with 45 percent and 27 percent of total 1990 European FDI, respectively. In Brazil, the U.K. led with 43 percent of total European 1990 FDI, and the Netherlands and Germany followed with 23 percent and 12 percent, respectively. Foreign investment has historically favored certain sectors in Brazil: automobiles (where 95 percent of domestic sales are generated by foreign companies), electronics and telecommunications (90 percent), pharmaceuticals (80 percent), and chemicals (72 percent). Chile presents yet a different pattern, with (as in Brazil) the United States as lead investor, but with European FDI led by Spain with 41 percent of the 1990 total. By contrast, Mexico's FDI is overwhelmingly led by the United States with 80 percent of total world FDI in 1990; Europe only accounts for 14 percent of investment, and is led by Germany, followed by France, the U.K., and Spain.[36] (See Tables 2.8 and 2.9)

### New Investment Strategies

European companies now operating in Latin America fall into two main categories: long-established large multinationals, ranging from Nestlé to Unilever, who already have a direct sales and production presence in most countries, and newer entrants such as France Télécom and Iberia, who were largely attracted by the recent wave of privatizations.[37]

In 1992, Latin America led the world in privatization, accounting for 35 percent of world total in value (up from 6 percent in 1988). Although Mexico was the leader, attracting some $20 billion from 1988 to 1992, Argentina sold major companies, including strategic ones such as YPF, whose 45 percent initial public offering brought in $3 billion.[38] Not including YPF, by June 1993, the privatization program had brought in revenues of about $5.5 billion in cash, $6.8 billion in debt paper at nominal value, and an additional $2.9 billion at market value, more than half of which represented foreign direct investment. Although, as of mid-1993, almost 42 percent of the shareholdings in controlling consortia of privatized companies was held by Argentina, Spain was the leading foreign investor with almost 15 percent, followed by the United States, Italy, and France. Foreign investment continues to rise and is expected to total $2 billion in 1994 alone.[39] Besides privatization, recent investment has been driven by factors affecting specific industries, such as deregulation and pent-up demand.

In addition to increasing its banking investments in North and South America, Spain has made major moves in telecommunications and airlines. Telecommunications, mostly state-owned in the 1980s, are being

**Table 2.8a  Argentina: FDI Flows (Millions U.S.$)**

|  | 1979–1982 | 1983–1986 | 1987–1990 | 1985 | 1986 | 1987 | 1988 | 1989 | 1990 |
|---|---|---|---|---|---|---|---|---|---|
| Belgium | 1 | 10 | -35 | 4 | 4 | -1 | -21 | -12 | -1 |
| France | 426 | 35 | 97 | 9 | 3 | 19 | 11 | 17 | 50 |
| Germany | 210 | 76 | 338 | 8 | 29 | 153 | 70 | 127 | -12 |
| Italy | 12 | 32 | 61 | 35 | -1 | 48 | 2 | -3 | 14 |
| Netherlands | 76 | 52 | 51 | — | 10 | 7 | 25 | -15 | 34 |
| Spain | 133 | 18 | 162 | 4 | 6 | 18 | 32 | 30 | 82 |
| Switzerland | n.a. | n.a. | n.a. | n.a. | n.a. | n.a. | n.a. | n.a. | n.a. |
| United Kingdom | 145 | 143 | 204 | 38 | 65 | 60 | 81 | 46 | 17 |
| Europe | 1,003 | 366 | 878 | 98 | 116 | 304 | 200 | 190 | 184 |
| USA | 1,577 | 437 | -138 | 73 | 233 | -86 | -224 | 8 | 164 |
| Japan | 113 | -26 | 44 | 4 | 6 | 14 | 16 | -14 | 28 |

**Table 2.8b  Brazil: FDI Flows (Millions U.S.$)**

|  | 1979–1982 | 1983–1986 | 1987–1990 | 1985 | 1986 | 1987 | 1988 | 1989 | 1990 |
|---|---|---|---|---|---|---|---|---|---|
| Belgium | 54 | 0 | 143 | 3 | -5 | -2 | 56 | 52 | 37 |
| France | 331 | 89 | 102 | 15 | 21 | -14 | 52 | -18 | 82 |
| Germany | 947 | 385 | 482 | 32 | 18 | 111 | 233 | 35 | 103 |
| Italy | 299 | 431 | 337 | 80 | 8 | 38 | 166 | 103 | 30 |
| Netherlands | 112 | 172 | 410 | -1 | 60 | 73 | 5 | 127 | 205 |
| Spain | 77 | 16 | 73 | 4 | 3 | 7 | 13 | 10 | 43 |
| Switzerland | n.a. | n.a. | n.a. | n.a. | n.a. | n.a. | n.a. | n.a. | n.a. |
| United Kingdom | 578 | 822 | 1,706 | 135 | 368 | 475 | 444 | 413 | 374 |
| Europe | 2,398 | 1,915 | 3,253 | 268 | 473 | 688 | 969 | 722 | 874 |
| USA | 1,991 | 705 | 5,378 | 106 | 31 | 669 | 1,403 | 2,252 | 1,054 |
| Japan | 1,063 | 659 | 958 | 180 | 62 | 10 | 374 | 324 | 250 |

*Source:* OECD, Paris.

**Table 2.9a  Mexico: FDI Flows (Millions U.S.$)**

| | 1979–1982 | 1983–1986 | 1987–1990 | 1985 | 1986 | 1987 | 1988 | 1989 | 1990 |
|---|---|---|---|---|---|---|---|---|---|
| Belgium | 5 | 9 | -20 | 1 | 7 | 26 | -11 | -54 | 19 |
| France | 94 | 12 | 113 | 2 | 1 | 38 | 7 | 12 | 56 |
| Germany | 204 | 233 | 431 | 23 | 10 | 131 | 38 | 102 | 160 |
| Italy | -1 | 2 | 30 | 0 | 1 | 2 | 12 | 15 | 1 |
| Netherlands | 12 | -6 | 14 | -1 | -8 | 2 | 12 | — | — |
| Spain | 189 | 27 | 109 | 4 | 6 | 21 | 27 | 15 | 47 |
| Switzerland | n.a. | n.a. | n.a. | n.a. | n.a. | n.a. | n.a. | n.a. | n.a. |
| United Kingdom | 126 | 130 | 74 | 48 | 40 | 186 | 102 | -262 | 48 |
| Europe | 629 | 407 | 751 | 77 | 57 | 406 | 187 | -172 | 331 |
| USA | 2,005 | 223 | 4,157 | 510 | -139 | 241 | 607 | 1,360 | 1,949 |
| Japan | 808 | 0 | 203 | -224 | 78 | -36 | 44 | 38 | 157 |

**Table 2.9b  Chile: FDI Flows (Millions U.S.$)**

| | 1979–1982 | 1983–1986 | 1987–1990 | 1985 | 1986 | 1987 | 1988 | 1989 | 1990 |
|---|---|---|---|---|---|---|---|---|---|
| Belgium | 20 | -1 | 5 | 1 | 2 | 1 | 4 | -3 | 3 |
| France | 22 | 12 | 62 | 0 | -1 | 12 | 14 | 17 | 19 |
| Germany | 21 | 4 | 16 | 2 | 2 | -4 | 6 | 7 | 7 |
| Italy | 0 | 2 | 5 | 1 | 1 | — | 5 | 0 | 0 |
| Netherlands | — | — | 39 | — | — | 2 | — | 8 | 29 |
| Spain | 114 | 112 | 215 | 11 | 23 | 18 | 42 | 90 | 64 |
| Switzerland | n.a. | n.a. | n.a. | n.a. | n.a. | n.a. | n.a. | n.a. | n.a. |
| United Kingdom | 101 | 105 | 285 | 48 | 18 | 58 | 111 | 82 | 34 |
| Europe | 278 | 234 | 627 | 63 | 45 | 87 | 182 | 201 | 156 |
| USA | 412 | 116 | 890 | 25 | 99 | -7 | 291 | 313 | 293 |
| Japan | 22 | 40 | 62 | 30 | 1 | 4 | 29 | -3 | 32 |

*Source:* OECD, Paris.

privatized throughout the subcontinent and present enormous potential due to the current low rate of telephone penetration. MERCOSUR countries, for instance, are close to South Korea in electricity consumption (averaging 1,600 kwh per capita, versus South Korea's 1,900 kwh) and in television set ownership, but they lag behind in telephones. Only 6 percent of the population in Latin America is connected by telephone, compared to 71 percent in the United States, 45 percent in Europe, and 16 percent in Asia. France alone has more telephones than all of Latin America.[40]

In parallel with AT&T's and Motorola's major equipment sales and investment in Mexico, Spain's Telefónica, France's Télécom, and Italy's STET have invested in the Southern Cone. With assets totaling $38.5 billion, generating almost 2 percent of Spain's GDP, Telefónica has major globalization objectives. Its impressive past performance is at risk under new EC directives abolishing monopolies in data transmission, electronic mail, mobile communications, private data networks (which represent 14 percent of Telefónica's revenues) and possibly international calls (another 12 percent of revenues). Telefónica's globalization initiatives in Europe, except for investments in Romania and Portugal, have been thwarted by stronger players, but it has been able to take advantage of Latin American privatization, although many of its acquisitions were in dismal shape. Its roster of Latin American holdings includes a 44 percent stake in Chile's Teléfonos, 20 percent of Entel (Chile's long-distance company), and 8 percent of Telefónica de Argentina. Even though a common language allows the company to maximize its telecommunications technology investment, the return so far has been uneven. Its $450 million investment in Chile, as might be expected, has so far been the most profitable because Teléfonos, at its 1989 purchase date, was already a well-run company. In Argentina, however, Telefónica found a company that had never been audited. After making radical moves, such as slashing the work force by 25 percent, it managed to make a profit, but it expects its effort to build up basic networks to be a multiyear commitment. Because of investment demands at home (the company has slated $53.5 billion through 2002 to bring Spain up to EC standards) and continued outlays in Latin America ($4.5 billion has been earmarked for Chile and Argentina over the next five years), Telefónica is expected to be more conservative through the rest of the decade.[41]

Apart from telecommunications, the other leading sector for Spanish investment (also driven by privatization and deregulation) is air transportation. Although it incurred persistent losses, the state-owned Iberia became the largest European carrier in Latin America as a result of an $800 million investment. Results so far have been highly problematic. Iberia's purchase of a 30 percent stake and management control of Aerolíneas Argentinas was plagued by losses, conflicts with local investors, and by strikes, and the airline has announced that it would sell its stock. Venezuela's Viasa, in which Iberia has a 45 percent stake and management control, is also incurring losses. By contrast, Chile's Ladeco, in which Iberia has a 35 percent stake but no management control, is profitable.[42] Iberia's current Latin American portfolio is highly uneven in size and performance. Scope varies from 8 billion revenue passenger kilometers (RPKs) for Aerolíneas Argentinas to only 884 million for Ladeco; load factors (percent of seats sold) are unacceptable, ranging from 64 percent for Aerolíneas Argentinas to a low of 57 percent for Viasa. Besides improving productivity, priorities such as establishing a common reservation system linked to Amadeus entail massive training costs.

Although survival in a deregulating Europe depends on alliances, Iberia's network is limited (pacts with Alitalia and Royal Air Maroc, and a route-specific alliance with Japan Airlines). It therefore hopes to gain a key advantage by being the first foreign carrier to be granted fifth-freedom rights in the United States, allowing it to set up its pan-American hub in Miami. The combination of a Miami hub and a Latin American network should be a positive factor, unless further investments stretch its resources beyond the extreme limits already reached.[43]

Concurrent with air transport investments, tourism has also attracted Spanish funds, but in a different geographical pattern. The leading location is Mexico (where the Sol-Melia group invested $1 billion in six hotels), given the volume and development stage of the local industry, second to oil in revenue generation. Secondary projects include the transformation of Buenos Aires's old port into hotels and shopping centers, with the hope that it will attract some $500 million in foreign investment.[44]

### Regional Reorganization Strategies

Among large European multinationals, the consensus is that, although MERCOSUR and other blocs are not "top of mind," business is ahead of government in its strategic response. This response is flexible and pragmatic, exploring all avenues on a case-by-case, country- and sector-specific basis. Historically, companies in such sectors as consumer goods or pharmaceuticals had to localize production because intraregional exports were not feasible due to labeling, packaging, health, trademark, or other regulations.

For Nestlé, among others, one objective is to "rationalize, specialize, delocalize." Nestlé/Argentina now has some imports from Chile, and it is exploring ways of exploiting "natural export advantages." For instance, Argentina is cost-effective in agribusiness, and in particular, has a comparative advantage in derived dairy products such as powdered milk, due to its relative efficiency and counterseasonality; it may therefore become in time an export base for Nestlé in these products to the rest of the region.

The same localized production pattern prevails in the cosmetics and household products sector. Although in detergents, Unilever currently dominates the Southern Cone with twenty-four plants in Brazil, two in Argentina, and one in Chile and Uruguay, it is interested in some rationalization of supply. Similarly, Reckitt & Coleman, a subsidiary of the U.K.-based Reckitt and Coleman plc, has been in Latin America for seventy years and has direct production in all countries, with particular strength in Brazil, Argentina, Chile, Mexico, and Colombia. Although historically barred by legislation from shipping finished household products, it does supply some waxes and plastics on a multicountry basis.

These companies may be starting some consolidation on the supply side, but the vast majority of their brands remain local. McCann Erickson, which handles accounts such as Nestlé, L'Oréal, American Home Products, Nabisco, and Gillette, reports little demand so far for regional advertising campaigns. Latin American markets remain, by and large, characterized by strong brand loyalty and the dominance of long-established local brands.

Although Gessy Lever in Brazil is working on harmonization, those of its brands that sell well in several markets were not developed as regional brands; rather, they are quasi-global brands such as Dove bath soap (strong in Brazil, Argentina, and Chile, but also sold under the same brand name in Italy and the U.K.) or Lux (with a global scope). Because of brand loyalty in detergents, Omo is sold only in Brazil, not in the rest of the Southern Cone. The Lever portfolio may include some potential panregional brands (Le Sancy bath soap has half of the Chilean market and is sold in markets as diverse as Kenya and India), but the company has undertaken no systematic effort toward panregional segmentation.

The situation is entirely different in the automobile sector. Even in the largest market, Brazil, a relatively small proportion of the population can afford a car, and the need to increase exports is clear. Although the Brazilian auto industry generated almost $3 billion in revenues in 1992, it still has insufficient economies of scale to compete globally, with only 1.2 million units per year versus 15 million in the United States or Europe.[45] Some auto parts suppliers are setting up export programs to complement their domestic production and improve economies of scale.

The combination of a highly inflationary economy and a low level of productivity has led to inefficient operating patterns and contributed to relatively high labor costs. Average hourly compensation is about 1.4 times in Brazil and over twice in Argentina what it is in Mexico. Priorities for the industry in the Southern Cone are therefore cost competitiveness and productivity enhancement. Improving the local supply is crucial in Brazil, since the industry has a 70 percent local content (for decades, foreign parts were not allowed to be fitted on locally made cars). Accordingly, Autolatina (a Ford-Volkswagen joint venture, now split again except for trucks), through an eighteen-point supplier program, has seen significant improvement in recent years and also reports customer satisfaction levels of 90 percent among new car buyers.

Although market development levels vary widely (inhabitants per car range from 8 in Argentina, to 12 in Brazil and 50 in Colombia, versus 2 in the United States), the industry is also targeting an emerging pan-regional, low-end segment. In 1993, Autolatina initiated a six-month program to reintroduce the VW Beetle (or "Fusca") seven years after production stopped in Brazil. The car is also produced in Mexico. With a few changes, such as new catalytic converters, the cars are priced competitively in Brazil at $7,200. Predictably, both GM and Fiat also launched "popular cars" at similar price levels. A record 568,000 vehicles were sold in the first half of 1993 (a 44 percent increase over the first half of 1992).

This success may be due in part to macroeconomic action. The Brazilian industry successfully appealed to the government to reduce its tax burden: A tax of 35 percent of retail price now applies only to upscale models, while "popular cars" are taxed at 13 percent (versus 6 percent in the United States and 8 percent in Japan). Brazil's automakers are also aligning themselves with the EU in demanding some protection for the rest of the decade. Although the EU set volume limitations on Japanese imports at 8 percent of European vehicle sales through 1999, Brazilian industry and unions want (in addition to import duties on foreign cars) an import quota of a maximum of 7 percent of domestic sales through 2000.[46]

In Argentina, although producers have been hampered by what has been termed "Argentina costs" (a fiscal and regulatory burden that included payroll taxes at the 49 percent level) as well as by a strong peso, they are also expanding domestically and regionally. A pending labor reform should mitigate rigid work rules and help lower operating costs. Meanwhile, the auto industry is performing well, with output estimated at a record 380,000 to 400,000 units in 1994, compared with 342,000 units in 1993.

Although Argentine producers continue to be protected from non-MERCOSUR imports by a 30 percent tariff, they fear dumping from Brazil as the customs union eliminates many internal tariffs in January 1995. However, they have already experienced intra-MERCOSUR trade increases and, like their Brazilian counterparts, see significant potential in panregional models.

Sevel, for instance, a $2 billion associate company of the SOCMA group, formed by the 1980 merger of Fiat Automotores and Safrar Peugeot, leads with approximately half of the Argentina market. The company has seen its trade with MERCOSUR increase from $507 million to $571 million in 1992 to 1993, and it is expanding both in Brazil and Uruguay. In the low-end segment, Sevel produces the successful Fiat Vivace in

Argentina, priced at $7,300, and expects that a popular regional car in the future will be the Fiat Uno 1000, now produced in Brazil. One of Sevel's objectives for 1995 is to establish the Fiat 178 (to be produced jointly in Argentina and Brazil) as a regional automobile.[47]

In summary, therefore, the strategies of multinationals are sector-specific. Some rationalization of supply is being initiated, but the structure of demand and distribution remains fairly localized. Although some global brands are sold on a multicountry basis, there has been no major move to develop panregional brands in consumer products. In contrast, a low-end multicountry segment does appear to be emerging in the automobile sector (driven in part by the need for economies of scale and by the MERCOSUR integration).

## Latin American Business Strategies

As with European business, there has been no universal Latin American response to the emerging trade blocs. Company strategies differ by sector and region. External trade expansion depends more on quality improvement and portfolio diversification than on trade-bloc formation, but internal trade and investment also show different patterns by region and market size.

### Trade Patterns

External trade by the ALADI countries greatly overshadows intraregional trade (which dropped from 14 percent to less than 13 percent of total trade in the 1980s before rising again in the 1990s).[48] However, a fundamental weakness of ALADI's external trade portfolio is its nondiversification. Of the top thirty-five exporting firms in Latin America, twenty-four are locally owned, but only two are noncommodity exporters (see Table 2.10). Other exports range from oil and mining to agribusiness. No significant portfolio change can be expected until local quality levels match world standards.

The evolution of internal trade in the last fifteen years shows a consistent pattern: Smaller countries maintain a greater share of their trade with ALADI than do the larger states. The latter have increasingly globalized rather than regionalized. Chile's, Brazil's, and Mexico's exports to ALADI as a percentage of total exports *declined* from 1980 to 1991, and Argentina's and Venezuela's barely increased. Tariff cutting in the MERCOSUR zone propelled internal trade from $4.1 billion in 1990 to $9.5 billion in 1993, but the share of Brazil's exports to MERCOSUR, although it tripled since 1990, still takes only 14 percent of total.[49] (See Figure 2.3)

In addition, strong new connections exist outside blocs, such as those between Argentina and Chile. Chile itself, already considered a First World country, constitutes a powerful alternative approach to the fledgling trade blocs within the region.

Table 2.10   Latin America's Top Thirty-Five Exporting Firms, 1992

| Company | Country | Exports (US$ mil) | Sector |
|---|---|---|---|
| PDVSA* | Venezuela | 13,958 | Petroleum |
| Pemex* | Mexico | 10,009 | Petroleum |
| Codelco | Chile | 3,021 | Mining |
| Ford | Mexico | 1,400 | Automotive |
| Vale do Rio Doce* | Brazil | 1,394 | Mining |
| General Motors | Mexico | 1,358 | Automotive |
| Ecopetrol* | Colombia | 1,317 | Petroleum |
| CVG* | Venezuela | 1,205 | Metallurgy |
| Telmex | Mexico | 915 | Telephone |
| Minpeco* | Peru | 855 | Mining |
| Petrobrás | Brazil | 736 | Petroleum |
| Federación Nacional de Cafeteros* | Colombia | 711 | Food |
| Enami* | Chile | 677 | Mining |
| Southern Peru Copper* | Peru | 674 | Mining |
| YPF* | Argentina | 625 | Petroleum |
| Fiat | Brazil | 570 | Automotive |
| Sucocítrico Cutrale* | Brazil | 462 | Food |
| Industrial Minera* | Mexico | 461 | Mining |
| Met-Mex Peñoles* | Mexico | 454 | Mining |
| Volkswagen | Mexico | 431 | Automotive |
| Mexicana* | Mexico | 428 | Airline |
| Embraer* | Brazil | 401 | Aeronautics |
| IBM | Mexico | 372 | Electronics |
| Ford | Brazil | 368 | Automotive |
| Citrosuco Paulista* | Brazil | 365 | Food |
| Usiminas* | Brazil | 357 | Steel |
| Siderúrgica de Tubarão* | Brazil | 353 | Steel |
| Ceval Agroindustrial* | Brazil | 346 | Food |
| Alcoa | Brazil | 333 | Aluminum |
| Somisa* | Argentina | 330 | Steel |
| Occidental* | Colombia | 325 | Petroleum |
| Shell | Colombia | 321 | Petroleum |
| MBR* | Brazil | 314 | Mining |
| Albrás | Brazil | 306 | Aluminum |
| Cargill | Argentina | 294 | Food |

*Source:*  Economist Intelligence Unit, *Seizing Free Trade Opportunities in the Americas,* September 1992.
*Note:*  *Locally owned.

Figure 2.3   Intra-MERCOSUR Exports as Percent of Total

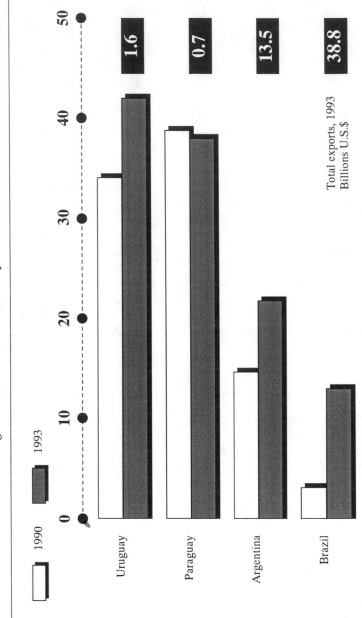

Total exports, 1993
Billions U.S.$

*Sources:* IMF, 1994; *The Economist*, August 13, 1994, p. 59.

Unlike its neighbors, and thanks to early deregulation and privatization, Chile has achieved a diversified export profile and remarkable economic growth. Its copper production has doubled since 1973, making Chile the world's leader, but copper's share of total export earnings has dropped from 82 percent to 42 percent. Overall exports jumped from $3.8 billion in 1985 to $9.6 billion today, and the country's GDP growth has averaged 6 percent annually since 1986. Chile has now become an exporter, not only of fish, fruit and wine, but also of banking, printing, engineering, and other services.[50]

Chile is developing global trade patterns, but it is also moving into the ALADI and, especially, the MERCOSUR countries. Chile's treaty with Mexico resulted in a doubling of their modest bilateral trade; tariff-cutting agreements with Argentina also resulted in a doubling of their trade to over $1 billion in 1992.[51] As in Brazil's case, the growth in Chile's exports may lead to a trade imbalance. In addition, there are tensions in the agribusiness sector between the two countries' producers of wine and fruit.

Chile's investment moves are even more aggressive than its export strategies. In the early 1990s, Chilean investment in Argentina rose tenfold, to $500 million in 1992. Argentine investment in Chile was less than a tenth of that. Most of these flows are concentrated in the energy sector. A $1 billion joint venture will provide 8 million cubic meters of Argentine natural gas a day to Chile. Chilean firms (Endesa, the largest electricity generator, and Chilectra Metropolitana, a Santiago-based utility), having paid $500 million for the Argentine utility Edesur, now supply a large part of the Buenos Aires market. Chile is also investing in the retailing sector in Argentina by setting up supermarkets, and in the mining sector, where the Argentine parliament has recently set up tax incentives for foreign investors.[52] Chile, however, continues to hedge its regional bets. As noted above, although increasing its links with MERCOSUR, it has also been admitted into APEC and has been invited to join NAFTA.

## Latin American Company Strategies

In this context of "multiple speed" regional integration, the strategies of Latin American companies differ broadly by sector and country.

### Privatized Acquisitions
In countries such as Argentina, large local companies are major players in the purchase of state assets. Strategies range from "grabbing what you can and sorting it out later" to focused investment in core businesses. The most aggressive buyer in Argentina, for example, was Perez Companc, which managed to spend $980 million for stakes in telephone companies, utilities, oil fields, refineries, and a pipeline as well as road and train concessions.

Some analysts are concerned, however, about Perez Companc's high debt load (at least $350 million), its overly dispersed holdings, and its over-payment for some assets.

In Argentina's oil, gas, and construction sector, Sociedad Comercial del Plata invested less and tended to acquire assets that reinforced its core energy and construction businesses. It is divesting some unrelated pur-chases, such as its share of Telefónica, which sold at a substantial profit. In steel, construction, and engineering, Techint spent over $500 million for steelmaker Somisa, a phone company, oil fields, gas and electrical distri-bution, and road and rail concessions. Although some acquisitions repre-sent a diversification strategy, Techint's goal is to channel them into its construction and engineering businesses. Astra was the most focused, in-vesting almost $350 million in its core energy business, bringing its sales to an estimated $640 million in 1993. Like Comercial del Plata, the group has started restructuring, selling its stake in a cellular phone company, and rationalizing its engineering interests.[53]

## Media Regionalization

The sector that has clearly placed itself at the vanguard of regionalization is the media industry. Brazilian publisher Abril and broadcasting compa-nies such as TV Globo have moved across borders and language barriers with Spanish versions of Brazilian products, from comic books to televi-sion programs; conversely, Mexican "telenovelas" have become the first Latin American TV import to Brazil. In the last two years, Televisa, Mex-ico's major media company, spent $550 million to take partial control of Univisión. Televisa went on to buy 49 percent of a Chilean network and a 76 percent share in Compañía Peruana de Radiodifusión. In print, it spent $130 million to acquire Editorial América, a group of eighty regional mag-azines, from Spain's Grupo Anaya. Similarly, Brazil's Abril group launched *Panorama*, a monthly business magazine in Spanish, on the Argentine mar-ket in 1992.[54]

## Other Sectors: Mixed Patterns

In consumer goods, Latin American companies are largely adopting the same approach as their European counterparts. The giant Bunge y Born has historically followed a localized production and country-specific brand policy. In beverages, Argentina's Quinsa Group has started a geographic expansion of its core business by entering the Chilean market in 1991 but believes that building a regional brand would be very costly, given local-ized market preferences; after its Quilmes brand (the leader with a 55 per-cent share of the Argentine market) tested negatively in Chile, Quinsa en-tered the Chilean market with another brand.

In high technology, the few local players are pursuing both global and regional policies. Brazil's "technology showcase," the aircraft manufacturer

Embraer, suffered significant losses in recent years, due in part to cuts in the Brazilian military budget, but also to the world civil market slowdown. (Its civil aircraft sales represent 70 to 80 percent of total.)

For its EMB-145 fifty-seat jet aircraft, Embraer has now expanded its global alliances, including links to Spain, Belgium, the United States, and France; these complement an earlier agreement with Italy's Alenia on the AM-X aircraft as well as subcontract work for Boeing and McDonnell-Douglas. At the regional level, Embraer has also established cooperation programs with Argentina and Chile's ENAER.

Embraer plans to continue a market-niching strategy with the twin-engine commuters (especially the EMB-145), which represent the largest product line in its portfolio, and will also expand its turboprop trainer family. Its biggest target for commuters are in the United States and Europe, but the Pacific Rim and Australia are also growing in importance.


## CONCLUSION

A comparison of trade bloc formation in Europe and Latin America reveals some similarities as well as sharp divergences. On both sides of the Atlantic, a centrally planned integration process is giving way, because of market and political factors, to a fuzzier, multitiered, and multipolar set of hybrid groupings that may evolve according to different timetables. For a number of reasons, the European model is, in its scale, scope, and evolution, largely inapplicable to Latin America. Vast development disparities, a large variance between natural economic clusters and political blocs, and the distorting effect of NAFTA, with its powerful "call of the North," all combine to distinguish the Latin American situation from the European one.

From a business standpoint, the economic links between the two regions reflect the worldwide shift from interregional trade to investment. The initial European response to Latin American integration efforts was the appearance of new investment (focusing, for Spain and other countries, on certain sectors such as telecommunications, banking, and transportation, made recently attractive by privatization and deregulation). The second European response to integration was the approach of established multinationals, which are beginning to rationalize supply but still think that panregional brands are largely not viable because of localized market preferences.

Latin American bloc–driven strategies are as diverse as their groupings. Although intraregional trade remains small in comparison with external trade, it has begun to show improvement in certain locations, whose linkages may (Brazil-Argentina) or may not (Chile-Argentina) be related to trade blocs. Investment flows follow the same patterns, with stronger linkages in the Southern Cone than in the northern blocs.

There are increasing indications that there may be a future "shake-out" between current blocs; some are already fragmenting, others are likely to be absorbed by NAFTA, and stronger ones such as MERCOSUR are hampered by different levels of development, scale, and commitment among members as well as by competing trade and investment flows.

In summary, Latin America's competitiveness and its progress toward becoming an equal partner of Europe appear to depend less on the formalization of government-driven groupings than on a sustained and universal commitment to the stabilization and market liberalization strategies already initiated by the leading countries.

## NOTES

Françoise Simon thanks Ambassador Arnoldo Listre, consul general of Argentina, and Ambassador Marco Meira Naslausky, consul general of Brazil, as well as Arnaldo Musich of Techint, Fulton Boyd of Boyden do Brasil, and Donald Nicholson of PROFIT/Deloitte Touche for their invaluable help in facilitating a series of interviews in Buenos Aires and São Paulo in August 1993. In addition, she expresses her deep appreciation to the following individuals for their kind assistance in granting her interviews: Ambassador Jorge Herrera Vegas and Minister Guillermo Harteneck in Argentina, and chief executive officers or senior executives of the following companies: Aerolineas Argentinas, Autolatina, Bunge y Born, Ciba-Geigy, Citibank, Embraer, Ernst & Young, Gessy Lever, McCann Erickson, Nestlé, Quinsa Group, Reckitt & Colman, Rede Globo, Sociedad Comercial del Plata, SOCMA, Techint, Telecom Argentina, Varig, and Caesar Park/Westin Hotels.

Susan Kaufman Purcell thanks Ambassador Angel Viñas, head of the Delegation of the European Communities to the United Nations; John Kriendler, the Deputy Assistant Secretary General for Political Affairs, NATO Headquarters: and Francisco Bataller M., principal administrator of the European Communities, for generously giving of their time in arranging interviews for her during her visit to Brussels, January 23–29, 1993. She also thanks the many officials of the EU as well as the European and Latin American ambassadors to the EU with whom she spoke, for sharing with her their insights and ideas and for the extensive documentation that they provided.

1. Kenichi Ohmae, "The Rise of the Region State," *Foreign Affairs* 72, Spring 1993, pp. 78–87.

2. *Eurecom* (monthly bulletin of EC economic and financial news), July/August 1994, p.2.

3. "The EC: Back to the Drawing Board," *Economist*, July 3, 1993, pp. 5–19.

4. Ibid.

5. *Target 92*, October 1992 (Newsletter on the Single Market), p. 1.

6. "Switzerland and the EC: The Difference," *Economist*, December 12, 1992, p. 59.

7. "Europe's Open Future," *Economist*, February 22, 1992, pp. 47–48.

8. "Yankees Go East," *Business Week*, January 18, 1993, p. 26.

9. *América Economía*, September 1995, pp. 26, 76.
10. *Economist*, June 18, 1994, p. 5, and August 13, 1994, p. 59.
11. *U.S./Latin Trade*, August 1994, p. 51.
12. "Economic Integration in the Southern Cone," *North-South Focus*, University of Miami, December 1992, pp. 1–6.
13. *U.S./Latin Trade*, August 1994, p. 51.
14. *Financial Times*, August 5, 1994, p. 4, and August 12, 1994, p. 4.
15. *Economist*, June 18, 1994, p. 5.
16. *Americas Trade and Finance*, June 1994, p. 12.
17. "To NAFTA and EMU, a Child," *Economist*, July 17, 1993, pp. 63–64.
18. Ibid.
19. Angel Viñas, "Spanish Policy Toward Latin America, from Rhetoric to Partnership," Iberian Studies Institute, University of Miami, May 1992, p. 18.
20. Francisco Bataller M., "La Transformación Política de América Latina y la Contribución de la Comunidad Europea a la Democratización y a la Protección de los Derechos Humanos en la Región," in Alberto Herrero , ed., *Los Derechos Humanos en Latinoamerica: Una Perspectiva de Cinco Siglos*, Cortes de Castilla y León, Valladolid 1992, mimeograph, p. 11.
21. *New York Times*, June 13, 1994, p. D1.
22. "Latin America and Europe: Toward the Year 2000," IRELA, Dossier No. 40, September 1992, p. 21.
23. *Economic Panorama of Latin America 1992*, ECLAC (Santiago: United Nations), September 1992, p. 6.
24. Bear Stearns, *Global Development*, August 4, 1993, p. 2, KPMG, *Hemisphere*, 1993, pp. 8–11, and Salomon Brothers estimates, 1994.
25. "Latin America Survey," *Economist*, November 13, 1993, pp. 5–28, and Salomon Brothers estimates, 1994.
26. "Latin America Survey," and Salomon Brothers, 1994.
27. *Seizing Free Trade Opportunities in the Americas*, Business International Research Report, New York, 1992, p. 28.
28. "Public Services, Private Pesos," *Economist*, July 17, 1993, pp. 38–40.
29. *Seizing Free Trade Opportunities*, p. 26.
30. McCann Erickson Latin America–Caribbean, *Media Facts* 1992–1993, p. 4.
31. Jon Martinez, John Quelch, and Joseph Ganitsky, "Don't Forget Latin America," *Sloan Management Review*, Winter 1992, pp. 78–92.
32. *Seizing Free Trade Opportunities*, pp. 22–23.
33. McKinsey Global Institute, *Latin American Productivity*, Washington, D.C., June 1994.
34. *Latin American Weekly Report*, January 9, 1992.
35. *International Trade 1990–91*, vol. 1, GATT, Geneva, 1992.
36. Inter-American Development Bank and Institute for European–Latin American Relations (IRELA), *Foreign Direct Investment in Latin America and the Caribbean*, Madrid/Paris 1993.
37. This section and the next are based in part on a series of interviews conducted by Françoise Simon in Buenos Aires and São Paulo in August 1993.
38. "Selling the State," *Economist*, August 21, 1993, pp. 18–19.
39. "Privatization as a Catalyst for Foreign Direct Investment in Argentina," presentation by Guillermo Harteneck, Subsecretary for Investment, Argentine Ministry of Economy, conference on FDI relations with dynamic nonmember economies, OECD, Paris, July 12–13, 1993; also *Business Latin America*, May 16, 1994, p. 5.

40. Martinez, Quelch, and Ganitsky, "Don't Forget Latin America," p. 84.

41. Maria Pico, "Telefónica Pursues Overseas Opportunities," *Telephony*, August 3, 1992, pp. 9–10.

42. "El Conquistador," *Economist*, May 7, 1993, p. 77.

43. Martin Noble, "Iberia's Grand Strategy Takes Shape," *Aerospace World*, July-August 1992, pp. 41–44.

44. Martinez, Quelch, and Ganitsky, "Don't Forget Latin America," p. 87.

45. *World Motor Vehicle Data* (MVMA) 1992, and Autolatina internal documentation.

46. "The Bugs from Brazil," *Economist*, August 21, 1993, p. 54.

47. *Business Latin America*, May 16, 1994, p. 4. Also internal documentation from Sevel Argentina, S.A.

48. *Handbook of International Trade and Development Statistics*, United Nations, 1990.

49. IMF, 1994; also *Economist*, Aug. 13, 1994, p. 59.

50. "How Chile Busted Out of the Growth Basement," *Business Week*, December 28, 1992.

51. "Patchwork," *Economist*, May 15, 1993.

52. Ibid.

53. "Four Big Argentine Firms Stake Future on Role in Nation's Privatization Push," *Wall Street Journal*, March 10, 1993.

54. "Media: Rebuilding the Spanish Empire," *America Economía*, December 1992, pp. 9–10.

# 3

# Germany and Latin America
## *Wolf Grabendorff*

Aside from the United States, Germany is Latin America's most important economic partner. Yet it does not appear to have a very strong overall relationship with the region. Because of its postwar history, Germany has never developed a true Latin American "policy." Its priorities have centered, for obvious reasons, on relations with its Western neighbors and on its security relationship with the United States. In its policy toward the South, Germany has tended to concentrate on major actors, such as Egypt and India; it is in this latter context that one should view its relations with Brazil.

The absence of a defined policy does not mean that Germany lacks a visible profile in the region. But its profile is the outcome of a relationship that is much broader and far more complex than Germany's economic and diplomatic activities in the region would appear to demonstrate. Transnational actors such as political parties, churches, trade unions, and solidarity groups play a greater role in Germany's relations with Latin America than with any other part of the developing world. Germany's links with the region are much more solid and differentiated than those it maintains with Africa, the Middle East, or the Far East.[1]

Many Latin Americans worry that this presence could now be changing. Some observers suggest that except for its obligations within the European Union (EU), Germany will now give undivided attention to its eastern European neighbors and will have few human and material resources left to maintain its traditionally high profile in Latin America—a trend aggravated by the enormous costs associated with German unification.[2]

It would be ironic if the post–Cold War order were to result in Germany and the United States focusing most of their attention on their respective geographical neighbors: Eastern Europe and Latin America. Historically, these regions have had a very mixed relationship with their rich and powerful neighbors to the north and west. Both regions will in the future continue to face major political and economic changes and the need for reform. In order to meet those challenges, they may find it more promising to diversify their external links, moving away from excessive dependence on one partner.[3]

Why does Latin America still seem to have such a positive view of Germany? A number of reasons come to mind:

- Germany is seen as the economically and technologically most advanced European power.
- Compared to Britain and France, Germany is seen as having few responsibilities and even fewer priorities in the African, Caribbean, and Pacific (ACP) countries.
- Germany is thought to be relatively more supportive of a liberal trade regime than are many of its partners in the North.
- Germany is still seen as a country where economic development and social justice have been relatively well balanced.[4]

Such sentiments are widespread among Latin Americans. Although it is not clear to what extent they will shape the region's future relations with Germany, they certainly differ from Latin America's views with respect to the United States.

German interests in Latin America have been of a different nature than those of the United States. Historically, Latin America was perceived as a continent of unlimited economic possibilities. Its people—some of whom emigrated from Germany generations ago—were seen to abide by value systems similar to those of the German people. Hence, Germans have often found it easier to do business with Latin Americans than with others in the developing world. Dramatic political and economic reforms in much of Latin America over the past decade—democratization, market liberalization, and the promotion of the private sector—have increased Germany's feeling of kinship with the region. There is a growing impression among Germans that military dictatorships, human rights violations, and constant instability in the region belong to the past. Germans' and Latin Americans' perceptions of each other have drawn closer: Latin Americans are seen as less "exotic" in their economic and political behavior, and the Germans are seen as less perfect and, given postunification priorities, possibly less strong and resourceful than before.

In the evolving international system—in which military might has lost some of its importance compared to financial capacity, economic efficiency, and technological inventiveness—Germany is likely to remain an important partner for Latin America. This partnership will nevertheless be defined within and possibly be constrained by Germany's overall geopolitical agenda and its commitment to European integration. Germany will continue to take into account U.S. interests in Latin America, which now focus increasingly on trade rather than security concerns. But here again, a certain complementarity of interests is becoming visible, with stronger U.S. economic penetration in the Greater Caribbean and northern Latin America and, with the exception of Mexico, a concentration of German interests in the Southern Cone.

Hence, although German unification and Germany's growing responsibilities in eastern Europe seemed to promise a new, less intensive relationship with Latin America, it was not by accident that the first postunification visit abroad of a German chancellor was Helmut Kohl's October 1991 visit to Latin America. At the time, no German chancellor had visited Latin America since 1979.

## HISTORICAL DIMENSIONS OF THE RELATIONSHIP

Because Germany was never a colonial power in Latin America, early German–Latin American contacts must be traced to the waves of German immigration into the region that corresponded with the periodic economic and political crises in modern German history. Most Germans arriving in Latin America before the Second World War were motivated by a simple desire for land and work. They headed mainly for the Southern Cone countries. Later immigration waves, in contrast, were much more the direct result of political developments in Germany. During the late 1930s, most immigrants were German Jews and other political refugees, who settled mainly in Argentina, Mexico, and some of the Andean countries. The most recent tide of immigration occurred at the end of the Second World War. Although some immigrants were former Nazis, most were refugees from parts of Germany taken over by the Soviet Union and Poland.[5] Today, Latin America is home to about five million people of German origin. An estimated two million still speak German. In general, they have integrated themselves extremely well into their societies and, during the postwar era, in particular, they have helped German business interests to flourish in the region, especially in the Southern Cone countries.

The values of Germans who immigrated to Latin America some decades ago, or of those born in the region, tend to differ considerably from the values of German businesspeople, diplomats, and representatives of the German aid agencies active in the region, and Germany's image has not always benefited from the political opinions and social behavior of its expatriates. However, their contribution to economic and cultural development in certain regions of Latin America should not be underestimated nor should their function as a link between official German interests and those of the region itself. The last group of German immigrants settled in Latin America about half a century ago, so their impact on relations between the two regions is likely to decline in the future.[6]

The traumatic experience of the Third Reich is similarly distant in time, yet for many decades its legacy overshadowed relations between Germany and Latin America, and its impact is still felt today. Some Latin American countries, under pressure from the United States, severed diplo-

matic ties with Germany after 1941. Others declared war on Germany only
in 1945. The rupture in diplomatic relations led to the confiscation of most
German firms and financial assets in the region. In some countries, it also
led to a radical change in perception with regard to Germans living in
Latin America and toward Germany itself. Meanwhile, the German communities in the region were split between those in favor of, and those
against, the Third Reich. When diplomatic and economic relations with
Germany resumed in the early 1950s, most Latin American countries refused to compensate local Germans for the losses they had incurred during
the war. Yet the willingness of many countries to accept a large number of
German political and economic refugees was stressed by the Federal Republic as a very positive factor in the evolving pattern of the new relationship.

Postwar German diplomacy toward Latin America was heavily influenced by the Hallstein Doctrine: Any country that recognized the German
Democratic Republic (GDR) faced a possible break in relations with the
Federal Republic. Although the existence of two Germanies had little impact
on West Germany's relations with Latin America in general, it did make a
difference in some countries, such as Cuba and Mexico, and under some
regimes, such as the Allende period in Chile and the Sandinista period in
Nicaragua. The GDR invested considerable political and human capital in
developing strong relations with countries whose official ideological positions it considered useful to the advancement of the socialist cause. Its financial and material commitment was especially strong in Cuba.

The GDR was never a genuinely important political or economic actor
in Latin America, even after most countries in the region recognized it as
a sovereign state. On the other hand, West Germany was much closer to
the United States in all East-West–related conflicts in Latin America than
it would have been if there had been only one Germany. With unification,
the new Federal Republic assumed responsibility for the GDR's development projects in the region, notably in Nicaragua and Cuba, a problematic
legacy. (After the Soviet Union, the GDR was Cuba's most important trading partner and its largest supplier of aid and technical know-how.) The financial strains of unification, which will affect the German economy for
years to come, may prove very costly for Latin America, as Germany turns
its attention toward its own region.

## INTERESTS AND POLICIES

### Germany's Political Intentions

Germany has traditionally maintained a low profile in its political relations
with the region. In fact, German political scientists have repeatedly blamed
their government for its benign neglect of the region, for relying on the

already existing cultural, economic, and political bonds established at the nongovernmental level.[7] The increased political attention given to Latin America since 1989—demonstrated by the growing number of official German visits to the region—has two determinants: German interests in the region and the changing international context.

Latin America clearly is of interest to Germany, particularly given the potential for expanding existing economic and cultural links. However, Latin America remains a developing region marred by instability. Consequently, German policy toward the region is characterized by a combination of development cooperation and economic "partnership," which implies reciprocity and equality in economic relations. It has sometimes been difficult to reconcile these two sets of interests. Initiatives to promote social stability and peace have clashed with economic interests, for example, where arms trade with Latin American countries is concerned. On the political front, Germany's main interests with regard to Latin America are the following.

- The establishment of stable economic conditions, which is important given Germany's trade and investment links with the region.[8] Economic stability is also believed to constitute the basis for stable political systems.[9]
- Support for democracy and human rights, which not only reflects an ideological position, but also the desire among German politicians to maintain relations with countries that have similar political cultures and values.[10]
- Maintaining peace and political stability. Germany was a key supporter of the Contadora initiative and the Arias Peace Plan for Central America. One of the most pressing issues today is the drug problem and drug-related terrorism in Colombia, Bolivia, and Peru, particularly given the recent rapid increase in drug flows to Europe.
- Strengthening Germany's cultural presence in Latin America, partly because there are over five million people of German descent in the region and also because Germans desire to promote German as a major international language.

Germany's political profile toward Latin America has developed against the background of conflicting foreign policy interests, which are undergoing a process of redefinition within the overall context of national and European priorities. Political engagement in Latin America is constrained by the fact that the emerging democracies in eastern Europe are becoming a new priority on Germany's foreign policy agenda. The enormous financial burden this imposes on Germany (mostly in the form of economic aid) makes it difficult for Germany to seek greater economic exposure in Latin

America at the same time, since this would also involve financial obligations, as with Chancellor Helmut Kohl's promise to the Brazilian government to jointly fund a pilot project for the protection of the Amazon rainforest.

However, several factors linked to the recent changes in the international system have rendered political engagement in Latin America more attractive for Germany: First, the end of the Cold War opens new possibilities for strengthening political and economic relations between Latin America and the EU. The dominant European perception of Latin America as a sphere of U.S. influence is becoming obsolete. Moreover, given its own budgetary difficulties, the United States is increasingly keen to share the burden of development cooperation with the EU and its member states, particularly its largest contributor, Germany. Second, democratic consolidation in Latin America has strengthened German political interest in the region. To a degree, Germany feels morally obliged to support democracy and human rights worldwide in order not to jeopardize its international credibility as a democratic nation. The absence of democracy in the 1970s and early 1980s was one reason why Germany distanced itself from Latin America. Third, some German politicians consider themselves to be experts on democratic consolidation, given their experience with, and insight into, the political reform processes of eastern European countries; and many Latin Americans regard Germany's social market economy and its particular form of pluralistic democracy as a model for their own political systems.[11]

Because of their recent learning process, Germans now tend to demonstrate more tolerance toward others grappling with the difficulties of democratic transition and economic reform. Latin America has benefited from this in that Germany treats the region more realistically and with greater understanding than it did prior to unification.

Although political relations have not been strong at the governmental level, close political links exist between Latin American and German nongovernmental organizations (NGOs). The recent German government initiatives in Latin America suggest, however, that Germany is making new efforts to bring its official political relations in tune with the broad nature of its relations with the region in general. Germany's pluralistic structure allowed such transnational actors as political parties, trade unions, and churches to establish strong links independent of the government. Such ties were intended to strengthen Latin American civil society against dictatorship.

German political parties—the Christian Democrats, the Social Democrats, the Liberals, and the Conservatives—are courted by their Latin American counterparts, and their involvement in Latin America has served to bolster their international standing and to widen their political horizons.[12]

The parties enable the German government to keep in touch with opposition parties and political counterelites in Latin America. The relations of both German churches and trade unions with their respective counterparts in Latin America are also quite close.

German policy with regard to the region will have to take into account this divided structure. It may prove difficult to integrate the specific interests of various transnational bodies into the general profile of German official policy, however. The lack of a consistent perspective concerning political commitments in Latin America has often become an issue of conflict within Germany. Certain Latin American issues have also played an important role in the domestic political debate in Germany, particularly with regard to Bonn's stance on Central America and on the conservation of the Amazon rainforest. Any new policy toward Latin America will have to evolve within the context of these internal (as well as external) constraints.

## Economic Linkages

German business interests in Latin America date back to the early sixteenth century and precede any diplomatic or political ties between the two regions. During the colonial era, such interests remained very modest due to Spain's virtual monopoly over trade with the New World. Soon after independence, however, Prussian industries, and businesses in the prominent *Hansestädte* (foremost among them Hamburg) began a concerted effort to penetrate the markets of Latin America, which promised enormous opportunities and gains. The 1820s and 1830s saw the conclusion of a number of bilateral trade and shipping agreements, and business relations developed rapidly in the following decades. After trade and shipping followed investment, mainly in Mexico and the Southern Cone countries of Argentina, Brazil, and Chile.

For several decades, Germany's growing economic presence in the region was not matched by similar efforts on the political side. Only toward the end of the century did Germany increase its diplomatic efforts in Latin America, and then it did so mainly to protect existing business links against rising U.S. influence in the region and to support the interests of the growing number of German immigrants, mainly in southern Brazil.

By the beginning of the First World War, 10 percent of all foreign investment in Latin America was of German origin; these investments represented an estimated 15 percent of total German foreign direct investment (FDI). In 1914, Germany was the second largest supplier of goods to the continent after Britain. By 1938, it still held that position, but this time after the United States. After the Second World War, which seriously damaged German–Latin American political and economic links, the newly founded Federal Republic of Germany made efforts to regain lost territory and to establish a strong presence in the continent once again. Trade picked up in the 1950s, and German companies began to invest heavily in the region—mainly in Brazil and Mexico—during the "boom years" of the 1960s and 1970s.

Today, Germany is the region's second-largest trading partner after the United States. It is Latin America's most important partner in the European Union: its biggest EU donor (providing 30 percent of all EU official development assistance [ODA] to Latin America), its biggest EU investor (along with Britain), and its biggest EU trading partner. It holds a large portion of Latin America's foreign debt (almost 40 percent of EU bank claims in the region). One country in the region—Brazil—is Germany's main economic partner among less developed countries (LDCs) after China. São Paulo, with around 600 German companies, is home to the world's largest German industrial "enclave" outside Germany itself.[13]

Yet there have been signs in recent years that this important economic relationship is losing its strength. This loss is most pronounced in the area of trade. Although commercial exchanges between the two regions have grown in absolute value over the last decades, Latin America is clearly a business partner of declining relative importance to Germany. Germany has turned increasingly "inward": Compared to a few decades ago, it trades relatively more with its EU partners than with non-EU countries. Thus, the share of extra-EU imports in its total imports declined from 60 percent in 1960 to 45 percent in 1991. EU agricultural protectionism, discriminatory tariff structures, and preferential treatment for ACP countries have all had detrimental effects on trade with Latin America. Furthermore, the inward-oriented development policies followed by Latin American countries during the 1960s and 1970s hindered the region's ability to keep up with technological developments that would have enabled its exporting companies to remain competitive vis-à-vis emerging exporters in other parts of the world, notably Asia.

There is widespread fear among Latin American countries that this trend will be aggravated by recent developments in Europe: First, that the Single European Market (SEM) will lead to a further boost in intra-EU trade and that companies will have to continue to invest heavily in domestic capacity in order to remain competitive in the enlarged European market. Second, that German unification—particularly the task of modernizing the eastern *Länder*'s inefficient industrial sector—and the reconstruction of the eastern European and former Soviet economies is bound to swallow up a large chunk of western Europe's, and Germany's, capital and economic efforts over the coming years. This focus could weaken investment activity in other regions of the world—Latin America, among others—where German investment has traditionally been of considerable importance.

However, there are trends that point in another, more positive, direction. Many Latin American countries have adopted open-market, export-oriented development strategies and are offering increasingly attractive investment conditions to their external partners. After the "lost decade" of the 1980s, business confidence is slowly returning to the continent. The "emerging markets" of Latin America are also engaged in renewed and, it seems, more promising efforts at regional integration. The North American Free Trade Agreement (NAFTA) and the Southern Cone Common Market (Mercado Común del Sur, or MERCOSUR) offer new possibilities to foreign investors: more transparent trade and investment regulations and larger target markets, among other things. These are the developments on which Germany seems to be banking when it stresses its continued interest in strengthening economic relations with Latin America.

## Trade

For Germany, Latin America represents a trading partner of limited and declining relative importance. For Latin America, on the other hand, Germany is a key trading partner, whose relative importance, however, has also declined slightly in recent years. Germany's trade relations with Latin America are concentrated in a few countries of the region, notably Argentina, Brazil, Mexico, and Chile. Brazil has traditionally been Germany's primary trading partner in the region. It is still the main Latin American exporter to Germany; however, most of Germany's exports to the region now go to Mexico.

Trends in German export performance with regard to Latin America largely reflect the economic situation in Latin America itself. During the 1960s and 1970s, when most of the region showed high levels of economic growth, German exports to Latin America soared. From 1970 to 1980 alone, they increased almost fivefold in value terms. With the onset of the debt crisis and widespread economic collapse in the early 1980s, exports declined drastically; between 1980 and 1985, their value dropped by almost 50 percent. Since then, however, there has been an upturn in Latin American purchases from Germany, mostly as a result of trade liberalization and economic recovery in some key countries—Mexico in particular. From 1985 to 1991, German exports to the region grew by almost 100 percent in value terms. Hence, Latin America is once again developing into an attractive market for German exporters.

In relative terms, that market is still small. Only a tiny percentage of German exports go to Latin America: 1.6 percent in 1990, down from 3.8 percent in 1970. However, in 1991, the share increased slightly to a still very modest 1.8 percent, a reflection, nevertheless, of increased economic activity in Latin America.

Over the last decades, Germany has lost some of its market share in the region to other countries, notably to the United States. In 1970, almost 10 percent of Latin American imports came from Germany; by 1991, that figure had dropped to 6.4 percent. As Latin American economies have become increasingly dependent on the United States for their imports, German companies have lost market shares in all but one country of the region: Colombia.

More than 90 percent of Germany's exports to the region are industrial products. In line with the changing needs dictated by Latin America's industrialization process, such exports now consist less of consumer goods and more of intermediate and capital goods. Thus, in 1991, 52 percent of German exports to the region were made up of machinery and transport equipment. Given the characteristics of this product category (large orders, long-term finance), German exporters have stressed the resulting increased importance of adequate financing and export credit schemes, without which trade in such commodities may be seriously impeded.

In terms of German exports to Latin American countries, the main destinations are Mexico (33.2 percent), Brazil (24.5 percent), Argentina (9.1 percent), and Venezuela (8.2 percent). Future export promotion efforts by German companies will most likely concentrate on MERCOSUR and Mexico, which together account for around 70 percent of all Latin American imports from Germany. Germany will also continue to target the emerging markets of Chile, Colombia, and Venezuela, where recent export performance has been improving.

German imports from Latin America have grown steadily in absolute terms. In fact, Germany has for some years maintained a trade deficit with Latin America, buying more from the region than it sells to it. Over the last decades, however, Latin American suppliers have lost considerable market shares in Germany to suppliers from other exporting nations. Their share in total German imports declined from 4.7 percent in 1970 to 2.4 percent in 1991. This decline is partly a result of increased trade between Germany and its EU partners (particularly in agricultural products) and between Germany and other developed countries (Japan).

Latin America's share in total German imports from LDCs also declined: from almost 30 percent in 1970 to 12.5 percent in 1991. Clearly, the region has been unable to compete with the emerging export-oriented economies of the Asian continent. Few Latin American countries have been able to significantly diversify their export offer away from agricultural and mineral raw materials and toward competitive manufactures. More than two-thirds of Latin American exports to Germany still consist of food and raw material products, for which world prices have declined over the past two decades. Brazil is the only Latin American country with a relatively diversified export offer in its trade with Germany; it accounts for the majority of the region's manufactured exports to Germany. In general, Latin American exports to Germany remain much less diversified than its exports to the United States.

Nonetheless, Germany has remained an important market for Latin America. There has been only a slight decline in the share of Latin American exports destined for the German market: in 1970, 7.4 percent of the region's exports went to Germany; by 1991, that figure was 6.1 percent. After the United States, Germany is the second-largest market for Latin American products. The main Latin American exporters to Germany are Brazil (35.7 percent), Argentina (13.7 percent), Chile (9.4 percent), and Colombia (8.7 percent). Although Mexico ranks only sixth in importance, its share in the region's total exports to Germany has grown steadily over the last years.

## Investment

Although Latin America has become an increasingly marginal trading partner for Germany, it remains an important destination for German investment. Traditionally, German firms have maintained a strong presence in the region. Some of the biggest companies—Volkswagen, Siemens, AEG, Bosch, Bayer, Hoechst, and BASF—have been in the region for many years. Especially during the 1960s and 1970s, when most Latin American countries were pursuing inward-oriented development strategies, many German firms settled in Latin America in order to gain shares of the domestic markets. By 1988, an estimated 8.6 percent of total German foreign direct investment was located in Latin America, spread over more than 1,000 companies mainly located in Brazil, Mexico, and Argentina. The German automobile industry is particularly strongly represented by Volkswagen in both Brazil and Mexico. After the United States and Britain, Germany is the most important investor in the region.

Investment flows over the last decade reflect economic trends both in Latin America and, to some extent, in Germany itself: German companies invested almost 1.5 billion deutsche marks (DM) in Latin America in the years 1979 to 1982; that figure dropped to just over 700 million DM in the period 1983 to 1986. This decline was largely a result of declining investor confidence in Latin America's overindebted economies but also reflected sluggish economic development in Europe itself, which in the early 1980s experienced recessionary trends. In fact, German investment flows to *all* LDC regions dropped considerably in those years. German FDI flows to Latin America picked up again in the late 1980s, amounting to almost 1.4 billion DM in the period 1987 to 1990: a clear sign of the revival of many Latin American economies in those years, and of improved investment conditions for foreign companies in a number of countries, notably Mexico. Contrary to Latin American perceptions of increased German orientation toward eastern Europe, FDI flows to Latin America actually rose in the period 1990/91. Slight declines in 1989 and 1990 seem to be largely attributable to the economic situation prevalent in the countries where flows declined (Brazil in 1989 and Argentina in 1990) because in that same period, flows to Mexico increased by almost 60 percent.

Over 80 percent of all German foreign direct investment in Latin America is concentrated in three countries: Brazil, Mexico, and Argentina. Brazil accounts for the largest share (almost 50 percent), which has nevertheless declined from over 55 percent in 1981, reflecting persistent economic instability and slow progress in the implementation of lasting market reforms in that country. The value of German FDI stock in Brazil actually fell by 6 percent between 1981 and 1990, while stock values in Mexico and Argentina increased by around 60 percent each. These countries' shares in total German FDI stock in Latin America now stand at 19.6 percent and 12.5 percent, respectively. Moreover, although most recent FDI flows to Mexico have been in the form of "fresh" investment based on the attractiveness of new projects, much of the new money that went to Brazil in recent years is said to have resulted from debt-equity swaps.

In global terms, the German FDI stock in the region has grown by 7 percent over the last decade, a sign of continued interest of German investors in the three big Latin American economies, and in some smaller countries such as Chile and Colombia, which have both seen a 50 percent rise in stock values in the period 1981 to 1990. In the future, German interests will most likely continue to be concentrated mainly in the MERCOSUR countries and in Mexico.

Growing German confidence in the performance of some key Latin American economies is also reflected in its position on the region's foreign debt. In 1986, when the debt crisis was still at its height, Germany held around 9 percent of external commercial bank claims on Latin American countries. In the following years, the largest creditors to the region—the United States, Japan, and Britain—intensified their efforts to reduce their claims there, mainly through sales, write-offs, or swaps of loans for equity. Between 1987 and 1991, U.S. claims dropped from $75 billion to $41 billion; the U.S. share in total commercial bank claims on the region declined from 29 percent to 19 percent. In contrast, German banks increased their exposure, from $21 billion in 1989 to over $30 billion in early 1992. They now hold a 14 percent share of all commercial bank claims on the region: the third largest, after the United States and Japan.

## Prospects

Several key factors will shape economic relations between the two regions over the next decades: European integration, including the full implementation of SEM, the establishment of the European Economic Area (SEM, plus six of the seven countries of the European Free Trade Association, or EFTA) and, possibly, the move toward economic and monetary union;

economic reconstruction in eastern Germany and the countries of Central and Eastern Europe; and economic developments in Latin America, including the level of commitment toward and success in implementing market reforms, growth prospects for the region as a whole, and progress on regional integration.

German imports from Latin America will be affected both positively and negatively by the Single European Market. The medium- to long-term growth expected in EU member states as a result of SEM will boost demand for some imports: tropical products, fisheries, some metals and minerals and, above all, manufactures. However, since food and raw materials are generally not very income-elastic, demand for them will not increase much. Moreover, as regards manufactures, Latin America will have to compete for market shares with other external (mostly Asian) suppliers.

Trade liberalization within SEM may further boost intra-EU trade and lead to greater efficiency and competitiveness among European firms, resulting in a reduction in demand for imports from third countries. If integration efforts in Europe prove costly, and growth remains sluggish for some more years, protectionist sentiments may intensify. For Latin American exporters, gains in some product groups (coffee, meat, fish products, and some manufactures) will be largely outweighed by losses in other groups (oil products and processed minerals). Even if the net effect is positive in absolute terms, it will probably not change the current trend toward a declining relative performance of Latin American exports in the German market.

The outcome will ultimately also depend on German investment activity in Latin America. Many Latin American companies that have increased their exports to Germany in recent years are partly German-owned: Volkswagen (VW) Mexico, for example, exports around 2,000 auto motors to Germany every day. SEM has required many European firms to invest in their domestic capacity in order to remain competitive in the enlarged European market; but the data show that FDI flows to Latin America have, as yet, not been greatly affected by this.

Along with western European integration, Germany faces the enormous task of incorporating the eastern *Länder* into its productive and social apparatus. Moreover, it has assumed growing responsibilities in the reconstruction of the eastern European economies. Already flooded with immigrants from Eastern Europe, Germany has a vital interest in supporting growth and development in the region, thus reducing the pressure on its borders. This interest will affect its commitments in third countries, in terms of both investment and development aid. Countries like Hungary, the Czech and Slovak republics, and Poland—through their association agreements with the EU and ongoing market reforms—will prove attractive investment locations for German capital in the medium term, offering as they do cheap, educated labor, growing domestic markets, and relatively open access to EU markets.

However, it should be stressed that private capital always moves to where the greatest profits are. Ongoing political and economic turmoil in many countries of Eastern Europe have so far prevented the development of a friendly investment climate in the region. As long as Latin American countries remain attractive options for foreign investment, German FDI will continue to flow to them. The early 1990s might well prove to be a window of opportunity for the Latin American economies before Eastern Europe becomes a competitive region. Moreover, once Germany has overcome the worst and most costly part of its reunification process, investors will have renewed incentive to look overseas for fresh opportunities.

German unification may indeed also represent an opportunity for Latin American exporters. The former GDR imported few products from the region.[14] However, with rising consumption levels after unification, there are real possibilities for Latin America. Banana imports into eastern Germany, for example, have already increased considerably, although future prospects depend on developments in the EU banana regime. All of Central and Eastern Europe may in the future represent a growing market for some Latin American products, such as fish and tropical fruit. Conversely, the region may also become a strong competitor against Latin America in the European market, especially if it is granted wide preferential access for certain temperate agricultural products and textiles, which would hurt corresponding Latin American industries.

Against these odds stands the recovery of the Latin American economies. Appropriate fiscal and monetary policies, prudent management of foreign and domestic debts, market reforms, trade liberalization, and improved investment regulations in several Latin American countries are reviving foreign investors' interest in the region. As economies start growing, German export performance with regard to the region will improve. More trade will be followed by more investment, as German companies seek to serve growing markets from local subsidiaries. Eventually, this could benefit Latin American exports to Germany.

Regional integration initiatives will enhance the prospects for the region. In Mexico, the combined factors of economic recovery and NAFTA —which promises firms located in the region easy access to the huge North American market—have made that country an attractive investment location. German companies eager to exploit this opportunity are already investing heavily in Mexico. Many are settling into a recently opened industrial park next to the VW complex in Puebla, from which they will be directly serving the requirements of the huge VW production plant. The German automobile company will thus be able to comply with the strict norms on local content prescribed by NAFTA in order to gain access to the North American market. Similarly, MERCOSUR, if successfully implemented, will offer attractive investment opportunities for foreign firms, not the least of which is a huge domestic market.

Future economic links will depend on the specific actions taken by the German and Latin American governments to foster them. Germany must take full advantage of economic recovery in Latin America in order to avoid further marginalization in the markets of that region. Similarly, Latin American companies must target the European market more actively. Traditionally, their export promotion efforts have been concentrated far more on the U.S. than the European market.

In this respect, government-sponsored programs to boost business contacts and economic cooperation between the two regions are of vital importance. Such programs already exist in several countries. The German-Mexican Chamber of Commerce, for example, is actively involved in the promotion of Mexican exports to Germany, offering direct and often free assistance to Mexican firms who want to sell their products on the German market. In 1991, moreover, the German-Mexican "Commission 2000" was set up to identify problems in the bilateral economic relationship and suggest ways to foster economic cooperation in the future. As regards FDI relations, Germany has signed bilateral investment guarantees with both Chile (October 1991) and Argentina (April 1991).

Several German institutions are actively supporting private-sector links between Germany and Latin America. The German Investment and Development Association (Deutsche Investitions–und Entwicklungsgesellschaft, or DEG), for example, supports German FDI and joint ventures in the region, while the German Credit Association for Reconstruction (Kreditanstalt für Wiederaufbau, or KFW) provides export credits to Latin American importers as well as loans to finance joint German–Latin American technology programs in the region. Among other things, the KFW has supported projects aimed at the rehabilitation and modernization of degraded productive capacity and infrastructure, activities that are vital for the development of a competitive private sector.

Scientific and technological cooperation is actively supported by both sides. For Latin American firms, it means acquiring the technological know-how necessary for the growing domestic markets and for improving their competitive position in the international market. For German companies, who provide such technological know-how, it means increased business opportunities in the region.

In the 1970s and early 1980s, energy-related cooperation schemes were of the greatest importance. The biggest project involving such cooperation between a German and a Latin American government was the 1975 $3 billion nuclear deal with Brazil. Its centerpiece was the construction of eight nuclear reactors in Brazil, intended to help the country produce around 40 percent of its total energy supply locally by the year 2010. The agreement, which provided for joint German-Brazilian participation in all phases of the nuclear energy industry, involved intensive training of Brazilian professionals in nuclear technology and heavy participation of Brazilian industry, which would have enabled Brazil eventually to become an exporter of nuclear fuels and equipment. The deal was heavily criticized by the United States, which, focusing on the provision for enrichment and reprocessing facilities included in the deal, worried about the possibility that Brazil could become a producer of nuclear weapons. In the 1980s, problems also emerged between the partners when Brazil, encountering serious economic difficulties, faltered in its commitment to build all eight reactors—a condition for the previously agreed transfer of nuclear technology from Germany.[15]

Future technological cooperation will no doubt concentrate on less contentious areas, such as telecommunications or the environment. With respect to the latter, in particular, German companies are at the forefront of research, but Latin American industries will need to make rapid improvements if continued environmental degradation in urban and rural areas is to be avoided.

## Development Cooperation

German development assistance (GDA) has always been linked to the country's strategic, ideological, and economic interests. This link was perhaps most obvious in the 1960s, when GDA was mainly used as an instrument to support nonrecognition of the GDR, to impede the expansion of the noncapitalist systems in the LDCs, and to maintain export markets and raw material sources for the German economy. Today, ideological preoccupations have waned and, much more than in previous years, German development policy has its own officially declared priorities and technical standards. With the end of the Cold War, humanitarian and global concerns—such as the environment—are at the forefront of the German development debate, although economic interests continue to play an important role.[16]

German development policy is also influenced by the perceptions of the government in power, by the domestic economic situation in Germany, and by pressure from the LDCs themselves. Development assistance is discussed extensively among the German public, forcing politicians to take popular sentiment into account in their foreign policy formulations. Concerns about the environment, for example, or about human rights violations, are strongly reflected in official development policies vis-à-vis developing countries.

Such policies are designed and overseen by the Federal Ministry for Economic Cooperation and Development (Bundesministerium für Wirtschaftliche Zusammenarbeit und Entwicklung, or BMZ). Technical cooperation is mainly administered by the Association for Technical Cooperation (Gesellschaft für Technische Zusammenarbeit, or GTZ); financial cooperation by institutions such as the aforementioned KFW and DEG. Moreover, German political party foundations, church organizations, the German Volunteer Service, and many German NGOs receive official government support for their activities in the Third World. Around 70 percent of GDA is in the form of bilateral assistance; the remaining 30 percent is earmarked for multilateral assistance, such as contributions to UN agencies, EU programs, the World Bank, and regional development banks.

### General Priorities
Poverty alleviation, improvement of economic performance and competitiveness, education, and environmental protection constitute the main focus of German development assistance. In the poorest countries, GDA officials are mainly active in rural development, health care, family planning, and securing basic supplies, such as safe drinking water. In more advanced LDCs, activities include the promotion of private enterprise, support for structural-adjustment programs, and institutional development. In 1991, in accordance with stated objectives, 60 percent of German technical and financial cooperation funds went to the least developed countries (LDCs) with annual per capita incomes of less than $600. Few Latin American countries fall into this category, however.

Recognizing the limited potential success for projects undertaken in the absence of a conducive external environment, German development policy attaches increasing importance to the overall conditions prevailing in the recipient country for extending direct assistance. According to the guidelines of the BMZ, development assistance is conditional on:

- Respect for human rights (aid to Chile was frozen during the Pinochet era).
- Popular participation in the political process (German aid to Peru was frozen following President Alberto Fujimori's constitutional coup of April 5, 1992).
- A market-friendly approach to economic development (Cuba receives little aid, but aid to Nicaragua increased fourfold after the Sandinistas left office in 1990).
- The recipient government's practical attitude toward development, reflected, for example, in its own efforts to improve the situation of the poor.

When assessing the situation in a particular country, German development officials use these criteria as an "open-ended system": They not only look at the indicators as such (for example, the level of popular participation in a recipient country) but also at any visible changes in trends. Governments willing to improve their human rights record or to seriously consider the environment in their development strategies are likely to qualify for direct assistance even though their overall record on such issues remains far from ideal.

## Cooperation with Latin America

In 1991, 10.3 percent of German bilateral official direct assistance (ODA) went to Latin America. This percentage was considered to be rather low given the strong historical and cultural ties between Germany and Latin America and the latter's relatively more prominent role as an LDC trade and investment partner for Germany: In the period 1990 to 1991, for example, over 50 percent of German FDI flows to the developing world went to Latin America. Several factors may explain this phenomenon: Latin America is less underdeveloped than other areas, and it has traditionally been seen as the domain of the United States. Indeed, German initiatives in the region have sometimes led to severe tensions with Washington. Germany has sought to avoid such tensions wherever possible. In the 1960s and 1970s, in particular, political developments in Africa and Asia led Germany to worry more about communist infiltration in those regions and to focus its development assistance on them. Germany has also been pressured by its EU partners to assist the former British and French colonies and overseas territories in Africa and Asia.

The United States remains Latin America's largest single-country aid donor, accounting for 30 percent of all bilateral ODA received by Latin American countries in 1991. Significantly, Japan now ranks second, having increased its share from 13 percent to 20 percent over the last decade. Germany, traditionally Latin America's second most important aid donor, has moved to the third position, contributing 12 percent. It is still Latin America's most important EU donor, providing 30 percent of all EU member states' aid to the region.

Germany's direct assistance to Latin America largely reflects the above-mentioned priorities of German development policy. However, given the relatively advanced stage of development in many Latin American countries, the business element plays a significant role in Germany's development cooperation with the region. And the importance of such "special interests" as economic relations, concern for the environment, and the fight against drugs as well as political priorities have meant that a large chunk of German direct assistance to Latin America has been concentrated in the relatively affluent countries of the region—Brazil, Mexico, Argentina, Chile, and Colombia. Thus, in 1991, after Bolivia and Peru, Brazil received the most GDA, while Argentina ranked fifth. In Brazil, Chile, Colombia, and Venezuela, Germany provided between 36 and 59 percent (that is, a disproportionately high share) of total ODA received by these countries. In general terms, GDA in Latin America focuses on:

- Economic cooperation, including private-sector initiatives—support for small and medium-sized firms and joint ventures, export promotion, industrial and management training, and technology programs—and assistance to structural adjustment programs. The main recipients are Argentina, Brazil, and Mexico.
- Poverty alleviation, including primary health care and basic education. This type of aid goes mainly to the poorest countries, notably Bolivia, Peru, and Nicaragua.
- Fighting the drug trade. In Bolivia, Peru, and Colombia, Germany has supported programs to curb the cultivation of coca crops and their subsequent processing into cocaine.
- Democratization. Germany actively supports redemocratization and peace processes in Latin America, as evidenced by its generous contributions to such countries as Chile and El Salvador.
- Environmental protection. Germany has so far concentrated its efforts on the preservation of the Amazon rainforest, where it will be funding two-thirds of the first phase of the Brazil Pilot Program for the Amazon, a $250 million initiative jointly administered by the Brazilian government, the World Bank, and the EU.

The environment has assumed a dominant position in Germany's development policy with regard to LDCs in general, and Latin America in particular. In 1991 alone, 25 percent of all technical cooperation funding was dedicated to environmental projects. Moreover, all development projects are now assessed for their environmental impact prior to approval. Latin America, with its abundant natural resources and rapid population growth (which may affect future global consumption patterns), is high on the environmental agenda. It is therefore unlikely that German interest in the region will subside.

## Prospects

In the year 1990/91, German direct assistance to Latin America declined in absolute value. It also declined in relative terms, as total GDA to LDCs increased over the same period. However, throughout the late 1980s, German assistance to Latin America grew considerably, and it is therefore too early to determine whether the somewhat negative trend of 1991 will continue through the present decade. Germany's responsibilities in eastern Europe may mean that for the remainder of the decade, it will have to concentrate more of its technical and financial resources on that region. However, German government officials have repeatedly argued that their commitments toward Latin America will not be negatively affected by developments in Europe, particularly given Germany's focus on the environment.

Clearly, however, there will be no significant rise in Germany's contributions toward development in the South over the next few years. Slow growth and rising unemployment at home, and the enormous costs associated with unification, will probably prevent Germany from raising its contributions beyond the 0.4 percent of GNP that it currently sets aside for such purposes—although this is still double the percentage provided by the United States.

In Latin America, this trend has produced a certain sense of pessimism. Latin American countries, in the midst of painful adjustment processes, see that aid levels from the richer countries are stagnating. Moreover, their efforts to achieve export-oriented growth have been hampered by sluggish growth and continued protectionism in the North. At a time when many Latin American countries continue to be highly dependent on technical and financial assistance from the North, Germany will remain an important but probably not a growing source of such assistance.

## INSTRUMENTS AND ACTORS

Germany's relationship with Latin America can best be analyzed by isolating the three levels on which activity between Germany and the region takes place.

- The supranational/multilateral level. As an EU and NATO partner, Germany must integrate its Latin American policies into the context of overall EU–U.S.–Latin American relations, and the EU's North-South policies.
- The national level, including the national actors and bilateral instruments available to all internationally active states. Here, Germany has traditionally preferred to maintain a rather low profile with regard to Latin America.
- The transnational level, which is characterized by a variety of specific networks between German and Latin American civil societies: business networks, church organizations, political parties, trade unions, special interest associations, and solidarity groups. Since the 1960s, this transnational dimension, long underestimated and

underresearched, has become a key aspect of German–Latin American relations. Its actors do not project common or even similar German interests in the region. Rather, they compete with each other, reflecting the high degree of political pluralism in German society.[17]

## External Conditioning:
## The United States and the European Union

All postwar German governments, regardless of their political orientation, have been reluctant to challenge U.S. interests in Latin America, which have traditionally centered on security concerns, followed by economic relations, then by the promotion of democracy and human rights. In contrast, Germany has always regarded economic issues as being at the forefront of its ties with Latin America; it has no security issues with the region. Supporting democratic development and human rights has sometimes been easier for German governments than for other governments because they have had the instruments to deal not only with the region's governments, but also with opposition groups–even during times of military dictatorship. When German and U.S. perceptions of Latin American developments have conflicted, German politicians have made good use of the European context to voice those differences. At the same time, however, they have also been willing to discuss Latin American issues directly with the United States, mainly when differences of opinion were thought to endanger the overriding importance of maintaining the Atlantic Alliance.[18]

U.S.-German consultations, which traditionally focused on Cuba and Soviet-related issues, became especially important during the Central American crisis: In the Reagan years, the United States tended to view German political actors as intruders in an area that was seen essentially as a U.S. domain. With the end of the Cold War, these differences have almost disappeared. Friction in the context of the Atlantic Alliance could still arise with regard to trade and investment issues, or with regard to military training arrangements, which have been on the increase since the democratization process took hold in Latin America. Some countries of the region, especially in the Southern Cone, appear to be returning to pre–Second World War patterns of military cooperation and armament acquisition; in their endeavors to reform and improve their military establishments, they could find an efficient partner in the German *Bundeswehr*.

For historical reasons, Germany has been a motor of the European integration process in all of its stages, and it has been more willing than most EU member states to relinquish part of its national sovereignty in order to make such integration viable. It was therefore convinced that any demonstration of interest in Latin America should be of European, rather than purely German, nature. This became especially clear during the two major crises in EU–Latin American relations in recent years, namely, the Central American and the South Atlantic crises.

As regards Central America, Germany was instrumental in bringing about the San José peace process, convinced as it was that only Europe could offer the region a mechanism of conflict resolution that would be in the common Western interest but would not be dominated by the United States. In the case of the South Atlantic crisis over the Falkland Islands, it was difficult for Germany to fully support the British position, given its strong economic relations with Argentina and its conviction that all diplomatic means should be exhausted before military power was employed. Without doubt, however, Germany supported the process of finding a common European position on how to address the crisis.

Its preference for operating within a European consensus means that Germany—especially when compared with the United States—can only be a "limited" partner for Latin America. With regard to many issues concerning the region, it cannot decide independently, but must accept the majority voting process that has become the rule for deciding many issues within the EU. A case in point is the Union's recent reform of its banana import regime. The compromise reached between EU member states—it includes quantitative restrictions and a 20 percent tariff on Latin American "dollar bananas" in order to safeguard the competitiveness of the more expensive bananas from ACP and EU domestic producers—was clearly not in the interest of either Germany (since it consumes over a third of EU banana imports and previously had a zero tariff on them) or Latin America. The case demonstrated three things: First, that when German and Latin American priorities coincide, Germany is a good advocate of the region's interests in the EU context; second, that Germany has not yet been able to assist Latin America by correcting the EU bias in favor of the ACP states (former colonies of Britain, France, and, to a lesser extent, Belgium and Holland); and third, that the European integration process imposes policy constraints on Germany. Plans for closer collaboration on foreign policy issues through the European Political Cooperation (EPC) mechanism will no doubt strengthen the latter trend.

If the region's traditional low ranking in the EU's hierarchy of preferences is to be improved and Latin American issues are to be treated with the necessary political support in future EU foreign policy and foreign economic policy initiatives, an intra-EU alliance will have to be formed between Germany, Spain, Italy, and Portugal, the EU countries that maintain the strongest bilateral links with Latin America. To what extent Germany's new responsibilities with regard to Central and Eastern Europe or the Union's problems in the wider European and Mediterranean context will make such an alliance not only possible, but also effective, remains an open question.

## Bilateral Instruments

Compared to the United States, Germany's use of bilateral instruments in its relations with Latin America is much more diversified. German diplomacy has never attempted to monopolize German–Latin American relations. With the interruption of diplomatic relations after the First World War, and until 1951 (when the first embassy in Latin America was reopened in Brazil), many day-to-day contacts had to take other routes. Given the political instability in many Latin American countries, such a system proved to be an asset rather than a handicap and has been maintained over the past decades. Therefore, German commercial and business interests as well as the activities of German aid agencies are not coordinated by the embassies. Rather, they have their own representative and cooperative networks in each of the Latin American countries.

The twenty-two Goethe Institutes operating in the region, which offer a wide range of cultural activities, are an important bilateral instrument. Although they are funded mainly by the German Foreign Ministry, they form a private, independent organization. They defend their independence vigorously, and there have been frequent differences between the various institutes' and embassies' policies. It is also noteworthy that over fifty German schools operate in the region, and several exchange programs and German cultural foundations provide about 3,000 Latin American students with scholarships at German universities.

The German political foundations, which are closely linked to Germany's four largest parties, constitute another bilateral instrument, although they would be strongly opposed to being characterized as such.[19] However, their principal funding comes from the Ministry of Economic Cooperation and Development and from the Foreign Ministry. Since beginning their activities in Latin America almost thirty years ago, these foundations have contributed to democratization and increased popular participation in Latin America. Their impact on dialogue within and among Latin American political parties, trade unions, and cooperatives can hardly be overestimated. During the era of authoritarian and military rule, the foundations' offices and programs became important centers of action for opposition groups within civil society. They also contributed to a greater understanding of the region's problems among Germans and Europeans in general. Thus, the foundations can be regarded as a particularly successful instrument in North-South relations and cooperation.

Critics of the foundations' activities have been legion. Established elites in Latin America, often supported by the United States, objected to external "meddling" in their domestic political affairs. The United States alleged, for example, that some of the foundations working in Central America had a pronounced anti-American slant. Since the dissolution of the socialist regimes in Central and Eastern Europe, the foundations' attention has partly been redirected toward Europe, but there can be little doubt that the "Latin American connection" will be kept intact.

A little known, but nevertheless effective instrument of German interest in the region has been the German military. This statement refers not so much to weapons transfers (generally left to German or multinational firms) but rather to the area of military training. The German *Bundeswehr* is an army that, despite its origins in an authoritarian tradition, has become, over time, an accepted part of a modern society with few or no problems in the area of civil-military relations. A number of Latin American governments have therefore turned to Germany for assistance in reforming their militaries. The visit of the German defense minister Volker Rühe to various Southern Cone countries in February 1993 clearly demonstrated Germany's willingness to establish partnerships in the military arena.

## Transnational Actors

The line between bilateral instruments and transnational actors is blurred. With good reason, the political foundations are sometimes regarded as the executive arms of international party movements and therefore as part of the transnational network. From the German political perspective, however, the importance of the transnational actors rests in their relative independence from government interference, despite the substantial government funding many of these organizations receive. Even so, they are effective foreign policy instruments insofar as they strengthen German–Latin American relations, which they tend to do better the more they pursue their own corporate interests.

In this context, the oldest and most important of the German transnational actors is the German business community. Excluding the United States, no other country has so many national firms established in as many Latin American countries, not to speak of representative and trade offices. German industrial products, especially machinery and pharmaceuticals, have become household names for the Latin American consumer. Even in times of political strife and economic decline, German production in Latin America has hardly faltered. Moreover, the trend toward globalized production is leading major German firms to view Latin American growth prospects very positively. Some intend to install greater assembly capacity in the region.

The German Catholic and Protestant churches also play a major role in Latin America, where they are less noted for their pastoral engagement than for their social commitment. Both have their own extensive aid and voluntary services in the region and have probably channeled more money to the Latin American poor than all the official German cooperative efforts put together. Yearly fund-raising efforts provide several hundred million dollars to hospitals, schools, refugee camps, and soup kitchens annually. Together with the political parties and some of the solidarity committees, the churches have contributed extensively toward publicizing and address-ing the problems of human rights violations, repression, social injustice, hunger, and misery in many Latin American countries. Any German gov-ernment policy must take the moral impact of their work as much into con-sideration as the economic impact of the German business community.

Different types of solidarity committees emerged in Germany over the past decades. They were usually based on the attractiveness of certain de-velopment models (Allende's Chile or Sandinist Nicaragua) to particular segments of German youth; in response to the negative impact of civil war (El Salvador); or in response to the suffering of specific groups within Latin American society (Indians, women). Those groups with a certain tendency toward militancy have never been representative of mainstream German–Latin American relations, but they have certainly constituted a reservoir of mobilization in support of Latin American issues and a pool of information about Latin American developments in Germany. Today, sev-eral hundred groups exist; about half of them have their own programs in Latin America, though many of these are very small. Likewise, several German municipal councils maintain close relations with their sister cities in the region.

Looking at the wide variety of instruments and actors that shape the image of Germany in Latin America, and to a certain extent the view of Latin America in Germany, it becomes apparent why it has been so diffi-cult to identify specific Latin American policies followed by the various German governments over the years. The willingness to allow many sub-state transnational actors to operate in Latin America (and to fund them) has made official policy appear blurred and less than all-encompassing. In the absence of major crises, the German foreign policy philosophy with re-gard to Latin America has been to encourage good relations by allowing numerous actors to pursue their interests. As a result, Germany has main-tained a low official profile. To some extent, this was precisely the inten-tion of German foreign policy: Germany was eager not to generate conflict with the United States and to avoid a leadership position with regard to Latin America within the EU.

## CONCLUSIONS

The necessity of reevaluating (and financially supporting new) foreign pol-icy interests in the post–Cold War world will affect the complex relation-ship between Germany and Latin America. The self-imposed restrictions that resulted from Germany's being a divided and only partially sovereign nation particularly vulnerable to the fallout of the East-West conflict will be replaced by a clearer willingness on that nation's part to express and pursue its national interests. Germany will no longer look on Latin America as Washington's backyard. It will nevertheless accept the continuation of a strong U.S. interest in the Greater Caribbean.

German relations with the region have always been very differentiated. Over the last decades, Germany has clearly concentrated on certain preferred countries and economic sectors, and it has been criticized for this unbalanced approach: Germany was seen to be simultaneously too little (in Mexico) and too much (in Brazil) involved in the region. Such differentiation will probably characterize future relations as well. The special relationship that exists between Germany and Brazil because of strong economic and technological linkages is likely to continue, despite Brazil's rather slow process of economic and social reform. In the future, however, Germany and Brazil will, in the context of their own regional integration processes, have increased international responsibilities. These might, at some point, find expression in both countries joining the UN Security Council. Meanwhile, Brazil will remain a focus for German environmental concerns.

Apart from Brazil, Germany, given its traditionally close relations with Argentina and Chile, will be focusing on other countries of the Southern Cone, independent of their membership in MERCOSUR. Mexico will also be of special interest, due to increased German economic involvement there and to Mexico's own interest in stronger relations with Europe, mainly to counterbalance its increasing economic integration with the United States.

As democratization advances and social participation increases in Latin America, Germany will continue to see itself in a privileged position to communicate some of its own experiences in institution building and creating conflict-reducing mechanisms between different groups in society. Beyond that, Germany will also be willing to share its experience in the areas of decentralization, education, and regional integration with its Latin American partners. The evolving German international posture will probably become more cooperative, especially as regards those issues that are not only of global concern but have a direct effect on German domestic politics: the environment, drug trafficking, human rights, and extreme poverty. Germany may not direct much more aid, or more investment, toward the region. But Latin Americans will be able to count on its willingness to support more open trade and to share more responsibility for encouraging democracy and sustainable development than previously. In short, Germany will most likely—in a different sense than before 1989—remain a limited, but reliable partner for Latin America.

## NOTES

Special thanks to Anneke Jessen for her substantive contributions to, and editing of, this essay, which was written in the summer, 1993.

1. See Achim Schrader, ed., *Deutsche Beziehungen zu Lateinamerika, Regionalwissenschaft Lateinamerikas*, vol. 1 (Münster: Lateinamerika-Zentrum der Westfälischen Wilhelms-Universität, 1991), p. 8. Overviews of Germany's relations with the region are provided by Peter Hermes, "Aspekte und Perspektiven der deutschen Lateinamerika-Politik," *Europa-Archiv* 14 (1979), pp. 421–430; and Gerhard Henze, "Deutschland und Lateinamerika: Partner in einer sich wandelnden Welt," Achim Schrader, ed., *Deutsche Beziehungen*, pp. 11–29. For Latin American views, see Guillermo Moncayo, "Las relaciones políticas entre la República Federal de Alemania y América Latina," *Contribuciones para el Debate* 1/86, (Buenos Aires: CIEDLA, 1986), pp. 41–50; and Adriana Valadéz, "Las relaciones políticas y culturales entre Alemania y América Latina," *Foro Internacional*, 128–129 (Mexico, 1992), pp. 455–466.

2. On political and economic changes in Eastern Europe, and their impact on German–Latin American relations, see Dieter Benecke, "Relaciones entre América Latina y Alemania a la luz de los cambios en Europa Oriental," *Contribuciones* 4 (Buenos Aires, 1990), pp. 113–119.

3. See Violanda Botet, "Die deutsch-lateinamerikanischen Beziehungen in den neunziger Jahren," *Aussenpolitik* (I/93), pp. 44–54.

4. See Manfred Mols, "Das Verhältnis der Bundesrepublik Deutschland zu Lateinamerika: Defizite und Lösungsansätze," in Günter Kahle, Hermann Kellenbenz, Horst Pietschmann, and Hans Pohl, eds., *Jahrbuch für Geschichte von Staat, Wirtschaft und Gesellschaft Lateinamerikas*, vol. 25 (Köln-Wien: Böhlau Verlag, 1988), pp. 321–348.

5. For a historical overview of Germany's relations with Latin America, see Albrecht von Gleich, *Germany and Latin America*, Memorandum RM-5523–RC (Santa Monica, Calif.: Rand Corporation, June 1968).

6. See Wolf Grabendorff, "Los alemanes e Iberoamérica," *Humboldt* 93 (Bonn, 1988), pp. 26–45.

7. See Manfred Mols, "The Latin Connection," in Peter H. Merkl, ed., *West German Foreign Policy: Dilemmas and Directions* (Chicago: Chicago Council on Foreign Relations, 1982), pp. 92–123.

8. See Helmut Schäfer, "Grundsätze und Ziele deutscher Lateinamerikapolitik," in Albrecht von Gleich, ed., *Wirtschaftspartner Lateinamerika. Stand der Beziehungen und Erfahrungen aus der Praxis der deutschen Aussenwirtschaftsförderung* (Hamburg: Institut für Iberoamerika-Kunde, 1988), pp. 13–25.

9. See the report of the German Association for Research into Latin America (ADLAF) for the German Government: Dieter Benecke, Michael Domitra, Wolf Grabendorff, and Manfred Mols, *The Relations Between the Federal Republic of Germany and Latin America: Present Situation and Recommendations* (International Politics, Friedrich Ebert Stiftung Research Institute, 1984).

10. Violanda Botet, "Die deutsch-lateinamerikanischen Beziehungen," p. 44.

11. Ibid., p. 45.

12. On this issue, see, for example, Eusebio Mujal-León, "The West German Social Democratic Party and the Politics of Internationalism in Central America," *Journal of Interamerican Studies and World Affairs* 29, no. 4 (Winter 1987–1988), pp. 89–123.

13. On German industry in Latin America, see Hans-Günter Gehring, "Beziehungen der Wirtschaftsunternehman," in Achim Schrader, ed., *Deutsche Beziehungen*, pp. 117–139.

14. For trade relations between the former GDR and Latin America, see Karl-Christian Göthner, *El Comercio entre América Latina y Alemania Oriental en la Retrospectiva* (Hamburg: Deutsch-Südamerikanische Bank, October 1990).

15. For details of Brazil's nuclear policy, see Wolf Grabendorff, "Brazil," in Harald Müller, ed., *A European Non-Proliferation Policy* (Oxford: Oxford University Press, 1987), pp. 323–366.

16. For a historical overview of Germany's development assistance to Latin America, see Mechthild Minkner, *The Development Assistance of West Germany: An Overview with Special Reference to Latin America*, Occasional Paper Series, Latin American and Caribbean Center, Florida International University, Miami, September 1986. For an official review of German development cooperation with Latin America, see Federal Ministry for Economic Cooperation and Development (BMZ), *Concept for Development Cooperation with Latin America* (Bonn, December 1992). Cooperation with Argentina, Brazil, and Venezuela is discussed in detail in Edith Kürzinger, *Bilaterale Entwicklungszusammenarbeit mit ausgewählten Schwellenländern Lateinamerikas* (Berlin: Deutsches Institut für Entwicklungspolitik, 1987).

17. On transnational actors, see Klaus Bodemer, *¿Hacia una relación más transnacional? El rol de las organizaciones no gubernamentales (ONG) en la política alemana de cooperación con América Latina durante la Guerra Fría* (Montevideo: FESUR, 1992).

18. On U.S.-German relations and Latin America, see Peter Bazing, "Lateinamerika und die Beziehungen zwischen der Bundesrepublik Deutschland und den Vereinigten Staaten," *Europa Archiv* 5 (1983), pp. 149–156.

19. The Friedrich Ebert Foundation is close to the German Social Democratic Party (*Sozialdemokratische Partei Deutschlands*, SPD); the Konrad Adenauer Foundation is close to the Christian Democratic Union (*Christlich Demokratische Union*, CDU); the Friedrich Naumann Foundation is close to the Liberal Party (*Freie Demokratische Partei*, FDP); and the Hans Seidel Foundation is close to the Bavarian Conservative Party (*Christlich Soziale Union*, CSU).

# 4

# Spain and Latin America: The Resurgence of a Special Relationship

*Edward Schumacher*

International relations are not unlike human ones: the most complex are in the family. Five hundred years ago, Columbus planted the flag of Castile on American soil, and almost overnight Spain became the seat of the world's greatest empire and mother of most of what would come to be called Latin America. An absolutist parent, Spain imposed its language, laws, and culture on a region many times its own size. Three centuries later, Spain was spent, and her colonies, like rebellious teenagers, bolted. Liberation of the land, however, did not mean liberation of the soul for the Latin Americans. For nearly two centuries, despite occasional spurts of brilliance, both Spain and its former colonies floundered in a sea of insecurity, instability, and introspection. Each alternately reached out to the other for salvation and self-identification. As often as not, each rejected what it found.

Today, a new relationship is evolving, one that goes beyond the rhetoric of the psyche to the realities of mutual economic and political self-interest. Spain has emerged as a major player in the struggle to bring political stability and democracy to the Spanish-speaking New World. Economically, Spain's involvement is small compared to that of the United States, but it is remarkably dynamic, and it has taken the lead in involving the European Union in the region. Spanish aid, trade, investment, and finance have taken on new importance in Latin America.

Spain has benefited considerably in return. Its Latin relations have helped it make giant strides toward internationalizing its economy and enhancing its political position in the world. Threatened by European Community integration, Spanish companies have been strengthened by expanding into Latin America. Spain's special relationship with the region has given Madrid added political weight inside the European Community and with the United States.

The new relationship between Spain and Hispano-America has reached a level of maturity that allows for the expression of differences, which do exist. As Spain finds itself pulled toward Europe, Latin America finds itself pulled toward the United States. There is no doubt that Spain's most important interests lie with Europe. Latin America's lie with the United States, particularly after the expansion of the North American Free Trade Agreement became part of the hemispheric agenda resulting from the December 1994 Summit of the Americas in Miami. But the growing ties between Spain, and to a lesser extent Portugal, and Latin America are such that a nascent bloc, the Community of Ibero-American Nations, may be taking shape as political complement or political alternative to economic integration between Latin America and the United States.

Annual summits beginning in 1991 bringing together the heads of state of Spain, Portugal, and the nineteen Spanish- and Portuguese-speaking nations in Latin America are becoming institutionalized. The fledgling Ibero-American community is hardly an effective political alliance yet. But with nationalism and ethnic conflict on the rise throughout the world, ideological blocs may increasingly be giving way to cultural ones. In such a changed world, an effective Ibero-American community would have serious implications for the future of the Organization of American States and the position of the United States itself in the Western Hemisphere.

## *HISPANIDAD,* EUROPE, AND A BRIDGE: THE WEIGHT OF HISTORY

Relations between Latin America and Spain are heavily weighed by the baggage of history, not only of Spain with the region, but also of Spain with the rest of Europe.

The loss of most of its New World colonies in the first part of the nineteenth century was bad enough for Spain. But the loss of the remainder—Cuba and Puerto Rico—plus the Philippines in the Spanish-American War was a body blow that left the nation humiliated and without a sense of place in the world. Out of the ashes of defeat arose a movement led by the philosopher Miguel de Unamuno and the so-called Generation of '98 dedicated to shucking off the past and pushing Spain toward modernization. One tenet was the idea of *Hispanidad,* which even today forms the bedrock of Spanish policy toward Latin America.

Hispanidad sought to sidestep the problem of Spain's political and economic weakness in its relations with Latin America by stressing shared cultural values. But Spanish decline was such that by the end of the nineteenth century even such a largely benign policy faced rejection. New cultural and psychological complications had emerged. Affected by the British-propagated "Black Legend" of Spanish rapaciousness, and by faddish Northern intellectual theories denigrating Spanish and all Southern cultures as politically authoritarian and economically lazy, many Latin American intellectuals came to blame their nations' failings on Spain. The children pointed to the mother for the inheritance of the flaws they saw in themselves—a fatalistic religion, a paternalistic social structure, a greedy conquistador mentality, and an inability to be organized, efficient, and enterprising.

Such attitudes, which linger to this day, led Latin intellectuals to look to other European countries for ideas and inspiration. Great Britain attracted some, especially in Argentina, and Germany attracted others. But it was France, the self-proclaimed cultural capital of the world, and the romanticism of the French Revolution that were the real magnet. The very phrase "Latin America" was a French invention, designed to legitimize French aims of expansion in the region.

Still, Hispanidad was received with some sympathy, if only because Latin Americans were worried about their neighbor to the north, which was flexing its imperial muscles. But Hispanidad had different meanings for different intellectual and political groups in Latin America, and for good reason: It had different meanings in Spain. The countercurrents came to a head in the Spanish Civil War, which reverberated throughout Latin America as countries and individuals took sides. The official Spanish definition of Hispanidad fell to the fascist victor, General Francisco Franco, and it was decidedly different from the liberal, republican concept of the Generation of '98. Harking back to values thought to have served as the foundation of the Spanish empire, Hispanidad as propagated by the Franco regime's Hispanic Council was defined by a conservative Catholicism, a corporatist economy, and an authoritarian political system. The regime found adherents among some of Latin America's military and upper social castes.

To the United States, even though Spain maintained its neutrality during the Second World War, the Hispanic Council smacked of the fascism being fought in Europe. The Franco regime subsequently moderated its tone in Latin America, replacing the Hispanic Council in 1946 with the Institute for Hispanic Culture, but to no avail. Spain was kept out of the United Nations and was subjected that year to a U.S.-led trade embargo. Only six UN members voted against the embargo resolution, and they were Latin.[1] By 1950, they were joined by other Latin nations sorry for the old mother country and as a group prevailed in bringing the embargo to an end. The United States, increasingly obsessed with communism, soon further relented, and Spain was admitted to the UN in 1955.

The UN experience reflected how Franco's Spain was such an international pariah in the first years after the Second World War that Latin America was virtually its only escape hatch. Peronist Argentina was of particular importance, donating wheat and extending a line of credit. Spain was so poor that, as late as 1958, three Latin countries—Argentina, Venezuela, and Cuba—still had higher per capita incomes.[2]

Franco ruled Spain for more than thirty-five years, until his death in 1975. But although he found his closest allies among right-wing Latin American governments, the power of Hispanidad in its broadest conception was such that Spain remained a Latin obsession for all. A prodigious number of Spanish Republican exiles in Mexico, Argentina, and elsewhere helped assure the cultural connection, however politically hostile it might have been. Indeed, Mexico continued to stubbornly recognize the Republican government in exile until 1977, two years after Franco's death. But Franco himself proved that Hispanidad was first and foremost a sense of community that superseded ideology. He did so most strikingly in Cuba in the early 1960s. The United States led an international boycott, forcing almost all noncommunist governments in Europe, Latin America, and elsewhere to break relations with the communist government of Fidel Castro. Franco, despite his dependence by then on U.S. military bases and aid, refused. An undercurrent of Spanish anti-Americanism dating back to 1898 contributed to Spanish obstinance.

In the first years after the death of Franco, the former colonies remained more critical to political developments in Spain than the reverse. Spain's new king, Juan Carlos I, and its prime minister, Adolfo Suarez, traveled frequently to the region, seeking legitimacy in order to shore up the transition to democracy at home. But as Spanish democracy took root and flowered beyond all expectations, the roles switched. The old intellectual prejudices inside Latin America against Spain began to weaken. This reversal was stimulated in part by the charisma of the king, of Suarez, and of the prime minister, Felipe González. Each of them was young, dynamic, and handsome. The new Latin American democracies that emerged in the 1980s began reaching out to Spain for advice and inspiration, Spain's political and economic successes having put the lie to the notion that Latin America's problems were in some way genetic.

The cultural politics of Hispanidad in its purest form showed up in relation to the celebration of 1992, the quincentennial of Columbus's voyage to the New World. Beginning shortly after Franco's death, Spain had planned for the year to be a massive coming-out party for the new Spanish democracy. With Latin American backing, Spain won the right to host a world's fair—Expo '92, in Seville—and the 1992 Summer Olympics in Barcelona. Spain also financed and staged an intense barrage of quincentennial cultural events, symposiums, publications, and public-relations splashes in the years leading up to and during 1992, much of it in collaboration with Latin America and the United States. Hundreds of millions of dollars went into the effort, and the money was almost all Spanish. The early efforts met with mixed reviews from Latins. Countries with strong indigenous traditions, particularly Mexico, Guatemala, and Peru, were divided by the idea of celebrating the "discovery" of America. To its credit, the youthful, idealistic González government in Spain switched the theme to that of an "encounter" between two cultures. The quincentennial celebrations did not win over all Latin Americans, but on balance they gained Spain considerable good will, helping redefine and strengthen Hispanidad in a broad cultural context.

Inside Spain a separate, competing trend was developing: Spain was reaching out to Europe. Spain had retreated behind the Pyrenees during the Counter-Reformation and by the eighteenth century was largely outside the European mainstream. Spaniards suffered from an inferiority complex with respect to the rest of Europe, but many were also genuinely ambivalent over the extent to which Spain should belong. They wanted to remain apart from the political upheavals and social experiments of the continent. Aloofness from Europe was part of Spain's political makeup. Franco had emphasized Spain's uniqueness in the world. The country was neutral in this century's two world wars, and most Spaniards, whether on the right or the left, opposed Spanish membership in both the North Atlantic Treaty Organization (NATO) and the Warsaw Pact.

But the march of modernization and Westernization was inexorable. By concluding an agreement with the United States in 1953 to locate military bases on its soil, Spain reopened the political door to the West. A great inflow of European tourists and liberalized Spanish economic policies over succeeding decades set off an economic boom and resulted in new social, cultural, and trade ties to the rest of the continent. The centrist Suarez government formally applied in 1977 for membership in the European Community itself, a popular move because of the perceived economic benefits to Spain. Following an aborted coup in 1981, the succeeding Calvo Sotelo government went one step further and abruptly joined NATO, in part to protect the fledgling democracy by firmly placing Spain in the Western security camp as well. This act set off a domestic political storm, which resulted in a landslide victory for Felipe González's Socialists in 1982. After campaigning against NATO, however, González flipped his position once he was in power and in a hard-fought referendum won confirmation of Spanish membership. Behind the flip was González's conclusion that NATO membership would aid Spain's EC application and more generally guarantee his aspirations to convert Spain politically, economically, and socially into a solidly modern Western European nation. As González often put it, Spain had to join the "train of history" or be forever left behind.

The Socialist party came into office on a platform declaring Europe to be its first foreign-policy priority, and Latin America its second. With Spain's entry into the EC in 1986, the government declared that the two priorities were compatible and would be met in tandem. "Spain, from its new position, will continue to work for peace and democracy in Latin

America," Juan Carlos told the diplomatic corps "and will not relax its efforts to give ever greater meaning to our fraternal ties with the countries of Hispanic America."

There was, quite obviously, built-in tension in the government's policy. Earlier, Prime Minister González had floated the concept of Spain as a "bridge" between Latin America and Europe. Fostered by Foreign Minister Fernando Morán, the concept was based in part on a calculation that Spain's influence in Europe and with the United States would be proportional to the extent to which it exercised its special relationship with Latin America. It also was based on the old emphasis on Spain's uniqueness and on Hispanidad. The tension was immediately apparent concerning the Falklands/Malvinas. As Franco had supported Cuba against the United States, Calvo Sotelo supported Argentina in its war with Britain. González followed suit. He risked British ire and Spain's EC application by signing a joint declaration with Argentine president Raúl Alfonsín in 1984 condemning the British occupation of the Falklands and Spanish-claimed Gibraltar as "anachronistic colonial" behavior.

But the greatest test of Spain as a bridge came in Central America. González entered office as a member of the Socialist International's Committee of Solidarity with the Nicaraguan Revolution. Having traveled frequently in Central America, he saw the conflicts in Nicaragua and El Salvador as reflections of internal social sicknesses, as opposed to the Reagan administration's view of them as reflections of outside communist influences. In office, González proposed that Spain act as a mediator between the United States and the Sandinistas. After showing some initial interest, the Reagan administration, suspicious of the Socialists' intentions, rejected the proposal, but the Spanish government did not retreat. It publicly opposed the formation of the U.S.-backed Contras, condemned the mining of Nicaragua's harbors, and became the first Western nation to back the Contadora peace process. It also actively sought to involve the European Community. For its efforts, Spain was invited in 1984 to join the EC's first San José Conference with Central America. After becoming a full EC member two years later, Spain successfully pushed to make the conference an annual affair. In the end, the Central Americans themselves found a way to peace through the Esquipulas I and Esquipulas II agreements. But the San José conferences did provide moral support for the Contadora process, resulted in small amounts of additional economic aid, and kept the Community involved in the region. Through the EC and bilaterally, Spain, acting as a friendly member of the loyal opposition, sought diplomatically to moderate U.S. actions.

In recognition of its role, Spain was asked in 1989 by the Central American countries to take responsibility for the UN Observer Group in Nicaragua to demobilize the Contras and bring peace and elections into the country. In

1991, it again participated as a member of the UN Observer Group in El Salvador. Along with Colombia, Mexico, and Venezuela, Spain was a member of Secretary General Javier Pérez de Cuellar's "group of friends" who, at the end of 1991, helped bring about the signing of the accords ending the Salvadoran civil war, and Spain participated in the UN peacekeeping force there. Spanish generals commanded both UN contingencies.

Spain's role in Central America was thus considerable, but the concept of Spain as a bridge still died along the way. Early on, González recognized that the United States had legitimate interests in Central America, that it neither needed nor wanted any other country to act as a bridge, and that no peace was possible without U.S. acquiescence. The Latin Americans also looked askance at the concept. It smelled to them of old Spanish paternalism. It implied that Spain thought the Latin Americans could not speak for themselves. Finally, the strategy was confining to Spanish policymakers. Although González upheld the sovereignty of Sandinista Nicaragua, he publicly criticized many of its actions, an approach that did not square with the strict neutrality required of a country acting as a bridge between conflicting interests.

In 1985, Morán was replaced by the politically centrist Francisco Fernández Ordóñez, a Europeanist and supporter of NATO who was friendlier toward the United States. Nonetheless, he led Spain through the testy negotiations that resulted in a reduced U.S. military presence in Spain. He also remained dedicated to Hispanidad, as Spain celebrated the Quincentenary, Expo '92, and the Barcelona Olympics on his watch. But under him the concept of Spain as a bridge between Latin America and the United States and Europe was replaced with a more modest one of Spain as a catalyst for change and supporter of Latin American interests, particularly inside the European Community.

The shift was conceptually subtle but psychologically crucial. The last official vestiges of Spain's paternalism toward Latin America and of the idea of Spain as a country apart from the rest of Europe were swept away. Spain now thought of itself as a committed European country, albeit one with great interests in Latin America. The shift reflected as much Spain's aspirations in Europe as the limits of its influence in Latin America. Paradoxically the shift helped increase Spain's presence and influence in Latin America today.

## THE EUROPEAN UNION: THE KEY INSTRUMENT

The European Union is the single most important instrument of Spanish foreign policy in Latin America. It is also the Spanish resource in which Latins are most interested.

The European Union has been the focus of Spanish policy since the country's induction in 1986. Spain entered as the only "intermediate" state, one step below the "big" states of Germany, the U.K., France, and Italy, and as such it was given more voting weight and more offices in the various EU institutions than the remaining "medium-sized" and "small" states. By 1993, Spain had nearly completed its transition to full integration. It had largely caught up with the rest of the Union in implementing the original 148 White Paper measures setting up a common market, and it was in the middle of the pack in implementing the later 282 White Paper measures setting up a single market.[3]

One of the driving forces of Spain's EU policy has been economic self-interest. Spain has been a net recipient of EU aid. Private sector benefits have been even more important. European foreign investment washed into the country, quintupling from $2 billion in 1980 to $10 billion in 1990. The Spanish economy was the fastest growing in Europe between 1986 and 1991.

But the EU represents more than just marks and francs to Spaniards joining the EU has had tremendous psychological importance. It represents having arrived. It represents national pride and entering into the same company as France and northern Europe. Embarrassed by having lived under a military dictatorship for so many years, Spaniards have rejected the strident nationalism that Franco propagated, and overnight have become among the most dedicated Europeanists in Europe. Poll after poll has shown an overwhelming number of Spaniards willing to give up their army and forego much of their nation's sovereignty for greater European unity. The depth of such attitudes can only be tested in the event. But even as the Spanish economy plunged into recession in 1992 and 1993, in part because of the government's efforts to cut inflation and maintain the peseta in the drive to achieve European monetary unity, Spaniards, unlike the French, the British, and the Danes, remained remarkably united across the political spectrum in favor of the European Union, the Maastricht Treaty, and the continuing move toward European unification.

For Latin America, the European Community historically meant frustration. The Common Agricultural Policy restricted Latin food exports. What relief and aid the Community offered went mostly to neighboring Mediterranean countries and to the former colonies of Britain and France in Africa and Asia. The latter relationship was modified and formalized by the Lomé Conventions, which extended preferential treatment to the poorest countries of Africa, the Caribbean, and the Pacific. These policies were in place before Spain and Portugal became members of the Community, so Latin America was not a beneficiary of them. It was neither poor enough nor connected by past colonial history to the members of the Community.

Indeed, Latin America had barely existed as an EC concern. About the only institutional link was the modest San José dialogue with Central America. There were hardly any Latin American experts inside the secretariat, and the commissioner responsible for Latin America, Claude Cheysson, had little interest in the region. It was therefore a given that the Spaniards, because of their natural affinity, would move into bureaucratic positions dealing with the region. During the negotiations regarding its membership in the Community, Spain sought and got the key Latin American–related positions in the European Commission and the European Parliament, respectively the EC's executive and legislative arms. The most important of the positions, the Director for Relations with Latin America and Asia, went in 1987 to Angel Viñas, the executive adviser to the Spanish foreign minister.

What the Community did not expect was the determination and energy the Spaniards brought to their role. Spain began by instigating a review of EC policy concerning Latin America, and when the document prepared under Cheysson's guidance fell short of Spanish expectations, Spain forced it to be redrafted. The final policy guidelines issued in June 1987 by the European Council of Ministers, the EC's supreme body of prime ministers, broke little economic or political new ground, but they did constitute the first strategy paper committing the European Community to action in Latin America.[4]

Since then, the Union, almost always on Spanish insistence, has acted on a number of fronts. Early on, a budget line for Latin American cooperation was broken out, the tariff on green coffee was reduced slightly, and an informal ministerial dialogue was begun with the Contadora and Contadora support nations—Argentina, Brazil, Colombia, Mexico, Panama, Peru, Uruguay, and Venezuela—which in 1986 came together to form the Rio Group. More fundamental changes in relations with Latin America began after a new European Commission was appointed in 1989. Felipe González personally lobbied EC Commission president Jacques Delors and member states to pass the Cheysson portfolio to a Spaniard, Abel Matutes. The fact that Matutes was a successful businessman and a leader of the center-right Alianza Popular opposition party showed how Spain's determination to aid Latin America was a bipartisan, national concern.

Under Matutes, the European Community established for the first time a broad and serious institutional relationship with Latin America. The number of EU diplomatic delegations was expanded from four to the ten of today. The European Commission acquired observer status at the Organization of American States and set up cooperation mechanisms with such organizations as the Latin American Economic System, the Latin American Economic Integration Association, and the Inter-American Development Bank. Under the Rome Declaration of December 1990, the informal dialogue with the Rio Group, now expanded to include Bolivia, Chile, Ecuador, Paraguay, Costa Rica, and Jamaica as well, was upgraded to a formal annual ministerial meeting, complementing the ongoing San José dialogue.

At the same time, the network for nonpreferential agreements with Latin America was widened and EC development aid was reconceptualized in a way that benefited the region. The 1991–1995 EC guidelines for Asia and Latin America went beyond traditional technical and financial cooperation to include such matters as integration, education, the environment, urban problems, and the encouragement of private business. Because Latin America is considered to be less deserving of traditional aid than Africa and even Asia (Latin America receives 35 percent to Asia's 65 percent under EC guidelines), these new categories have opened up whole new areas of assistance to the middle-income Latin countries.

In addition, the Spaniards have been able to crack that most sacred of EC cows: import tariffs. In the European Community's "pyramid of privilege," Latin America is at the bottom. The Spaniards prevailed on the Community in 1990 to grant, as a drug-control measure, extremely preferential tariff treatment to Colombia, Bolivia, Peru, and Ecuador in the hope of stimulating other exports. In December 1991, most export products from Central America were given similar preferences. Then the Dominican Republic was (with Haiti) added to the list of Lomé Convention countries, the first Hispanic country to be included. It had been excluded even though it was poor and Caribbean.

In 1993, under Spanish prodding, the role of the European Investment Bank was broadened to include the financing of projects in Latin America and Asia. Future EU aid to Latin America will thus increasingly be in the form of loans. The addition of the finance arm means that, with the exception of balance-of-payments support, all the major tools of economic cooperation between the European Union and Latin America are now in place—a major accomplishment, considering Spain has been a member of the Union only since 1986.

Almost all of these initiatives met resistance, sometimes fierce, especially from Britain, France, and the Lomé countries. Britain and France sought to protect their aid and privileges from competing demands. Britain, for example, insisted each step of the way that any measure for Latin America be applied to Asia as well, even to the extent of maintaining the two as a single line item in the EC budget. But the Spaniards, gaining a reputation for bullheadedness, persevered, putting together a shifting alliance that usually included Italy and Portugal and, at different times, Germany, the Netherlands, Belgium, and others. The debates extended from the Council of Ministers, to the Commission, to the secretariat and into the European Parliament. Felipe González personally intervened with his counterparts at critical junctures, underlining the importance Spain gave to issues that for many of the others were more middling concerns.

Part of the Spanish ammunition was guilt. Spain was forced to join the European Development Fund in 1989 and to adopt the Community's official development aid (ODA) guidelines, which largely excluded Latin America. As a result, its contribution to the Community's ODA programs tripled between 1987 and 1991, from 8 to 25 billion pesetas, almost all of which went to Africa, the Pacific, and the non-Hispanic Caribbean.[5] Bilateral aid was affected as well. Between 1989 and 1990 alone, Spain's bilateral ODA more than doubled, from 31 to 65 billion pesetas, and almost all of the increase went to the EC-favored countries. Latin America went from being the recipient of 53 percent of bilateral Spanish ODA in 1989, to the recipient of just 27 percent the next year.[6] Although the actual amount of the aid Latin America received went up slightly, the plunge in percentage did not square well with Hispanidad in Latin America. Put together, Spain's overall aid expenditures—bilateral and multilateral—jumped from 41 billion pesetas in 1987 to 108 billion pesetas, or more than $1.1 billion, in 1991.[7] For the Spanish economy, that represented more than a doubling of ODA, from .1 percent of GDP in 1986 to .24 percent of GDP in 1992, which was still low compared to other industrial countries but more than that of the United States.[8] Spain, in other words, was paying the aid bill, but most of its monies were going to areas of little interest to the country. As a result, Spain believes it has a moral right to make demands on its fellow EU members, some of whom agree that the aid distribution is unfair.

Today, Spain is also counseling acceptance of the North American Free Trade Agreement (NAFTA), in the face of some hostility on the part of other EU members who believe that NAFTA constitutes trade diversion, not creation. Spain recognizes that the European Union itself is less than innocent in this respect and sympathizes with the aspirations of Latin countries to join NAFTA and other regional trade pacts, such as MERCO-SUR, made up of Argentina, Brazil, Paraguay, and Uruguay.

Curiously, the Latin Americans themselves have mostly sat on the sidelines with regard to the European Union. Either unable or unwilling to unite to speak with any force in Brussels, their efforts have been mostly haphazard individual ones. Argentina recently has taken to joining with Canada and Australia to confront the EU. Otherwise, most appear happy to let Spain do the battling for them in the Council of Ministers, the European Commission, and the European Parliament. The Latins have not pressed Spain to act on their behalf, although Latin governments generally have been appreciative of Spain's effort, especially given the obstacles built into the EU system of unanimous rule. Certainly no other nation in the European Union has taken on the Latin cause.

At times, however, Latin expectations have been higher than Spanish accomplishments, and this has resulted in some public grumbling. The

Spaniards in return complain that the Latins have not been nearly as resourceful as the Asians in pushing their exports, regardless of the hurdles they face. And there are occasions when interests diverge. Bananas are a case in point. Spain, seeking to protect its own banana production in the Canary Islands, has supported a controversial EU quota limiting cheaper and better Latin American bananas to 60 percent of the EU market, a blow to Latin growers. Some Latin governments have complained openly; Felipe González has defended the Spanish position unapologetically.

Future conflict, however, is less likely to stem from the problem of Latin American products competing with Spanish ones than from Spain's desire to protect another prime area of its interest, the Mediterranean, and especially Morocco. Located just twelve miles across the Straits of Gibraltar, Morocco is the source of growing illegal immigration and brewing security concern. The Mediterranean countries already enjoy certain trade advantages in the European Union. Spain has taken the lead in arguing that the Community go one step further and make Morocco an EU free trade area, with the aim of assuring Moroccan economic stability. With the exception of a few products, such as grapes, where it competes with Argentina and Chile, Morocco is not a direct competitor to Latin America. But there is a limit to the European Union's attention, generosity, and market. To the extent that Morocco—and other EU aspirants, such as Turkey and Eastern Europe countries—attract the Union's focus, Latin America will be left further in the cold.

Still, there is no doubt that Spanish leadership in the Union has been crucial in winning a number of measures advantageous to Latin America, which, although none is earth-shattering, taken together represent a reorientation of Europe toward the region. To be sure, Spain also has used its relationship with Latin America to gain political leverage inside the Community. But for Latin America, that is irrelevant to the benefits won.

In 1993, the European Commission was reorganized again. Matutes moved from the Latin American chair to energy. Another Spaniard, Manuel Marín, was given a redefined portfolio for development cooperation and humanitarian aid, taking over responsibility for all EU aid programs, including those involving Latin America, giving Spain even more influence in the field. By 1993, the Spaniards were already lobbying the European Union to prepare for radical changes in Cuba. González sent a commission of economic and aid experts led by former Finance Minister Carlos Solchaga to Cuba in the summer of 1993 to take stock of that country's needs, current and potential. Solchaga returned advising Cuba take a mix of economic liberalization measures to stimulate the economy and fiscal measures to protect the country's considerable social advances in areas such as public health and education. Opposed to the U.S. trade embargo as hindering change from within, the Spanish government began to consider ways to increase aid to Cuba as a means of encouraging a peaceful Cuban transition. Among the ideas floated was the radical one of designating Cuba a Lomé country, which would open the gates to EU aid and trade concessions. Such a proposal would surely spark furious debate in Europe, Latin America, and, not least, the United States. Whether Spain will make such a proposal remains to be seen, but it clearly sees itself continuing to work as a catalyst for change.

## THE BILATERAL ECONOMIC RELATIONSHIP

The concept of Hispanidad was devised in part to make up for Spain's economic weakness—the dirty little secret being that its economic presence in Latin America had dwindled so badly after 1898 that Spain had become a mere bit player. By 1960, less than 1 percent of Latin America's trade was with Spain. As the Spanish economy took off after 1960, however, the picture changed.

Spain's economy grew at an extraordinary 6.8 percent annual average between 1960 and 1975, far outstripping the rest of Europe. Spain took a dive during the uncertain years of the transition to democracy, then took off again in 1986, leading the rest of Europe with an annual average growth rate of 4.5 percent over the next four years. Spain fell into recession in 1992, along with the rest of Europe, but the relative trend remained unchanged. Spanish per capita income went from less than 60 percent of the EC average in 1960 to almost 80 percent in 1991, and the gap continues to close.[9] More graphically, the per capita income of Spaniards leapt from $5,991 in 1986 to $15,149 in 1992.[10] Spain is no longer a poor country. As a result, its bilateral aid, trade, investment, and general economic presence in Latin America has taken on new importance.

Spain developed a modern bilateral aid program in conjunction with joining the European Union. Before then, its administrative, financial, and legal infrastructure was so antiquated that such a program was not possible. A new organization, the Secretariat of State for International Cooperation and for Ibero-America, was formed inside the Foreign Ministry in 1985, and its very name underlined the importance of Latin America in Madrid's thinking. A hands-on aid organization, the Spanish Agency for International Cooperation, was founded three years later. Experts were hired, and procedures and laws were codified. In 1991, Spain joined the European Development Fund as well as the Aid Development Committee of the Organization for Economic Cooperation and Development (OECD).

As noted above, the total amount of Spanish aid nearly tripled between 1987 and 1991. Bilateral ODA to Latin America also increased, though at a more modest rate. Spain ranked fifth among EC donors in terms of the amount of aid to Latin America in 1991, but it ranked first by far in terms of the percentage of total aid expenditures there. In fiscal year 1990/91, Spain extended $212 million in ODA to Latin America, which represented 30 percent of its total aid expenditures. That same year, the United States provided $1.5 billion in aid, Germany $652 million, and Britain just $172 million.[11]

To help channel its growing range of aid to Latin America, the Spanish government devised a new strategy. Beginning in 1988, it signed a series of bilateral agreements, or General Treaties of Friendship and Cooperation, with Argentina, Mexico, Chile, Venezuela, Colombia, and Brazil. Another of these so-called framework agreements is being negotiated with Uruguay. These four- and five-year agreements cover nearly the full range of bilateral relations, including annual ministerial political consultations; cultural, educational, juridical, consular, and commercial cooperation; and development aid. The agreements offer a mix of soft credits for Spanish goods and services, investment loans, development grants, and technical assistance in such areas as public administration, health, education, urban development, technology transfer, and ecology. The bulk of the projected $15 billion in aid, however, is designed to promote industrial development, based on public and private investment targets. Two more limited agreements signed with Ecuador and Bolivia in 1989 and 1990, respectively, provide another $1.15 billion. Smaller agreements have been negotiated with Honduras and Nicaragua. To commemorate the five-hundredth anniversary of the voyage of Columbus to America, the Spanish government established the Quincentennial Fund in 1991, with another $500 million to be channeled through the Inter-American Development Bank.

More than altruism was at work here. Spain was motivated not only by its sense of responsibility, but by a wish to join the OECD "big boys" and by self-interest. Direct aid and the framework agreements are part of an overall political strategy of the González government to globalize the Spanish economy. Since 1988, Spain's Socialist government has been leading with the flag to expand Spanish investment and trade abroad.

The strategy was developed in part as a counterweight to the effects of the European single market on the Spanish economy. With few exceptions, Spanish companies are generally small, cautious, and internationally inexperienced. That leaves them vulnerable to European imports and corporate takeovers. To counter this weakness, and enable them to survive, many Spanish companies, urged on by the government, are attempting to broaden their bases and to internationalize. Latin America is a natural target. The framework agreements are the primary vehicle. In addition, the government has tied bilateral aid to the purchase of Spanish goods and services, under standard OECD and EU guidelines, and it has set out in the European Development Fund and the OECD AD Development Committee to win more contracts for Spanish companies so that they might gain more international exposure. The results have been impressive.

Spain's corporate presence in Latin America increased dramatically during a two-year blitz of foreign direct investment (FDI) in 1990 and 1991. Surpassing the EC average, Spanish FDI in Latin America doubled between 1989 and 1990, and then doubled again in 1991, to nearly $1.2 billion for those two years.[12] It has since settled back to more sustainable levels, dropping to roughly $230 million in 1992.[13] Much of the great spurt came from two government-controlled companies, Iberia Airlines and Telefónica, which were central to the government's strategy.

Iberia, Europe's fourth-largest airline, invested $800 million and quickly became a dominant carrier in Latin America. It gained management control of Aerolineas Argentinas and Venezuela's Viasa, buying 30 percent of the former and 45 percent of the latter. It also bought 35 percent of Chile's Ladeco. With hubs in Miami, Buenos Aires, and Santo Domingo, Iberia now has synergetic relationships and a broad web of routes throughout Latin America.

Telefónica, the Spanish telephone company, was even more aggressive. With $38 billion in assets (in 1991 dollars), Telefónica controls nearly 2 percent of the Spanish GDP. Between 1990 and July 1993, it invested $1.28 billion (in 1991 dollars) in Latin America, most of it during the two blitz years. It purchased 44 percent of Compañia de Teléfonos de Chile; 20 percent of the Chilean long-distance company, Entel; 60 percent of a Chilean telephone book company; 29 percent of Argentina's Telco-Sur; 6 percent of Venezuela's CANTV; and 79 percent of Puerto Rico's long-distance service. In 1994, Telefónica moved into Peru, buying 35 percent of Entel Peru, a telecommunications company, and 18 percent of Compañía Peruana de Teléfono, the national telephone company. The company has earmarked $4.5 billion for investment over the next five years to improve the Chilean and Argentine companies alone.[14]

Both Spanish companies were responding to particular challenges presented by EU integration at home. Airline deregulation has forced European carriers to scramble for partners to survive. The Latin American network gives Iberia unique added value. As a result, it is at the time of this writing engaged in advanced strategic conversations regarding the possibility of meshing globally with the German airline, Lufthansa, which is strong in other parts of the world. Telefónica, meanwhile, is being forced by EU directives to give up its monopoly at home in such services as data transmission, electronic mail, and mobile communications. Latin America, which has relatively few telephones, not only offers a fertile growth market, but by adding five million Latin American phones to its fourteen million in Spain, the company has obtained new economies of scale in negotiating with suppliers and for access to technology. As owner of the world's third-largest underwater cable system, it also has been able to divert telephone traffic between Latin America and Europe from U.S. cables to its own.[15]

The Spanish government's role was not limited to hands-off ownership; ministry officials intervened on the companies' behalf, as did González himself. Argentine president Carlos Saúl Menem telephoned González to push along the sale of Aerolineas to a reluctant Iberia. "It was practically a deal between two states," Argentine economy minister Domingo Cavallo said later.[16] But such nonmarket intervention can have its price. Iberia, whose heavy losses companywide in 1992 were being duplicated in 1993, has seen its projected profits from the Argentine purchase now turn into a projected five-year drain. The rushed deal at first unraveled in misunderstandings and recriminations over who was to pay for what. The Menem government returned as a 43 percent partner, but labor problems and poor management in the interim have resulted in poor service and a decrease in passengers. By 1994, Iberia, in management and financial turmoil in Madrid, was considering bailing out of Buenos Aires.

The Iberia experience in Argentina has helped fuel questions in Latin America as to whether these two Spanish state companies can accomplish the efficiencies privatization was meant to achieve. Both companies give mixed service in Spain itself. But the Spaniards generally are confident they will succeed where the local state companies failed, and on balance they deserve the chance. State-controlled or not, Iberia and Telefónica are still foreign companies and therefore not subject to the local political pressures that doomed the domestic state companies. Telephone service is improving where Telefónica operates: the Spaniards have cut bloated work forces, introduced new technologies, and raised telephone rates. Even Iberia has improved Viasa's computerized reservations system and begun to revamp its work forces. Telefónica's international operations produced 26 percent of the company's operating profits in 1992 and were projected to produce even more in 1993.[17]

Another Latin complaint is that the big Spanish investments smack of Spanish "colonialism." That the investments are in such politically sensitive sectors as airlines and telecommunications has probably prompted much of the resentment. That, however, is a complaint more appropriately directed at the Latin governments that make the sales. Partly as a result of cultural affinities, Spaniards were less afraid of the emerging Latin market and moved in faster than their U.S. and European competition to buy early at bargain-basement prices. But some perspective is called for. Although Spanish FDI in Latin America put Spain third among EC countries between 1985 and 1990, it generally pales when compared to U.S. FDI in the region outside the two blitz years and is less than that of Japan, Germany, and the United Kingdom.[18]

Nonetheless, from a Spanish perspective, the government's policy has been a success. Where Telefónica and Iberia have trod, private Spanish companies are following. The electricity-generating company, Endesa, joined with a French utility and an Argentine oil company in 1992 to purchase 51 percent of Edenor, the electrical-power provider for the northern half of Argentina, for $427 million. Another Spanish company, Unión Fenosa, is helping privatize El Salvador's electrical system. Cristalería Española, Perfumería Gal, and most of Spain's major publishers have expanded in Argentina and Mexico. Pescanova, a Spanish fishing company, took over fishing companies in Uruguay, Argentina, and Chile. Campofrio built a meat-packing plant in the Dominican Republic in 1990 and is planning to build a second one in Mexico. Repsol, a state-controlled mixed company, increased its oil exploration in Argentina with a projected $75 million investment in 1992 and constructed a $35 million paraffin factory in Mexico. Spanish insurance companies such as Mapre have long been active in Latin America.

The Spaniards also are investing heavily in tourism. Much of the investment has been in real estate, which does not count in official FDI figures. The investments include $1 billion earmarked by the Sol-Melia Group for hotels in Mexico. The Barceló Group has built four hotels in Santo Domingo. Grupo Once, an association of the blind that has a powerful industrial sector, has proposed a massive development of Venezuela's Isla Bonita. Spanish groups dominate the hotel sector in Cuba, either building new hotels or managing old government-owned ones. In the last five years, Guitart has invested some $100 million in Cuban hotels, followed by $48 million by Sol-Melia, according to the authoritative Research Institute of Cuba in Miami. (Cuba presents an interesting footnote. Spanish FDI in Castro's Cuba totals roughly $200 million, most of it in the last five years, according to the institute, which makes Spain the largest foreign investor in Cuba, followed respectively by Canada, Italy, and Mexico. In addition to Spanish investments in the tourist sector, a number of small and medium-sized Spanish companies in areas anywhere from generator manufacturing to trading have stayed on throughout the Castro years, leaving the Spaniards poised to exploit any changes in the island.)

So far, Spanish FDI has been concentrated in five countries: Argentina, Brazil, Chile, Mexico, and Venezuela. In addition to communications and transportation, the other sectors attracting the most Spanish investment are, one, energy and water and, two, finance. The latter alone accounted for nearly $200 million in FDI in 1991. Indeed, subtracting the investments made by Iberia and Telefónica, finance has accounted for nearly half of all FDI in recent years, as Spanish banks have expanded their presence proportionate to Spain's other economic activities.[19]

Spanish banks historically have been active in Latin America, mostly in trade financing and retail banking. They lent little during the great Latin debt buildup of the 1970s and were among the first to cut their losses when the Latin American debt crisis then hit in the 1980s. They refinanced more than $2.5 billion of Latin debt after 1985, but most of it was sold off or assigned, as the Spaniards were reluctant to reschedule debts with new loans. The Spanish banks were cash rich in the 1980s and could afford to take the hit. Protected from foreign competition, the financial sector has been one of the most profitable areas in the Spanish economy since the boom years began. European integration, however, is now forcing a liberalization in the domestic financial sector and exposing the banks to fierce competition from European intruders. In response to government prodding, the banks have begun to seek mergers and to globalize. The recently merged Banco Central Hispanico is now Spain's largest bank, and more than 41 percent—representing $2 billion—of its overseas assets were in Latin America in 1992. Banco Santander, the second-most-active Spanish bank in Latin America, has been regularly listed in recent years as one of the most profitable banks in the world, and Nomura Research reported that $100 million of its net profits in 1991 came from Latin America.[20]

Five of the six big Spanish banks are active in Latin America. At the retail level, they have a much greater presence than European and U.S. banks, a holdover from the days when they served immigrants and their descendents. The Spaniards are aggressively expanding their retail operations in Latin America by buying into or taking over local banks. Santander Chile is already the largest international bank in Chile, for example. Banesto owns a controlling share in Chile's Banco del Pacífico, which Central Hispano emulated in 1993 by purchasing 49 percent of Banco Higgins. In Puerto Rico, Santander owns the second-largest bank in assets, foreign or local. Central Hispano has just put together the third largest in Puerto Rico, and Banco Bilbao Vizcaya, in a joint venture with the Royal Bank of Canada, is coming on as a major contender. Bilbao Vizcaya and Banesto have purchased minority shares in Mexican banks, and other Spanish banks are actively seeking to follow suit.

Spurred in part by the framework agreements, the banks have returned to the lending market, particularly for privatization projects. Santander participated in 1991 in the $100 million privatization of Bancomer, one of Mexico's largest privatization deals. Banco Bilbao Vizcaya, the leading Spanish bank in world peseta financing, has extended $500 million in loans to the Mexican energy sector under the Mexican framework agreement. The Spaniards, however, remain cautious lenders in relation to U.S. and other European banks.

A new area into which the Spaniards have moved since 1990 is securities, reflecting their growing sophistication. Banesto launched a successful

Mexican investment fund, Fonméxico, on the Madrid stock exchange in 1991 and was working on an Argentine one in 1992. Santander put together the Emerging Mexico Fund. Both Banesto and Santander have been involved in a number of Latin share offerings, and Santander has been lead manager or comanager on a number of major Latin Eurobond issues. It also has been lead manager of numerous Brazilian bond issues and an active trader of Latin American government debt. Santander traded $12 billion in Latin debt in 1991 alone. So-called Matador bonds are a new Spanish financial instrument being offered the Latins. Appearing for the first time in 1987, these novel bonds are medium- and long-term foreign bonds issued in Spain in pesetas. Santander was the lead manager on three Matadors. BEX International, part of the government-owned Argentaria group, led a fourth and comanaged a fifth with Deutsche Bank, as the use of such bonds continues to grow.[21]

The Spanish banks have been most active in Chile and Argentina, due to the liberalization of markets there and the official encouragement, credit guarantees, and taxation agreements provided by the framework agreements. Mexico represents a major new market as its financial sector begins to open up. Spanish bankers also say that a visit by King Juan Carlos and Queen Sofia to Mexico in 1991 helped create a welcome atmosphere, underlining the critical role played by both the throne and the state in Spain's economic expansion in Latin America. The surprising levels of Spanish banking activity in Puerto Rico is the result of another kind of diplomacy. Not only is Puerto Rico economically open and attractive, but in declaring Spanish as an official language and reaching out to Spain through a highly active economic office in Madrid, it generated a chauvinistic response by the Spanish government, which has been encouraging the Spanish banks to move onto an island once thought to be exclusively in the U.S. zone of economic influence.

The last important area of economic relations between Spain and Latin America is trade, and it too has been growing. During Latin America's "lost decade" of the 1980s, total trade between Spain and the region dropped from $5.25 billion in 1980 to a low of $3.18 billion in 1986.[22] By 1990, however, it was back to 1980 levels and has continued to grow strongly. Total trade went from $5.3 billion in 1990 to $5.9 billion in 1991 to $7 billion in 1992. Latin America enjoyed a surplus of $1.4 billion of that 1992 commerce.[23]

Oddly, however, trade between Spain and Latin America declined in relative importance for both. As a percentage of Latin America's total trade, Spanish trade remained minor, declining slightly from 2.8 percent in 1980 to 2.1 percent in 1991.[24] As a percentage of Spain's total trade, the decline was even greater. Latin America declined from 9.6 percent of Spain's total trade in 1980 to 4.3 percent in 1992.[25] For both, trade with the rest of the world grew even more than with each other, especially Spain's trade with Europe.

But such relativity may be seen in different lights. Viewed in the European context, Spanish trade with Latin America is quite important. Among the EC-12 in 1991, Spain accounted for 11.5 percent of the imports from Latin America and 8.7 percent of the exports to Latin America. Only Germany was a significantly larger trading partner; Spain's trade with Latin America was on the same order of magnitude as that of Britain, France, Italy, and the Netherlands, who were clustered around second place, particularly in exports. The cluster's share of exports, for example, ranged from the Netherlands' 13.5 percent to Britain's 10.8 percent, sandwiching Spain's 11.5 percent.[26]

Trade content mostly follows traditional North-South patterns: Spanish manufactured goods and machinery in exchange for Latin raw materials and foodstuffs. Mexico has long been Spain's primary trading partner in Latin America, in part because of Spanish imports of Mexican oil. In 1991, Mexico accounted for 30 percent of Spain's trade with the region, followed by Brazil (17 percent), Argentina (14 percent), Chile (9 percent) and Venezuela (6 percent).

Spain's economic presence in Latin America—its aid, investments, finance, and trade—is likely to continue to grow. The Spanish economy shrank by 1.1 percent in the first three quarters of 1993, and the government entered a new period of uncertainty. In elections in June 1993, the Socialists were returned to office, but as a minority government for the first time in their eleven years in office. The effect of these political and economic developments on Latin American economic relations will be limited, however. The making of international economic policy is a multipartisan affair in Spain. Even the conservative opposition Popular Party and the major regional parties participate. Despite cutbacks in many areas, the 1993 budget approved by the government actually included an 11 percent increase in official development assistance, as Spain continues to try to reach OECD levels of giving.

One effect of the economic crisis has been a more than 30 percent devaluation of the peseta since September 1992 vis-à-vis the dollar. This decline should boost trade, stimulating Spanish exports while only minimally depressing demand for needed raw materials from Latin America. More fundamentally, trade growth is responding to structural trends in the Spanish economy. Although Spanish trade tripled in the 1980s, it still lags far behind the EU average as a percentage of GDP. Exports, for example, averaged 24 percent of GDP in 1991 in the EC-12, but little more than 12 percent in Spain. Spanish trade will continue to grow as part of Spain's overall EU convergence. To help Spain catch up, the government in 1992 announced a five-point plan to stimulate both trade and investments. In addition to the trade credits of the framework agreements, the plan includes commercial and financial measures, tax incentives, and information and training provisions.

After the blitz of 1990 and 1991, FDI reverted to more normal levels in 1992 and likely will grow at a more steady rate from now on. It will be less political and more governed by the internal corporate strategies of private companies, particularly the banks. Anecdotal evidence suggests that the economic crisis also has not slowed the plans of many of the Spanish banks to continue expanding in Latin America, if only out of necessity. For Latin America, the more the better.

## IBERO-AMERICA: THE BEGINNING AND THE END

Some dreams may be meant to come true. The Conde de Aranda, the brilliant minister of Carlos III, was the first to propose a community of Hispanic nations, but those nations were still colonies and he was way before his time. Today, his dream may finally be becoming reality.

Instigated by Spain as a corollary to its quincentennial efforts, the Ibero-American nations have been meeting in annual summits since 1991. The summits are in part an attempt to establish a still-to-be-defined Ibero-American commonwealth. To avoid costs and pomposity, there is no permanent secretariat, lending an informality to the proceedings that the participants prefer. But interest is such that attendance by the heads of government of the nineteen Ibo-American nations, plus Spain and Portugal, has been near perfect.

The first summit, held in Guadalajara, Mexico, in 1991, adopted the Guadalajara Declaration, which set forth the basic principles that the assembled were to share: democracy, human rights, and collaboration to achieve economic and social development. The second summit, held in Madrid in 1992, demanded the Uruguay Round of GATT be concluded, established university scholarships, set up a fund to aid indigenous groups, and called for sustainable development and common social policies. Felipe González also announced the imminent launch of Spain's first communications satellite, Hispasat 1A, which was to beam three hours of shared educational programming daily throughout the Ibero-American community, though he spoke too soon. The satellite was launched, but its antennas were askew, negating all television transmission. Spain has since launched a second satellite.

The third summit, held in Bahia, Brazil, adopted the Salvador Charter calling for the eradication of poverty and again demanded a GATT agreement, underlining the Latins' insistence on opening trade as an avenue to development. The summit also turned political, calling for the United

States to lift its thirty-two-year-old economic blockade of Cuba and proposing that the UN Security Council be enlarged.

The summits have achieved little of real substance, but this statement misses the point. It was unthinkable before they first met that the twenty-one nations could even be brought together. Having done so, they are overcoming at least three major obstacles to creating an effective Latin alliance: historical distrust, limited experience in teamwork, and the absence of a common external threat to act as glue. Institutionalization is under way as a result of the bevy of ministerial and technical meetings that must take place before each summit. Two fundamental shifts in world history are helping them: The passing of the Cold War has opened the way for new alliances. And with the exception of Cuba, all of the Ibero-American nations for the first time share the same political and economic values.

The summits have set in motion a number of small steps that together add up to a giant stride forward. The potential of the yet-to-be-formed Community of Ibero-American Nations is extraordinary. The twenty-one nations represent 500 million people in a land area of 20 million square kilometers and a combined economy of more than $1 trillion. These nations are rich in human talent and natural resources. But the challenges they face are equally extraordinary. The per capita income of the Ibero-American community is only some $3,000, compared to an average six times that in the European Community and the European Free Trade Association.

The British Commonwealth was formed while there was still a British empire. The idea of an Ibero-American Community is the outgrowth of an entirely different experience, of a sense of equality among nations. Unlike the polyglot European Community, the Ibero-American community has the distinct advantage of a shared culture and two related languages. And even that small language gap has been closing: Brazilian president Itamar Franco announced in Bahia that the teaching of Spanish was being made mandatory in Brazilian schools.

With the passing of ideological clashes, and with the crumbling of national boundaries in the former Soviet bloc, ethnicity has returned as a major factor in world politics. What new cultural and ethnic alliances will emerge—or whether the existing Arab, Moslem, and other such alliances will strengthen—remains to be seen. But by speaking out on Cuba and UN Security Council membership, the Ibero-American community is already speaking with a single voice on sensitive political issues. It represents a challenge to the Organization of American States (OAS) and, to a lesser degree, to the United States for influence in Latin America. The United States applied for observer status at Bahia and was refused, in part because the Latins do not want to create another OAS, which the United States dominates. The Latins also see the OAS as too bureaucratic; too diffuse in geographical focus, with the presence of Canada and the Caribbean; and too rigid, operating like a mini–United Nations when the real United Nations is where most of the important action takes place. There may always be a need for the OAS, if only as a place for Latin America to encounter the United States, but Latins feel a need for their own separate caucus. The Rio Group could become that caucus, but until now neither it nor the San José Conference has moved much past being a point of dialogue with the European Community. The subregional economic groups—MERCOSUR, the Andean Pact, and others—are limited in size and scope. The Ibero-American community offers the advantages of a defined ethnic base, a broad umbrella approach, and a sufficiently large shared voice.

The inclusion of Spain and Portugal in the Latin American community is certainly odd, but the Latins see this European connection as a counterweight to the United States, even if neither Iberian country is a powerhouse. Spain is also a catalyst that has forced the Latins to overcome their inability to work together. The Spaniards insist that they are not trying to challenge what even they admit is the natural preeminence of the United States in Latin America. At the Bahia summit, the Spaniards were instrumental in promoting a compromise in the heated debate over the controversial Cuba amendment that resulted in omitting any direct mention of the United States or Cuba. For the Spaniards themselves, meanwhile, inclusion in both the Ibero-American summits and the European Union has created some predicaments, as over the competing Latin and EU candidates for the directorship of the UN Food and Agricultural Organization. After some hesitation, Spain backed the Latin American candidate.

However the Ibero-American community develops, the fact that the recent summits have taken place at all reveals a good deal about the state of Spanish–Latin American relations, which have not been better or more promising in five hundred years. The Oedipal thrashing of the past has been replaced by familial peace. A common history, language, and culture add a certain romantic element that is not to be underestimated in its power. There continue to be conflicts, but that is normal in any family.

Who benefits the most? In many ways this is an irrelevant question. Both sides are acting out of realistic self-interest and both are accruing practical benefits. Economically, the benefits are to be seen in growing trade, aid, investment, and finance. Politically, they are evident in both sides' projection onto the world stage. Latin America has a lawyer inside the European Union and elsewhere; Spain has a weightier calling card because of its client.

But perhaps the most important benefit is a psychological one. Each continues to see itself in the other. The stunning success of Spain's transition to democracy and free-market economy has diminished Latins' fears that they were somehow genetically doomed to failure. The growing success of Latin America's young democracies and budding economies has added to Spain's new sense of ethnic self-assurance as a modern European nation. If the relationship has served only to give each the confidence to confront the future, then it has accomplished a lot.

## NOTES

1. The six were Argentina, Costa Rica, the Dominican Republic, Ecuador, El Salvador, and Peru.
2. Eric N. Baklanoff, "Spain's Emergence as a Middle Industrial Power: The Basis and Structure of Spanish–Latin American Economic Relations," in *The Iberian–Latin American Connection: Implications for U.S. Foreign Policy*, Howard J. Wiarda, ed. (Boulder, Colo.: Westview Press for the American Enterprise Institute, 1986), p. 134.
3. By September 1992, Spain was last among the EC-12 in the implementation of the original 148 White Paper measures, but it already had put into force 64 percent of the measures, compared to a 75 percent average among the EC-12 and 90 percent by the leader, Denmark. Moreover, Spain was closing in fast on the rest.
4. Angel Viñas, "Spanish Policy Towards Latin America: From Rhetoric to Partnership," an Occasional Paper of the Iberian Studies Institute, University of Miami, May 1992, p. 17.
5. "Previsiones de la AOD Total de España, 1987–1990," Planes Anuales de Cooperación Internacional, 1987 a 1991, Secretario de Estado para Cooperación Internacional y para Ibero-América, reprinted in Luis Yáñez-Barnuevo, "La Participación de España en la Cooperación Internacional para el Desarrollo," *Documentación Administrativa*, vol. 227 (Madrid: Instituto Nacional de Administración Pública, July–September 1991), p. 35.
6. Carlos Alonso Zaldívar and Manuel Castells, *Spain Beyond Myths* (Madrid: Alianza Editorial), p. 405.
7. "Previsiones de la AOD Total de España, 1987–1990."
8. *Anuario Internacional, 1992* (CIDOB: Barcelona, 1993), p. 80.
9. Commission of the European Communities, "Real Convergence Process in the European Community," reprinted in Zaldívar and Castells, *Spain Beyond Myths*, p. 90.
10. Roger Cohen, "Spain's Progress Turns to Pain," *New York Times*, November 17, 1992, p. D17.
11. Organization for Economic Cooperation and Development." 1992 Development Cooperation Report." Tables 41–42. (Paris: OECD, 1992).
12. Christian L. Freres, "Investing in Latin America," *The Ibero-American Community: A Latin Finance Supplement*, October 1992, p. 9.
13. "Inversiones Españolas Directas en el Exterior," *Boletín Económico*, Información Comercial Española No. 2359, March 1–7, 1993, p. 491 (conversion at 100 pesetas = $1.00).
14. Alberto Martínez Fernández, Director, Gabinete de Prensa, Telefónica, in written responses to author's questions, March 15, 1993. Also, "Telefónica de España Raises Stake," *Wall Street Journal*, July 7, 1993, p. A7.
15. "El Buen Resultado de Una Aventura Exterior," supplement in *Expansión*, March 3, 1993, pp. 1–3.
16. Thomas Kamm, "Argentine Airline Sale Shows Privatization Is Hardly a Cure-All," *The Wall Street Journal*, May 20, 1993, p. 1.

17. "El Buen Resultado de una Aventura Exterior."
18. Freres, "Investing in Latin America," p. 8.
19. Ibid., p. 16.
20. Ibid., p. 24.
21. Ibid., pp. 21–27.
22. Ibid., p. 7.
23. "Inversiones Españoles Directas."
24. Freres, "Investing in Latin America," p. 7.
25. Ibid., and Inversiones Españolas Directas."
26. "Performance of European Community Countries in Imports from Latin America," and "Performance of European Community Countries in Exports to Latin America," EUROSTAT, *External Trade and Balance of Payments, Statistical Yearbook,* 1992.

# 5

# Eastern Europe and Latin America

## Eusebio Mujal-León

This essay examines the relationship between Eastern Europe and Latin America from a variety of perspectives. The first section explores the evolution of commercial links between Eastern Europe and Latin America over the past decade and examines the prospects for their expansion. The other sections of the essay consider the Eastern European–Latin American relationship from a more dynamic perspective. The second section examines the relationship in terms of the rival claims Eastern Europe and Latin America make to a "special" relationship first with the European Community and, more recently with the European Union (EU) and considers the impact of probable EU enlargement on trade between Latin America and the Union. Finally, the third section focuses on Latin America and Eastern Europe as emerging financial markets. It analyzes their success in competing for capital and considers their future prospects in this regard.

### COMMERCIAL LINKS BETWEEN
### LATIN AMERICA AND EASTERN EUROPE

The direct economic relationship between Eastern Europe and Latin America has not been particularly significant, and it is difficult to imagine that there could be a substantial improvement in the levels of exchange between the two regions over the next decade or two. Historically, there was virtually no relationship between Eastern Europe and Latin America, with the obvious exception of Cuba. This began to change somewhat in the late 1960s and early 1970s, as the East European countries (and the Soviet Union) expanded their political and diplomatic representation in Latin American capitals. Along with this came the first tentative steps toward the expansion of economic links between the two regions.[1] On this front, Poland and Romania—by 1974, they had opened diplomatic and commercial offices in Latin American countries—led the way.[2]

A dual (and almost schizophrenic) perspective animated Eastern European involvement in Latin America during the Cold War. One part was political, and it stemmed from the logic of bipolar competition and alignment with the Soviet Union and focused on those countries where nationalist radical/revolutionary regimes were in power. The other part was economic, and it reflected the search for markets and supplies of raw materials and energy. The distinction between these political and economic perspectives may be illustrated by comparing the allotment of East European economic aid and credits to Latin America between 1971 and 1984. Of the more than $2.7 billion offered during these years, nearly $1.1 billion went to Central America. Since this subregion's combined GDP (in 1982) was less than two-thirds that of Colombia,[3] there can be little doubt the motivation was primarily political. By contrast, only $1.1 billion (directed mostly toward Argentina, Brazil, Colombia, and Peru) was made available to the entire South American continent.

East European trade with Latin America grew slowly during the 1970s, but it never amounted to very much in either absolute or relative terms. Reviewing the figures on a country-by-country basis for the period 1974 to 1982, we find that the average share of trade for most countries was quite low. Thus, Argentina traded 1.3 percent of its exports and 1.7 percent of imports with Eastern Europe; Bolivia, 2.2 percent and 1.2 percent; Brazil, 4.3 percent and 1.4 percent; Colombia, 3.0 percent and 1.4 percent; Mexico, .4 percent and .4 percent; and Peru, 4.4 percent and 1.3 percent.[4] The countries with the highest shares—Peru and Brazil—bought machinery and heavy equipment from Poland and Czechoslovakia, while selling foodstuffs and minerals. During the mid-1980s, Peru also signed a series of countertrade agreements with the Soviet Union and East European countries that resulted in increased exports of its textiles and footwear.

The East European–Latin American trade picture did not improve at all during the 1980s. The debt crisis contracted the Latin American economies and also reduced the trade appeal of East European countries, which had their own hard currency problems. The collapse of the Communist regimes in 1989 certainly did not help matters in the commercial field, but it is important to note that stagnation and decline in the East European–Latin American trade relationship had set in *before* the Berlin Wall fell.

The cases of Czechoslovakia, Hungary, and Poland—which I shall focus on because they are the countries with the greatest economic potential in the East European region—are instructive in this regard.[5] (See Table 5.1) Exports from Czechoslovakia to Latin America declined in both absolute and relative terms between 1981 and 1991. The value of exports went from $129 million in 1981 to $106 million in 1985 before dropping to $92 million in 1991; the Latin American share of these exports declined

**Table 5.1　Selected Eastern European Countries' Trade with the World, European Community, and Western Hemisphere, 1985–1991**

**(Millions U.S. $ and Percentages)**

| | Exports | | | Imports | | |
|---|---|---|---|---|---|---|
| | 1981 | 1985 | 1991 | 1981 | 1985 | 1991 |
| *Poland* | | | | | | |
| Total | 13,249 | 11,489 | 15,804 | 15,475 | 10,836 | 17,886 |
| EC | 2,575 (19.4) | 2,597 (22.6) | 7,055 (14.6) | 2,476 (16) | 2,111 (19.4) | 9,744 (54.4) |
| Western Hemisphere | 144 (1.0) | 204 (1.7) | 254 (1.6) | 700 (4.5) | 276 (2.5) | 230 (1.3) |
| *Hungary* | | | | | | |
| Total | 8,717.1 | 8,542.7 | 10,513.7 | 9,146.4 | 8,228.2 | 11,312.1 |
| EC | 1,502.9 (17.2) | 1,368.3 (16.0) | 4,163.1 (39.6) | 2,164.4 (23.6) | 1,776.0 (21.5) | 4,737 (41.8) |
| Western Hemisphere | 64.3 (1.0) | 55.2 (1.0) | 45.6 (0.4) | 321.3 (3.5) | 248.6 (3.0) | 192.0 (1.7) |
| *Czechoslovakia* | | | | | | |
| Total | 5,852.4 | 11,385.9 | 10,921.3 | 5,656.1 | 11,151 | 10,239.6 |
| EC | 1,629.3 (27.8) | 2,597.4 (22.8) | 4,435.9 (40.6) | 1,750.1 (30.9) | 2,518.7 (22.6) | 3,287 (32.1) |
| Western Hemisphere | 129.7 (2.2) | 106.9 (1.0) | 92.8 (1.0) | 223.2 (3.9) | 270.1 (2.4) | 231.1 (2.3) |

*Source:* IMF, *Direction of Trade Statistics Yearbook.*

from 2.2 percent in 1981 to 1.0 percent in 1985 and held steady at this mark in 1991. The total volume of Czechoslovak exports grew by 86 percent during this ten-year period; however, the value of exports to Latin America declined by 28 percent. Czechoslovak imports from the region showed a broadly similar pattern. Although 1991 showed a small increase in the dollar value of imports over the total ten years earlier, the actual share of Czechoslovak imports from Latin America declined from 3.9 percent to 2.3 percent. This decline occurred even as the volume of Czechoslovak imports was increasing by 81 percent (in dollar terms) between 1981 and 1991. During this period, Czechoslovakia's principal trading partners in Latin America on the export side were Brazil and Mexico. On the import side, Brazil was the leader, averaging $81.5 million for the five-year period, followed by Argentina with a $56 million average. The Brazilian performance on the import side was perhaps the most notable; it sold products totaling $108 million to Czechoslovakia in 1989 and $104 million in 1991.

Hungary showed a similar pattern in its trade relations with Latin America. The total value of exports grew from $8.7 billion in 1981 to $10.5 billion in 1991 (a 21 percent increase), but the value of exports from Latin America declined (from $64 million in 1981 to $55.2 million in 1985 and to $45 million in 1991); the Latin American share of East European imports, which was 1.0 percent in 1981, dropped to 0.4 percent of the total in 1991. (By contrast, the Hungarian share of EC trade more than doubled, from 17.4 percent in 1981 to 39.6 percent in 1991—a development shared by all the East European countries, and one to which we shall turn in the second section of this chapter, when we examine the "rival" claims of the two regions.) Hungarian imports from Latin America also declined. From a total of $321 million in 1981, they dropped to $248 million in 1985 and $192 million in 1991. While Hungarian imports grew by 23 percent during the ten-year period, the Latin American share in this category dropped from 3.5 percent in 1981 to 1.7 percent in 1991. As in the case of Czechoslovakia, Brazil was Hungary's major export/import partner in Latin America. Its exports to Hungary averaged $29.3 million between 1985 and 1991, with highs of $42.9 and $40.0 million in 1986 and 1989, respectively. On the import side Brazil was again a major partner, selling more than $154 million of goods in the Hungarian market in 1991. According to data released by the Central Statistical Office in Budapest, Brazil ranked eleventh and fourteenth in terms of volume of imports to Hungary in 1980 and 1988, respectively.[6]

The evolution of the Polish trade relationship with Latin America generally confirms the more general East European pattern. The only difference lies on the export side, where the Latin American share of Polish exports grew in absolute and percentage terms from 1981 to 1985 (from $144 million and 1.0 percent to $204 million and 1.7 percent), and then more or less held even (in terms of share) at 1.6 percent in 1991. Even as the general volume of Polish imports rose by nearly 16 percent in the 1981 to 1991 period, however, those from Latin America declined sharply. Their value (and share) dropped from $700 million (4.5 percent) in 1981 to $276 million (2.5 percent) in 1985 and $230 million (1.3 percent) in 1991. Here again, the only Latin American countries to emerge as major trade partners were Brazil and, to a much lesser degree, Argentina. Poland sold Brazil goods valued at $189 million in 1991 and bought nearly $164 million worth of products. The bulk of Polish exports to both countries was in machinery and equipment. Argentine exports (which totaled $26 million) consisted mostly of feed and soybeans.

So far we have considered the trade relationship between the two regions from the perspective of the East European countries. The pattern indicates the declining importance of Latin America (with the possible exception of Brazil) for Eastern Europe over the past decade. What can be said about the Latin American side? How important (in terms of value and percentage) was trade with Eastern Europe for such major Latin American countries as Argentina, Brazil, Chile, Colombia, Mexico, Peru, and Venezuela? The countries in question break down into two categories for the years 1981 to 1991: (1) those countries for which trade with Eastern Europe represented *less than 1 percent* of their volume of exports and imports; and (2) those countries whose export/import shares ranged between 1 and 5 percent. In no case, with the possible exception of Brazil, was there significant trade volume.

Countries of the first category are Chile, Mexico, and Venezuela. Their trade with Eastern Europe has been negligible. This region accounted for only .2 percent of the Mexican exports in 1981 and .04 percent in 1991. Chilean exports to Eastern Europe amounted to only $5.8 million in 1991, one-eighth of the 1981 total. Chilean imports from Eastern Europe were scarcely visible, totaling a mere .02 percent in 1991. The pattern was very similar in the case of Venezuela—only .1 percent of its exports went to Eastern Europe. At no time in the last fifteen years has the East European share of Latin American exports been very high. The 1.2 percent share for Chile in 1985 was the highest for any individual Latin American country in the 1980s. Among the countries in this first category, only Mexico has thought seriously in the last few years about ways to expand its trade and investment relationship with Eastern Europe. Thus, under the government of Carlos Salinas de Gortari, Mexico helped found the European Bank for Reconstruction and Development (EBRD), a decision that qualified it to bid on procurement contracts in Eastern Europe.[7]

Countries in the second category include Argentina, Brazil, Colombia, and Peru. Their trade with Eastern Europe is slightly more robust, but not especially noteworthy—again, with the possible exception of Brazil.

First let us take up the case of Peru. The dimensions and significance of its trade with Eastern Europe are difficult to assess. According to the IMF Direction of Trade Statistics, imports from Eastern Europe were negligible (they ranged from .4 percent in 1981 to .2 percent in 1991), while exports to this region fluctuated. The problem with direction of trade data (aside from the general unreliability of Soviet-bloc figures) is that Peru and several East European countries signed countertrade agreements during the mid-1980s that boosted exports; these figures were not included in the IMF data. Whatever the case, the Council for Mutual Economic Assistance (CMEA) share of Peruvian exports (including the Soviet Union), which had declined from a high of 8 to 9 percent in the 1970s to less than 4 percent in 1981,[8] picked up in the wake of the countertrade agreements.[9] Thus, according to UN Trade Data, exports to Eastern Europe, which between 1983 and 1985 represented an average of 1.5 percent of total exports, doubled to 3 percent in the period 1987 to 1990. During this period, Peru diversified its exports to Eastern Europe, adding textiles and footwear to existent shipments of minerals, coffee, and feed. Although Peru has had a niche in the East European market (primarily in Poland and Czechoslovakia), there is little chance its share will expand, given that nearly 50 percent of its exports in 1990 were to Yugoslavia. In any case, Peru's major export partners have been the United States (40 percent), the EU (24 percent), other Western Hemisphere countries (17 percent), and Japan (15 percent). Peruvian imports from Eastern Europe, it should also be noted, have been very low dating back to the 1970s. According to the UN Trade Data, the East European share of imports averaged a miniscule .6 percent in the years between 1982 and 1991.

During the 1980s, Argentina had a positive balance of trade with Eastern Europe and even more so, of course, with the former Soviet Union, to which it shipped vast quantities of grain. According to the IMF Direction of Trade Statistics, Argentine exports to Eastern Europe totaled $139.7 million in 1981, $260.6 million in 1985, and $151.5 million in 1991. These figures represented 1.5 percent, 3.1 percent, and 1.1 percent of its external trade, respectively. Feed, leather, soybeans, and fish (usually in that order) represented the principal Argentine items of export during the 1980s; they accounted for over 90 percent of the total.[10] The import side of the Argentine–Eastern European relationship was anemic, oscillating between .9 percent in 1981 and .5 percent in 1991. An additional perspective on what these figures represent may be gained by comparing these figures to those for exports/imports to Spain and the European Community. Argentine exports to Spain in 1991 totaled $562 million (a 4.3 percent share), while imports accounted for $276 million (3.5 percent). Exports to the EC were $4.2 billion (31.9 percent of the Argentine total), and imports from the Community were worth over $2.3 billion (28.8 percent).

Colombia has also ranked as one of Eastern Europe's larger trade partners in Latin America, but even the most cursory examination of the dimensions of its exports/imports suggests how weak the relationship has been. Exports to Eastern Europe totaled $92.3 million in 1981 (a 3.1 percent share), but declined to $63.1 million in 1985 (1.8 percent) and fell to $48.8 million in 1991 (.7 percent).[11] This situation compares unfavorably with the general volume of reported Colombian exports, which increased 225 percent during the same period. According to statistics released by the Colombian Ministry for Economic Development, Poland, the former German Democratic Republic, Czechoslovakia, and Hungary ranked twenty-second, twenty-third, thirty-fourth, and forty-first, respectively, among its trading partners in 1989.[12] Of Colombia's exports to these countries, coffee represented 84 percent of the total in 1989.[13] If we again use Spain and the EC as points of comparison for Eastern Europe, we find that Colombia had a stronger bilateral export relationship with Spain ($84 million in 1981, a 2.9 percent share, and $154 million in 1991, a 2.3 percent share) than with all of Eastern Europe combined, not to mention the EC—to which Colombia exported over $1.8 billion (a 28.1 percent share in 1991) and from which it imported goods worth nearly $1.2 billion (20.9 percent) in 1991.

Of the countries we have discussed in this section, Brazil is the only one that can claim to have had a *meaningful* trade relationship (in both absolute and relative terms) with Eastern Europe during the 1980s (see Table 5.2). A look at the export side reveals sales of more than $1.1 billion (a 4.9 percent share) to Eastern Europe in 1981. The volume of exports to Eastern Europe declined, however, during the next decade. By 1991, sales to this region accounted for only $586 million or 1.8 percent of Brazil's total export trade.[14] This figure, while certainly not insignificant, must be measured against the nearly 40 percent increase in the *total* value of Brazilian exports that occurred during this period. Eighty-five percent of Brazilian exports to Eastern Europe went to three countries—the former Czechoslovakia, Hungary, and Poland. The bulk of these was in the categories of minerals and agricultural products. Feed, iron ore, coffee, and tobacco made up more than four-fifths of these exports in 1991. Cocoa and processed foods, which had constituted an important component of Brazilian goods sold in Eastern Europe (more than $100 million annually in 1983–1985 and 1987), did not figure as prominently in the ledger later in that decade or so far in this one. During the 1980s, Brazil also exported significant quantities of textiles, yarns, and fabrics to Eastern Europe. Sales of these products, which rose to $108 million in 1984 and then declined, have not recovered. Looking toward the future, it should be noted that although East European production of these products

**Table 5.2**   **Brazil: Trade with Eastern European Countries, Spain, and the European Community, 1981–1991** (Millions U.S. $ and Percentages)

| | Exports | | | Imports | | |
|---|---|---|---|---|---|---|
| | 1981 | 1985 | 1991 | 1981 | 1985 | 1991 |
| Totals | 23,329 | 25,641 | 32,424 | 24,075 | 14,335 | 224,409 |
| Eastern Europe | | | | | | |
| Bulgaria | 71 | 48 | 55 | — | 3 | — |
| Czechoslovakia | 132 | 53 | 104 | 36 | 5 | 27 |
| GDR | 140 | — | — | 82 | 102 | — |
| Hungary | 160 | 124 | 137 | 11 | 19 | 22 |
| Poland | 507 | 161 | 260 | 89 | 155 | 208 |
| Romania | 131 | 76 | 30 | 48 | 27 | 22 |
| Subtotals | | | | | | |
| Eastern Europe | 1,141 (4.9) | 576 (2.2) | 586 (1.8) | 319.6 (1.3) | 311 (2.2) | 279 (1.2) |
| Spain | 368 (1.6) | 533 (2.1) | 826 (2.5) | 107 (0.4) | 61 (0.4) | 231 (1.0) |
| EC | 6,409 (27.4) | 6,896 (26.8) | 10,476 (32.3) | 3,422 (14.2) | 2,100 (14.6) | 5,128 (22.9) |

*Source:* IMF, *Direction of Trade Statistics Yearbook.*

is quite high, Brazilian goods have had a comparative advantage.[15] Footwear is another sector where Brazil, which is the largest exporter in Latin America and whose footwear industry grew by 24 percent between 1970 and 1989,[16] may be able to carve a market niche for itself in Eastern Europe. Viewed from the import side, the Brazilian relationship with Eastern Europe has been more modest. Indeed, the value of imports declined by 12.5 percent between 1981 and 1991, and Eastern Europe accounted for only 1.2 percent of total imports in the last year.

The data collected and analyzed in this section confirm the absence of any *meaningful* trade relationship between Latin America and Eastern Europe during the 1980s and early 1990s. They suggest that the opportunities for expanded trade between the countries of Latin America and Eastern Europe will be very modest. Such opportunities as develop will probably focus on the area of tropical foodstuffs and other primary commodities. In the medium term, there is not much prospect for an expansion in the export of Latin American manufactured products to Eastern Europe. Some entrepreneurs have argued that there exists a complementarity between the economies in the two regions and that the restructuring of the East European economies will open the doors to new possibilities for trade.[17] This is possible, but only in the very long term. Of the Latin American countries surveyed, Brazil is the only one that penetrated the East European market in any significant way, but the bulk of its exports have been in the mineral and agricultural-product categories, and even the dollar value of these has declined in the last few years. Ultimately, whether Brazil can recover its export share in these products, while also recovering its markets for textiles and other manufactured goods, is not altogether clear. Whether entrepreneurs in Brazil or other Latin American countries develop a niche in Eastern Europe will very much depend on how the two regions develop their relationship through the EU.

## LATIN AMERICA, EASTERN EUROPE, AND THE EUROPEAN UNION

Half a world away from each other, Eastern Europe and Latin America are, like many other developing regions, nevertheless linked through competition for expanded trade, investment, and aid from Europe. In the years after its creation in 1957, the European Community became an economic superpower, one of the most dynamic points of reference for the international economy. Although slow to develop the foreign and defense policy mechanisms that would allow it to play a more significant role on the international political stage, the Community was far more active and successful in creating a dense network of preferential trade arrangements with various regions of the world. These efforts have not simply reflected a European desire to maintain vague cultural or historical links. They have also been premised on the need to find markets (export growth has been crucial to European expansion in the postwar period) and to assure stable supplies of energy and raw materials.

Standing at the apex of the trade-preference hierarchy have been the African, Caribbean, and Pacific (ACP) countries—former Belgian, British, Dutch, and French colonies in various parts of the world—which, via the Lomé and Yaoundé conventions, have been guaranteed duty-free access for commodities, principally agricultural products and minerals. Mediterranean states have been in the second rank of the preference pecking order. Although the institutional relationship between them and the EU is in flux (and has always been difficult to define with precision), these countries have had a special link to the Union. Bound to the EU by strong economic ties and significant immigration flows, the region has offered Europe a direct window onto the Third World and its cauldron of demographic pressure and political instability. Finally, at the far end of the preference hierarchy are the Asian and Latin American countries that have participated in the Generalized System of Preferences (GSP) and have had a far more restricted access to European markets.

Latin America has not had an easy time developing a relationship with the EC/EU.[18] Excluded from the provision of the first Lomé Convention (1967), Latin American nations issued the *Carta de Buenos Aires*, a call for expanded economic and political dialogue with the EC. Although the EC and several Latin American countries subsequently signed commercial cooperation agreements, these did not bring very significant results. The early 1980s brought signs of change and greater engagement in the relationship. The European Community, having successfully consolidated its integration and having played an important role in the Iberian transitions to democracy, was now more ready to become active in a continent where the United States had long been considered dominant. For their part, the Latin Americans, wishing to diversify their political and economic dependence, looked eagerly toward the Community.

During the 1980s, various events (the Falklands/Malvinas War, the Central American imbroglio, the debt crisis, the democratization processes, and the enlargement of the Community through the inclusion of Spain and Portugal) encouraged this *reencuentro* between the EC and Latin America.[19] And there were visible results. Political dialogue assumed a much higher profile. The San José framework of meetings helped insert the EC into the Central American arena. The EC organized periodic high-level ministerial meetings with the principal Latin American countries. In June 1987, after significant internal debates, the EC Council of Ministers finally approved a strategic plan for the development of relations with Latin America that included new programs for expanding industrial, scientific, and technological cooperation. During the late 1980s, implementation of these directives led to the creation of "business councils" and the Business Cooperation Network to foster intraregional entrepreneurial links as well as the establishment of the so-called Economic International Investment Partners (ECIIP) whose principal objective has been to encourage the creation of small and medium-sized joint ventures. European development aid to Latin America—from both bilateral and EC sources—also increased significantly when compared to the amounts made available in the late 1970s and early 1980s, but it was still below the shares of other, more privileged, Third World partners.

If political/institutional links between Latin America and the European Community may be said to have improved during the 1980s, the same could not be said about commercial or trade relations. These relations continued a decline that had begun in the early 1970s.[20] Between 1981 and 1991, the Latin American share of EC exports dropped sharply (from 3.5 percent to 2.1 percent). So did its share of imports, which fell from 3.4 percent in 1981 to 2.1 percent in 1991. Even Spain, which had a more articulated and nuanced Latin American policy than other EC members, experienced a similar decline in its trade with (though not its investment in) Latin America. The dollar value of Spanish exports to the region rose slightly from 1981 to 1991 (from $1.95 billion to $1.98 billion), but the Latin American share declined from 9.5 percent to 3.4 percent. Spanish imports showed a similar pattern: Their dollar value grew by nearly $400 million in those years, but the share declined from 11.7 percent to 4.4 percent.

Behind these aggregate figures, of course, lies a more complicated reality. The composition of EU imports from Latin America has changed over the last decade—the proportion of manufactured goods has more than doubled.[21] Brazil and Mexico have also improved (if only marginally) their EU market share in manufactures.[22] And the EU remains an important trade partner for the Southern Cone countries.[23]

There is still no way around the fact, however, that the Latin American share of EC (and world) trade declined significantly during the 1980s.[24] More than the debt crisis weakened the purchasing power of Latin America during the 1980s. The decline in the Latin American share of the EC market also reflected the long-term drop in the prices of many nonfuel primary commodities that have remained the staple of Latin American exports to the Community.[25] Moreover, although it is true that the dollar value of manufactured products exported by Latin America to the EU has risen over the past decade, the increase has not been sufficient to offset the losses incurred through the fall in commodity prices.[26] Weakened by these developments, the Latin American commercial relationship with the Community has also had to withstand the diversionary effects of the sharp increase in intra-EC trade during the 1980s.

Another even more decisive blow struck against Latin American aspirations for a closer relationship to the Community occurred with the collapse of the Soviet empire in Eastern Europe in late 1989 and culminated in the disintegration of the Soviet Union itself two years later. These events recast the map of Europe and, in the process, they also helped deflect attention and resources from the anticipated "deepening" of the Community that was to have taken place in the late 1980s and early 1990s. These events also compelled a realignment of EC external relations, placing Eastern Europe at the core of Community concerns. Even had it wanted to do so, the EC could not have remained unengaged from the East European struggle with the twin challenges of democratization and economic reconstruction. The geographic proximity of Eastern Europe and the consequences of political and social instability there have been on the minds of all the Union partners, but it has been Germany, with its frontline strategic interest in assuring political stability and economic development in *Mitteleuropa*, which has had the most to gain or lose in the region.

Although the long-term perspective for Eastern Europe (and particularly for Hungary, Poland, and the Czech and Slovak Republics—referred to as the Visograd 4) almost certainly involves membership in the Union, plenary integration is not around the corner. There has been no specific commitment from the Union on when the East European countries will join. Not only is the Union wrestling with its own set of problems, many of its members fear too great a liberalization of trade with Eastern Europe, not to mention enlargement eastward. The southern European countries fear the eastward diversion of aid, development funds, and investment. Other countries (including Belgium, France, and Portugal) are concerned that trade liberalization will reduce their exports within the Union. Even Germany could not ignore the economic effects of East European wage levels that are between one-tenth and one-twentieth its own.

And yet behind these anxieties lies the inescapable reality that the European Union has a strategic interest in the transformation of Eastern Europe and the consolidation of democracies and markets there. Eastern Europe has already significantly shifted its trade in the direction of the Union; and despite protectionist pressures within the EU, the value of Polish, Hungarian, Czechoslovak, Romanian, and Bulgarian exports to the Community grew by 27 percent in 1990, 18 percent in 1991, and 20 percent in 1992.[27] More recently, the German recession and the overvaluation of East European exports have weakened exports from the region, but these are conjunctural phenomena. The trend toward greater integration between East and West Europe will not be reversed, and it will have a strong effect on trade. Figure 5.1 indicates that Eastern Europe and Latin

Figure 5.1 EC's External Trade by Selected Regions and Regional Growth Potential

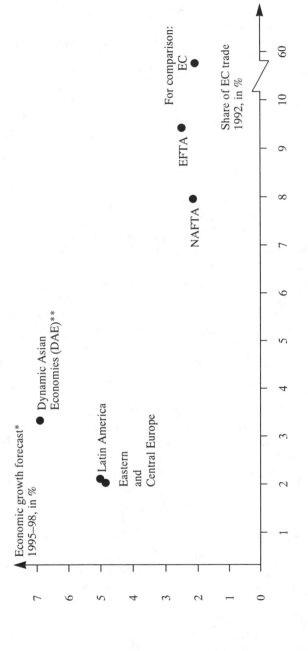

*Source:* Commerzbank, 1993.
*Notes:* * Based on IMF and own estimates.
        ** Korea, Taiwan, Hong Kong, Singapore, Thailand, Malaysia.

America had similar shares of EU trade in 1992, but we can anticipate an expanded commercial gap to develop between the two regions in relation to the Union. One study, which analyzed the geographical composition of East European trade, predicted that Czechoslovak, Hungarian, and Polish export/imports to the EU would surpass those from nearly fifty years ago only in the next century.[28]

The European Union has much to gain from expanded commercial links with Eastern Europe, particularly the Visograd 4. Critics of trade liberalization focus on the problems posed by rising East European exports in agriculture, textiles, and steel. But there is another side to the equation. Trade and integration with the European Union represent the best chance for stabilization and growth in Eastern Europe. The European Union will certainly benefit from the expansion of markets there. And this is not a dream for the distant future. It has already begun to occur. Compared to 1988, EU exports to Eastern Europe have grown by 130 percent, while imports from the region, which have also risen substantially, did so by only 82 percent.[29] Some critics have exaggerated the dangers posed by trade liberalization. After all is said and done, trade with Eastern Europe makes up only 1.7 percent of total Union trade.[30] Even in the area of agriculture, the dangers have probably been overstated. Although it is true that, especially if they modernize and increase productivity, Eastern European producers will eventually be able to compete with their counterparts in southern Europe (farmers in Greece, Ireland, Portugal, and Spain would be the most negatively affected), EU taxpayers and consumers would arguably gain from lower prices and reduced subsidies. Moreover, one unpublished OECD study has suggested that the Union has even gained competitive position in so-called sensitive areas.[31]

Nevertheless, the promise of unimpeded access to Union markets will take time to be realized. The EC signed association agreements with Czechoslovakia, Hungary, and Poland in December 1991 and Bulgaria and Romania in late 1992 that provided for the abolition of most quotas and the removal of many tariffs within a five-year period. But these agreements left barriers to trade in "import-sensitive" products, including iron and steel, chemicals, textiles, and clothing.[32] They also limited increases in East European exports of meat, fruit, dairy products, and vegetables to only 10 percent a year over the next five years.[33] More recently, in April 1993, the Union sent a clear signal to East European farmers when it temporarily banned imports of livestock and dairy products because of an outbreak of hoof-and-mouth disease in the former Yugoslavia. A surge in steel imports in 1992 also triggered restrictions (and, in some cases, anti-dumping duties) against Czechoslovakia, Hungary, and Poland.

Moreover, as we shall discuss in detail below, European investment in Eastern Europe has not flowed as quickly as some had anticipated. Uncertainty regarding accounting and banking rules, tax codes, labor laws, and pension and unemployment systems has been a major factor in this regard. Thus, while it is true that Italian and German investment in the region rose markedly in 1992,[34] agencies such as the European Bank for Reconstruction and Development (EBRD) and the European Investment Bank (EIB), which were specifically created to speed up the integration of Eastern Europe, have had difficulty finding projects worthy of support.[35] By mid-1993, the EBRD had disbursed investment credits worth only ECU 126 million in the region; for its part, the EIB had released only 20 percent of the ECU 925 million assigned for East European countries. EU aid to Eastern Europe had also leveled off. Although the EU was fairly generous in the aid it provided Eastern Europe during the first two years of the post-communist era, the aid budgets for 1992 and 1993 increased by only 10 percent. The aid picture to Eastern Europe will undoubtedly remain cloudy as the battles over distribution of structural and cohesion funds to the less-developed regions within the EU extend into the rest of this decade.

Regardless of the pace of East European integration into the expanded European area, the revolutions of 1989 decisively altered the terms of reference for the competition between Latin America and Eastern Europe for a "special" relationship with the Union. If the processes of democratization and economic reform now under way in Eastern Europe come to a successful conclusion (and there are, of course, important obstacles that must still be overcome),[36] they will be accompanied by the progressive incorporation of Eastern Europe into the Union preference schemes. The effects of this on Latin America could be significant—at least in terms of its future commercial relationship with an expanded Union.

Enlargement of the EU and the progressive incorporation of East European countries will likely result in trade diversion away from extra-European imports and toward intra-European trade. The Spanish example during the 1980s is again instructive in this regard. Whereas in 1985 the EC accounted for 52.1 percent and 36.8 percent of Spanish exports and imports (respectively), five years after Spain joined the Community the EC share had risen to 72.1 percent of exports and 59.3 percent of imports.[37]

Although there is some possibility that Latin American countries, especially those that benefit from a counterseasonal growing cycle, could increase their exports of some foodstuffs (especially tropical fruits and cereals) to both Eastern and Western Europe over the next few years, gains in this area would be easily offset were the EU to adopt a more restrictive trade regime vis-à-vis other Latin American imports and/or to grant preferential access to certain East European products.[38] We can also anticipate much sharper competition between Latin American (primarily Argentina and Brazil) and East European (Hungary and Poland) exporters of meat and meat products. Although both sides can expect to feel the continued impact of quotas and restrictions imposed by the Common Agricultural

Policy, it is more likely that East European vendors would have the advantage in this category. For its part, Latin America will have the clear edge over Eastern Europe in raw materials (its principal competitor will be Russia) and in petrochemical products. Among energy resources, only coal will place Poland and Colombia into direct competition.

The main areas of competition between Latin America and Eastern Europe will focus on semifinished manufactured products (SITC 6) and machinery (SITC 7). It is in the latter category (involving electric machinery and transport equipment, for example) where competition is likely to be most intense between producers in the two regions. Significantly, this is an area where foreign investment may also play an important role. So far, Latin America has maintained a comparative advantage over Eastern Europe in certain product lines (such as textiles, paper, leather, plastic materials, and chemical products);[39] but in a more protectionist climate, this would be very difficult for Argentina, Brazil, or Chile (the ABC countries) to hold, much less to expand their share of the East or West European markets in manufactured goods. Already in 1990, the Visograd 4 countries exported a significantly higher proportion of goods in SITC 6–8 (the percentages were 24.7, 13.0, and 17.6, respectively) to the European Community than the six major Latin American countries,[40] whose share was 16.9 percent, 7.2 percent, and 2.8 percent. A similar trend was evident in relation to Germany—the major trading partner for countries in both regions. Between 1989 and 1991, Argentine, Brazilian, and Chilean manufactured exports to Germany grew by 26 percent, but those of the Visograd 4 countries increased by nearly 116 percent. Even more significant, if we compare the first six months of 1991 and 1992, the manufactured exports of the ABC countries fell by 8 percent, while those of the Visograd 4 group increased by 27 percent.[41] The news was also bad for the ABC countries in the semifinished goods category. Whereas the value of such exports to Germany by the Visograd 4 countries increased 60 percent between 1989 and 1991, sales by the ABC countries—whose total exports in this category were, in any case, less than half the Visograd 4 amount—actually declined 2 percent. A similar trend was evident in terms of German imports. Between 1989 and 1991, the ABC share of German imports actually declined (from 2.4 percent to 2.0 percent), while those of the Visograd 4 countries increased from 1.7 percent to 2.6 percent.[42]

On balance, the conclusion seems inescapable that the progressive incorporation of Eastern Europe into the Union sphere of influence, while expanding commerce in some areas, will more likely have a negative effect on the broader trade relationship between Latin America and the EU over the longer term.

## THE EMERGENCE OF LATIN AMERICA AND
## EASTERN EUROPE AS FINANCIAL MARKETS

There is a third dimension to the relationship between Latin America and Eastern Europe—their recent emergence as financial markets and their competition for capital investments. Though members of distinct economic blocs, Latin America and Eastern Europe shared certain economic characteristics during most of the twentieth century. Both regions could be said to have been at the middle level of economic development, and they both tried to modernize their economies through the use of import-substitution models of industrialization.[43] More recently, Latin America and Eastern Europe have been compelled to undertake major structural reforms and to seek integration into the international economy; both regions are today in the throes of a painful transition to more open economies. Whether they succeed in these efforts will depend on many factors, but among the most important will be their capacity to attract and hold foreign capital and investment.

There has been an enormous increase in capital flows (primarily private) to Latin America in the last few years. The figures are nothing short of impressive. An estimated $100 billion moved into the region between 1990 and 1992. In 1991 alone, $40 billion entered the economies of Mexico, Chile, Brazil, Argentina, and Venezuela.[44] Given these numbers, it is not surprising that, for the first time since the onset of the debt crisis, the balance sheet for Latin America showed positive net resource transfers in 1991 and 1992. The region is on track to receive $40 to 45 billion in such transfers during 1993, with about $25 billion entering Mexico, $7 billion Argentina, and $3 to 5 billion Venezuela.[45] According to Salomon Brothers, for the year 1991, the bulk of these investments was in loan and bond financing in the international capital markets (52 percent) and in foreign direct investment (FDI) (32 percent), with another 17 percent directed toward portfolio investment. Much of the investment came in response to the numerous privatizations in the region. Mexico led the way in this respect with nearly $20 billion from sales of state-owned enterprises. An important part of this capital, it should also be noted, came from Latin American investors who had abandoned the region in the early and mid-1980s. Estimates of the amount of capital held abroad by residents have ranged between $200 and $400 billion. By late 1987, it was estimated, $84 billion in Mexican and $58 billion in Venezuelan capital had fled.[46] Some of this money began to return in the late 1980s. Between 1989 and 1990, approximately $14.1 billion returned to Chile, Mexico, and Venezuela,[47] and the Mexican government estimated an additional $5.5 billion returned in 1991.[48]

The massive infusion of capital represented an impressive turnaround from the situation in the early 1980s when the Latin American economies, with their currencies overvalued, public-sector deficits rising, international competitiveness in decline, and inflation climbing out of control, became unable to service the foreign debt which they had built up during the 1970s. The resulting crisis led to a sharp decline in international lending. In the period 1983 to 1988, voluntary credits and bonds to the region totaled only $7 billion.[49]

The situation began to change in the late 1980s, as many Latin American governments implemented macrostabilization programs with a focus on price and market reforms and undertook major restructuring and privatization initiatives. High on the agenda in the first phase was an effort to reduce budget deficits, to enhance the fiscal capacity of the state, and to liberalize both trade and the labor market. The second phase focused on privatization, which created ample opportunities for foreign investors to purchase what were, in effect, undervalued offerings. Progress in dealing with debt renegotiation and the increase in export activity drew increased attention to investment opportunities in Latin America. The success and apparent seriousness of economic reform programs there (this occurred at a time when interest rates were low in the United States, and neither Europe nor the United States could shake an economic recession) were also important in encouraging investors during the late 1980s and early 1990s.

Whether there will or can be continued vigorous growth in capital flows to Latin America through the mid- and late 1990s is unclear.[50] Up to this point, much of the investment to the region has been attracted by the high short-term rates of return; but, according to the Inter-American Development Bank, "in the future, capital inflows are likely to reflect a longer-term link with company earnings and the real growth of the economy."[51] Much of the portfolio investment has been speculative in nature and can be expected to migrate to other markets when returns decline. A panic on the Argentine stock exchange in mid-August 1992, for example, sent values plummeting by nearly 40 percent.[52] The more recent 30 percent devaluation of the Mexican peso underscores the potential volatility of the situation.

Many investors in Latin America are still uncertain as to the long-term commitment of many governments to economic reform and modernization. The social and political costs of these programs are great; and there is a danger that "adjustment fatigue" could set in and destroy investor confidence. In a more positive vein, Latin America has a number of large local or subregional markets,[53] and the five or six countries that have attracted the bulk of foreign investment have made (and are making) great strides in the modernization of their infrastructure, and they have eliminated or substantially reduced restrictions on capital movements and foreign-exchange markets. Another important development in Latin America has been the reform of the pension laws. The institution of privately funded programs for health, disability, and life insurance will further enhance the total demand for Latin American capital markets.[54] Approval of the North American Free Trade Agreement (NAFTA) and the successful conclusion of the Uruguay Round of the GATT talks sent strong and positive signals to investors interested in Latin America. But there can be little doubt that, as it searches for capital to meet its developmental needs, Latin America will have to compete with other potential borrowers. Among these will be the more developed economies of Eastern Europe.

In the wake of the revolutions of 1989, capital flows to Eastern Europe have been fairly modest. The reasons are not hard to decipher. The rates of return have been higher and institutional environments safer in other parts of the world. Even if significant distortions and controls existed in Latin America and elsewhere, at least markets did not have to be invented, an efficient banking system created, and a set of property and tax laws devised from the ground up. The state dominated domestic output in Eastern Europe; it was responsible for 65.2 percent of GDP in Hungary (1984), 81.7 percent in Poland, 96.5 percent in the former German Democratic Republic (1982), and 97.0 percent in Czechoslovakia (1986).[55] Because it has involved a redefinition of the very role of the state, the scale and scope of privatization in Eastern Europe has been enormous. At issue has been nothing less than the creation of the institutional framework without which markets (and democracy) cannot function and which are necessary to attract investors. Such issues as the development of legal and regulatory frameworks, the establishment of procedures to resolve lost property and restitution claims, the organization of unemployment insurance and other forms of social compensation, and the revision of the tax codes have had to be addressed in an atmosphere of social and economic uncertainty.

Hungary has certainly been the leader in Eastern Europe in terms of borrowing on the international capital markets and attracting foreign investment. These markets lent Hungary $4.7 billion in 1989 and $1.8 in 1991. Hungary's FDI stock is estimated to be $4.5 billion, an amount that places the country above the 1989 level for several Latin American countries, among them Argentina and Venezuela.[56] Ranking just below Mexico in the March 1993 *Institutional Investor* credit rating, Hungary raised $1.9 billion in 1991 and $1.7 billion in 1992[57]—most of which went to purchase privatized state properties. By late 1992, about 160 state-owned companies had been sold to foreign investors. Among the major investors in Hungary have been multinational corporations, such as Ford (with an initial $83 million investment), Suzuki ($30 million, in a joint venture), General Motors ($66 million, in a joint venture), and Nestlé ($38 million, in a joint venture).[58] More recently, Audi has invested in an engine-assembly plant outside of Budapest.

Broadly speaking, Hungary has provided the most favorable institutional environment for foreign investors in Eastern Europe. Among its major attractions has been the provision whereby the corporate income tax rate for foreign investors could be eliminated for up to ten years. This situation occurred in the case of GM, which joined forces with a Hungarian enterprise (Raba) in upgrading a plant that will produce Opel Astra automobiles for the Hungarian market and engines for West European markets. Surprisingly, in the first postcommunist years, U.S. firms have been more active than German ones in Hungary. Through 1991, approximately 60 percent of foreign investment in Hungary came from U.S.-based firms (much of it focused on technology-intensive industries or on the production of high-income consumer goods) and more than 75 percent of total U.S. investment in Eastern Europe was located there.[59] On the other hand, Hungary has not had much luck with its registered bond issues in the United States. American institutional investors have much preferred Mexican "Yankee" bonds over Hungarian "Paprika" ones.[60]

At least one part of former Czechoslovakia has also been relatively successful in securing external investment. By the end of 1992, the Czech Republic (which had only twice the population of Slovakia) had received more than 90 percent of the nearly $2.3 billion invested in the formerly unified country. Analysts estimated there was another $3 billion in foreign investment approved but not yet disbursed for the Czech lands. Two of the most prominent foreign investors have been Volkswagen, which entered into a partnership with Skoda Cars, and K-Mart, which acquired two department stores in an $118 million investment.[61] Attracted by substantially lower wages, German firms have also been very active in the Czech lands. Through 1991, Germany was the source of more than half of all foreign investment there; only 25 percent came from U.S. firms. Not least because it has moved much more slowly with respect to privatization, Slovakia has been far less attractive to external capital. Hoping to prompt such interest, Premier Vladimir Meciar took the occasion during a May 1993 visit to Austria to announce a series of incentives (including tax allowances) for foreign investors.

Of the Visograd 4, Poland has done least well in the scramble for foreign investment. It has the largest potential market in East and Central Europe, and as Table 5.3 indicates, its rates of return on bank debt have been very high. Nevertheless, the threat of political instability and a reversal in the privatization strategy has scared investors. The volume of investment has been "less than a third that of Hungary (which has one-quarter the population)."[62] In one interview, then minister of privatization, Janusz Lewandowski, indicated that Poland had attracted approximately $1.3 billion in foreign capital through participation in 8,800 joint ventures. But these amounts, he recognized, were far below the Hungarian totals, adding that many of the Polish joint ventures "mainly existed on paper . . . and fewer than 100 of them were of any real importance to the our economy."[63]

**Table 5.3    Emerging Market Debt: Highlights of Total Rates of Return, 1991–1993**

|  | 1991 | 1992 | 1993 6 Months annualized |
|---|---|---|---|
| **Mexico** | | | |
| par bonds | 48.7% | 16.9% | 33.1% |
| discount bonds | 30.0 | 10.5 | |
| **Argentina** | | | |
| bank debt (GRA) | 75.0 | 33.3 | 45.5 |
| **Brazil** | | | |
| MYDFA bank debt | 30.6 | 2.7 | |
| Exit bonds | 48.2 | -1.0 | |
| IDU bonds* | | -20.8 | 68.9 |
| **Nigeria** | | | |
| par bonds** | | 9.3 | 36.7 |
| **Philippines** | | | |
| par bonds* | | 12.1 | |
| **Poland** | | | |
| bank debt (DDRA) | 42.7 | 18.9 | 60.5 |
| **Venezuela** | | | |
| par bonds | 48.1 | -3.7 | 48.6 |
| debt conversion bonds | | | |
| (DCBs) | 30.7 | -16.0 | 58.2 |

*Ten months in 1992; **Eleven months in 1992.
*Source:* Goldman Sachs.

From this general overview of capital flows, it becomes evident that over the past few years Latin America has had the comparative advantage over Eastern Europe (and the Visograd 4) in attracting foreign investment. Although there are many reasons for this relative success, three factors stand out. First has been the existence of a legal infrastructure and a capitalist culture. Despite the cycle of loan defaults and the like (all of which logically make investors jittery), Latin America has well-codified rules and regulations regarding investment and industrial development. Whatever the potential for political and social instability in individual countries, the Latin American region lacks the culture of "socialist envy" that is still very much perceptible in Eastern Europe. Latin America (particularly the larger economies) also has a longer trajectory of involvement with global economic actors. Second, through trade and mineral resource exploitation as well as the activities of multinational corporations, Latin America has been for a long time incorporated into the international economy. The East European economies, by contrast, maintained a much higher degree of autarky and isolation. The third reason pertains to the commitment to privatization and economic reform. Virtually all Latin American governments have systematically enacted reform and stabilization programs. Since 1989, Mexico, Argentina, and Venezuela (among many others) have alleviated concerns over their debt, signing accords with foreign banks to exchange bad debt for new issues of government bonds backed by U.S. Treasuries as collateral. Privatization has advanced far more fitfully in Eastern Europe; the banking sector is still saddled with bad loans from the communist era; the corporate bond market is weak and illiquid; and, there are still significant restrictions on foreign ownership. In all, there have been powerful reasons why investors (including those from the European Community) have so far tended to favor Latin America over Eastern Europe.

There is no crystal ball available that would allow us to predict which region or specific countries will come out ahead in the competition for capital in the years ahead. (See Figure 5.2 for one economic forecast of consumer prices and GDP) The overall situation in the international capital markets will certainly play a major role in this regard. Although some analysts believe there will be a real tightening of conditions in that market over the course of the next decade, which could negatively affect both Latin America and Eastern Europe, others believe that a major contraction is not likely to occur. Market terms for borrowers may be affected, but with gross international bond financing totaling $256 billion and international bank lending another $820 billion (in 1989),[64] there should be plenty of capital available.

An analysis of country-risk rankings and economic projections for 1993–1994 (Tables 5.4 and 5.5) reveals some interesting cross-regional comparisons. In terms of risk, the top countries in both regions clustered into several categories. The leader was Chile, which ranks thirty-ninth. Mexico and Colombia among the Latin American countries and Hungary and the Czech Republic among the East European ones cluster between forty-sixth and forty-ninth. The next category—countries ranked in the top 40 percent—included Venezuela, Argentina, and Brazil from Latin America, and Slovenia from Eastern Europe. Romania and Poland brought up the rear. Their political risk component was significantly higher than for

Figure 5.2  Eastern Europe's Economies, 1990–1997

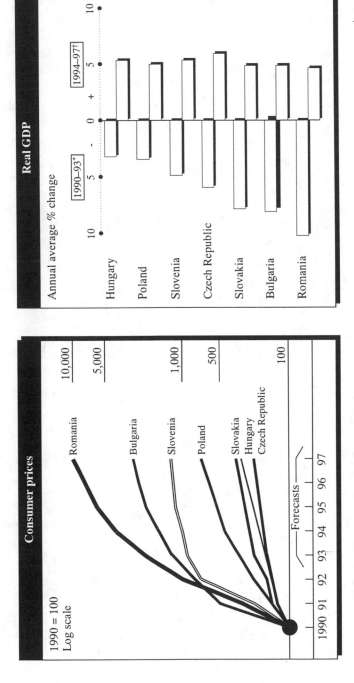

*Source:* PlanEcon. © 1993 The Economist Newspaper Group, Inc. Reprinted with permission.

**Table 5.4 Country Risk Rankings: Latin America and Eastern Europe, 1993**

| Rank 3/93 | Country | Total Score | Economic Performance | Political Risk | Debt Indicators | Access to Bank Lending | Access to Short-Term Finance | Access to Capital Markets | Discount on Fortaiting | Credit Rating | Debt in Default or Rescheduled |
|---|---|---|---|---|---|---|---|---|---|---|---|
| **Latin America** | | | | | | | | | | | |
| 39 | Chile | 65.70 | 7.33 | 14.47 | 8.76 | 4.57 | 6.00 | 7.00 | 7.61 | 3.85 | 6.12 |
| 46 | Mexico | 55.11 | 6.46 | 13.19 | 9.07 | 0.92 | 5.50 | 7.00 | 7.27 | 1.92 | 3.77 |
| 49 | Colombia | 62.08 | 5.47 | 12.55 | 8.92 | 1.07 | 5.60 | 4.00 | 5.45 | 0.00 | 9.84 |
| 58 | Venezuela | 44.68 | 5.34 | 12.34 | 9.04 | 0.47 | 4.50 | 5.00 | 4.55 | 1.92 | 1.50 |
| 62 | Argentina | 42.20 | 5.16 | 9.79 | 8.58 | 0.00 | 4.50 | 5.00 | 3.18 | 0.00 | 5.99 |
| 66 | Brazil | 40.04 | 3.66 | 8.30 | 9.16 | 0.22 | 4.00 | 4.00 | 3.18 | 0.00 | 7.51 |
| 75 | Costa Rica | 36.45 | 4.78 | 9.36 | 6.13 | 1.58 | 4.00 | 2.00 | 0.00 | 0.00 | 5.58 |
| 87 | El Salvador | 32.68 | 3.60 | 7.87 | 9.35 | 0.00 | 1.00 | 2.00 | 0.00 | 0.00 | 8.85 |
| 128 | Peru | 22.90 | 3.42 | 4.68 | 9.08 | 0.00 | 3.50 | 2.00 | 0.00 | 0.00 | 0.23 |
| **Eastern Europe** | | | | | | | | | | | |
| 47 | Hungary | 54.92 | 5.90 | 12.55 | 8.62 | 0.00 | 5.00 | 6.00 | 4.55 | 2.31 | 10.00 |
| 48 | Czech Republic | 54.89 | 7.08 | 10.85 | 9.57 | 0.00 | 6.00 | 5.00 | 4.09 | 2.31 | 9.99 |
| 63 | Slovenia | 42.19 | 4.84 | 10.43 | 9.47 | 1.09 | 3.00 | 4.00 | 0.00 | 0.00 | 9.36 |
| 74 | Romania | 36.94 | 3.42 | 7.02 | 10.00 | 0.00 | 3.50 | 3.00 | 0.00 | 0.00 | 10.00 |
| 78 | Poland | 35.78 | 4.91 | 8.72 | 9.35 | 0.00 | 5.50 | 4.00 | 0.45 | 0.00 | 2.84 |
| 132 | Yugoslavia | 21.96 | 1.61 | 0.43 | 9.47 | 1.09 | 0.00 | 0.00 | 0.00 | 0.00 | 9.36 |
| 133 | Latvia | 21.70 | 2.55 | 6.38 | 0.00 | 0.00 | 1.00 | 3.00 | 0.00 | 0.00 | 8.77 |
| 134 | Lithuania | 21.36 | 2.42 | 6.17 | 0.00 | 0.00 | 1.00 | 3.00 | 0.00 | 0.00 | 8.77 |
| 149 | Russia | 18.13 | 2.17 | 4.68 | 0.00 | 0.00 | 0.50 | 2.00 | 0.00 | 0.00 | 8.77 |

*Source: Euromoney 1993*, six-month country risks survey. Reprinted with permission.
*Note:* Rankings are based on 169 countries.

**Table 5.5   Country Economic Projections, 1993/94**

| Rank 3/93 | Country | Economic Performance | Overall Economic Performance 1993 | Overall Economic Performance 1994 | Average GNP Growth Forecast 1993/1994 % | Real GNP Growth Forecast 1993 % | Real GNP Growth Forecast 1994 % |
|---|---|---|---|---|---|---|---|
| **Latin America** | | | | | | | |
| 33 | Chile | 7.30 | 58.00 | 61.00 | 5.90 | 6.00 | 5.80 |
| 42 | Mexico | 6.50 | 52.00 | 53.00 | 3.30 | 2.90 | 3.60 |
| 51 | Colombia | 5.50 | 46.00 | 43.00 | 3.60 | 3.30 | 3.80 |
| 53 | Venezuela | 5.30 | 43.00 | 44.00 | 4.20 | 4.10 | 4.20 |
| 55 | Argentina | 5.16 | 41.00 | 43.00 | 0.00 | 4.30 | 4.00 |
| 84 | Brazil | 3.70 | 29.00 | 31.00 | 1.50 | 1.20 | 1.70 |
| 62 | Costa Rica | 4.80 | 39.00 | 38.00 | 3.60 | 3.50 | 3.60 |
| 86 | El Salvador | 3.60 | 30.00 | 29.00 | 3.90 | 3.60 | 4.20 |
| 92 | Peru | 3.40 | 25.00 | 31.00 | 3.00 | 2.30 | 3.60 |
| **Eastern Europe** | | | | | | | |
| 47 | Hungary | 5.90 | 46.00 | 50.00 | 1.90 | 0.70 | 3.10 |
| 35 | Czech Republic | 7.10 | 55.00 | 60.00 | 2.20 | 1.30 | 3.00 |
| 63 | Slovenia | 4.80 | 37.00 | 42.00 | -0.20 | -2.20 | 1.80 |
| 95 | Romania | 3.40 | 28.00 | 28.00 | -2.90 | -4.50 | -1.30 |
| 59 | Poland | 4.90 | 38.00 | 42.00 | 2.60 | 1.90 | 3.30 |
| 144 | Yugoslavia | 1.60 | 13.00 | 14.00 | -7.70 | -11.70 | -3.60 |
| 115 | Latvia | 2.50 | 19.00 | 23.00 | -5.20 | -7.00 | -3.40 |
| 122 | Lithuania | 2.40 | 19.00 | 21.00 | -8.90 | -10.60 | -7.20 |
| 129 | Russia | 2.20 | 17.00 | 19.00 | -8.90 | -11.70 | -6.10 |

*Source: Euromoney 1993,* six-month country risks survey. Reprinted with permission.
*Note:* Rankings are based on 169 countries.

their regional counterparts. Poland had the additional problem of having failed to reschedule its debt.

If we turn to economic projections for 1993/94 (see Table 5.4), we find a similar cluster pattern. Among the Latin American countries, Chile, Mexico, Colombia, Venezuela, and Argentina led the way in terms of economic performance (they ranked thirty-third, forty-second, fifty-first, fifty-third, and fifty-fifth). The Czech Republic and Hungary were the strongest East European performers, ranking thirty-fifth and forty-seventh. Poland and Slovenia place fifty-ninth and sixty-third, while Romania is ninety-fifth. Brazil, which had an annual inflation rate of over 1,000 percent in 1992, ranked eighty-fourth on the worldwide list.

Whether the pattern of capital flows to either Latin America or Eastern Europe will be altered over the next decade depends on the success individual countries have in addressing a number of challenges. The first set of challenges are infrastructural. These relate not only to the legal framework for the resolution of property claims and liabilities but to the restrictions and incentives that governments place on investments as well as to the legal protection accorded them.[65] Uncertainty in the first arena, for example, has led some East European countries (notably Hungary) to offer more generous terms to investors in terms of tax liabilities than do their Latin American counterparts. A related infrastructural imperative relates to the development of adequate telecommunications; road, railway, and sea transportation systems; and supplier networks. Latin American countries have had a relative advantage in this regard, but as anyone who has done business in the region well understands, transportation and communication delays and problems abound. Eastern Europe (especially Hungary and the Czech Republic) has made great strides in the last two years; its physical proximity to the European Union will facilitate the rapid development of these infrastructures.

The second set of challenges refer to the economy and, more specifically, to the commitment national governments make to continued privatization and reform. In response to the structural reforms undertaken in the last few years, there have been tremendous capital flows into Latin America. Flows into Eastern Europe, while less dramatic, have still been substantial. But investors are still finicky. Privatization still has a long way to go in several East European countries. Various schemes have been advanced to accelerate the process (among them, mass privatizations through vouchers). Their procedures are not only complex; the risks are also high, "especially if the changes do not result in improved enterprise performance."[66] But it is far more than a problem of transferring property ownership. Eastern Europe lags behind in terms of a financial network. Not only are banks still burdened by debts accumulated (and largely ignored) under the communist system, but the stock exchanges and other financial instruments are at a very early stage. The situation in Latin America (and, of course, it varies from country to country, as it does in Eastern Europe) is slightly different. By and large, the region has moved rapidly in the privatization area, and financial infrastructures (especially in the larger countries where much of the investment has gone) are relatively more broad-based and experienced than the East European ones. There is little doubt, however, that "policy slippages" could result in "sudden and large reversals of private capital flows."[67] Moreover, the massive infusion of foreign capital itself can have palpably negative effects, increasing the money supply and thus encouraging inflationary pressures. In this context, the temptation to devalue will be strong, but such a decision usually brings only short-term gains in competitiveness and undermines broader investor confidence.

The third challenge these countries confront is political. It relates to the delicate balancing act that governments in both regions must maintain between economic rigor, on the one hand, and the need to retain popular support, on the other. The euphoria of 1989 has long since passed, and in many Latin American as well as in the East European countries economic reforms have had a steep social price. Unemployment has risen substantially and will probably continue to do so in the face of additional structural reforms and the flexibilization of the labor market. Over the next few years, elections throughout Latin America and Eastern Europe will provide a barometer of just how popular various governments and their policies are. Corruption scandals in Latin America and the difficulty political parties have had in consolidating their structures in Eastern Europe will have the most lasting impact on the political scene.

How Latin American and Eastern European countries resolve the terms of their association with their neighboring regional trade blocs will clearly have an important effect on the volume of capital flows. Notwithstanding the turbulence of the Mexican financial markets in January 1995 and the knotty political-social situation there and in other Latin American countries, however, overall capital flows into the region are not likely to diminish. Over the longer term, NAFTA should provide additional impetus to such flows, and it should also synergize various subregional trade blocks, most especially MERCOSUR which has a population base of over 200 million people and whose intraregional trade has grown over 300 percent in the last five years. The progressive incorporation of other countries (such as Chile) into NAFTA will provide additional incentives in terms of trade and investment opportunities. There are, in sum, several large markets in Latin America that stand ready to attract investors through 1990s— if the right mix of political will, economic reform, and social equilibrium can be found.

Eastern Europe is Mexico to the European Union. The EU may be an occasionally reluctant suitor to its neighbors eastward, but it cannot afford to avoid engagement, and ultimately marriage, least of all with the Visograd 4. Once a definite timetable is set for accession, this will provide a strong boost to the commercial relationship; it will also invigorate major investment flows from investors seeking routes of access to the large and wealthy European markets. Analysts anticipate economic recovery to be well under way in Eastern Europe by the end of the decade. One group forecasts nearly 5 percent growth on average for the region between 1994 and 1997,[68] with the Czech Republic, Hungary, Slovenia, and Poland likely to have the strongest growth rates.

Capital flows toward Eastern Europe (in the form of investments and aid) are likely to intensify in the decade ahead as the EU deepens its commitment to the modernization of Eastern Europe. The stability of Eastern Europe and its modernization have become the most significant strategic concern for the members of the Union. Whatever arguments or disputes there may be within the EU about the pace and timing of East European accession, there can be little doubt the countries of Eastern Europe will sooner or later join the train of regional integration. Of course, there are and will be protectionist pressures, and the road to a new version of the Treaty of Rome will not be smooth. Neither Germany nor its neighbors, however, wish to risk the problems that would be unleashed if democracy and the market do not take hold in the region. In short, a strategy of investment and modernization in Eastern Europe, which aims at eventual accession, will be a crucial component of EU foreign policy.

## CONCLUSIONS

This chapter has focused on a variety of ways in which Eastern Europe and Latin America interact and relate to each other. In the first section, I examined the commercial relationship between the regions and found that whatever trade had developed in the early 1980s had collapsed by the latter part of the decade. There seems to be little chance of this relationship recovering or, even more unlikely, expanding in any meaningful way in the near to medium term. In the second section of this chapter I analyzed the interaction of Eastern Europe and Latin America through the prism of relations with the European Union. I found that the progressive incorporation of Eastern Europe into the Community will likely have a negative effect on the broader trade relationship between Latin America, on the one hand, and the EU and Eastern Europe, on the other. Latin American exports of semifinished manufactured products in SITC 6–7 will be most affected by this process. Finally, in the third section of this chapter, I analyzed the Latin American–East European relationship in terms of their competition for capital flows. The evidence suggests that, although over the course of the next decade investments should continue to move in the direction of Latin America (albeit without the intensity of recent years), the volume of such flows to Eastern Europe is likely to increase substantially. Because the two regions offer different kinds of opportunities (Latin America has larger markets, Eastern Europe will serve as a sourcing base), they are not likely to compete directly with one another for capital investment. Prospects for both regions depend, of course, on the sorts of policies followed by their respective governments. The victory of the former communists and their allies in the December 1993 Polish parliamentary elections as well as the success of their Hungarian counterparts in the May 1994 elections (they received over 30 percent of the vote and handily outdistanced the ruling conservative party) should remind us of how much the transition to the market has hurt ordinary citizens in Eastern Europe. But beyond the specific policies adopted or the pace and timing of continued economic reform, we should keep in mind that the European Union has a strategic interest in what happens in Eastern Europe. And this will guarantee an intensified flow of aid and investment through the rest of the decade.

## NOTES

I benefited greatly from the comments of the study group and the editors of this volume. My particular thanks to Françoise Simon for her suggestions and assistance.

I also thank Vasco Rato, Melissa Pantel, Matthew Marshall, Barbara Donovan, and Alejandro Foxley for their invaluable assistance with the research for this chapter. Thanks are also due to Vikas Seth for helping to clarify some of my ideas and to Kim Chan, Eric DiMicelli, and Jeffrey Lee of the Columbia University School of Business for sharing the results of a paper they prepared on emerging markets in Eastern Europe and Latin America.

1. Unless otherwise noted, trade data are drawn from the International Monetary Fund's *Direction of Trade Statistics Yearbook*.

2. The discussion in these first paragraphs draws on Michael Radu, "Eastern Europe and Latin America," in Eusebio Mujal-León, ed., *The USSR and Latin America—A Developing Relationship* (Boston: Unwin & Hyman, 1989), pp. 254–1270. In light of subsequent events, it becomes apparent that the title of the book could have used a question mark.

3. Ibid., p. 259. For the GDP figures, see Inter-American Development Bank (IADB), *Economic and Social Progress in Latin America: 1992 Report* (Washington, D.C.), p. 286.

4. United Nations, *Yearbook of International Trade Statistics* (New York: United Nations, 1983).

5. Figures are drawn from the International Monetary Fund, *Direction of Trade Statistics Yearbook* (Washington, D.C.) for the years 1988 and 1992. Slightly different figures are contained in the UN trade data charts. Unless specifically noted, references throughout this paper are to the IMF's direction of trade figures.

6. See the *Statistical Pocket Book of Hungary* (Budapest, 1988), p. 187.

7. Esperanza Durán, *Mexico's Relations with the European Community*, Working Paper No. 33 (Instituto de Relaciones Europeo-Latinoamericanas [IRELA], 1992), p. 43.

8. See Ruben Berríos, "Relations Between Peru and the Socialist Countries," in Augusto Varas, ed., *Soviet–Latin American Relations in Latin America* (Boulder, Colo.: Westview Press, 1987), pp. 211–229, esp. pp. 212–219.

9. For a discussion of this issue, see Robert K. Evanson, "Soviet Trade Relations with Latin America" in Varas, *Soviet–Latin American Relations*, pp. 238–239.

10. This information is drawn from UN trade data (see Note 4).

11. The source for Colombian data is the IMF *Direction of Trade Yearbook*. The UN trade data indicate a slightly stronger export performance for Colombia in relation to Eastern Europe. Between 1986 and 1990, exports to Eastern Europe averaged 2.7 percent, before falling to 1.1 percent in 1991.

12. Ministerio de Desarrollo Económico, *Comercio Exterior de Colombia* (1992).

13. Ibid. The UN trade data for 1990 and 1991 indicate a decline in coffee exports to Eastern Europe. Coffee is still by far the largest export commodity, but in 1991 fruits made up 35 percent of the total share.

14. The UN trade data indicate Brazilian exports to Eastern Europe of $922 million (1987), $777 million (1988), $825 million (1989), $593 million (1990), and $353 million (1991). The latter figure represented 1.1 percent of total commodity exports.

15. IADB, *Economic and Social Progress,* Appendix Table 7, "Revealed Comparative Advantage in Latin America's Top 12 Manufacturing Exports," p. 266.

16. Ibid., p. 221.

17. See, for example, Guillermo Caballero Vargas, "Europa del Este: Un Nuevo Mercado para los Productos de América Latina," (interview) in *Pensamiento Ibero-Americano* (Madrid), special issue on "La Nueva Europa y el Futuro de América Latina" (1991).

18. See Aida Lerman Alperstein, "Evolución histórica de las relaciones comerciales entre América Latina y la CEE," *Comercio Exterior* (Mexico), Vol. 41 (February 1991), pp. 177–185, and Fundación Friedrich Ebert, *Relaciones Económicas entre América Latina y la Comunidad Económica Europea* (Documentos y Estudios No. 59) [Madrid, 1988].

19. For a balanced and realistic assessment, see Angel Viñas, "Community Relations with Latin America: Past, Present and Future," in Armand Clesse and Raymond Vernon, eds., *The European Community After 1992: A New Role in World Politics?* (Baden-Baden: Nomos, 1991), pp. 348–359.

20. See IRELA, *Economic Relations Between the European Community and Latin America: A Statistical Profile* (Working Paper No. 31), 1992.

21. See Françoise Simon's and Susan Kaufman Purcell's contribution to this volume (Chapter 2).

22. See IADB, *Economic and Social Progress*, p. 270.

23. In 1991, the EC accounted for 31.9 percent, 32.3 percent, and 31.9 percent of Argentine, Brazilian, and Chilean exports, respectively. Comparable figures for Colombia and Peru were 28.1 percent and 24.6 percent. For Mexico and Venezuela, by contrast, they were 8.5 percent and 10.3 percent. There was less of a discrepancy on the import side, where the range for all seven countries was between 17.8 percent for Peru and 28.8 percent for Argentina.

24. Argentina accounted for .0033 of EC exports in 1981 and .0030 in 1991, and for .0044 of EC imports in 1981 and .0016 in 1991. For its part, Brazil accounted for .0097 of EC exports in 1981 and .0074 in 1991, and for .0053 of EC imports in 1981 and .0038 in 1991.

25. See United Nations *World Economic Survey—1992* and the Comisión Económica para América Latina y el Caribe (CEPAL), *Notas sobre la Economía y el Desarrollo*, No. 537/538 (December 1992), table 13, p. 51.

26. For the destination of Latin America's exports of manufactures in 1990, see the IADB, *Economic and Social Progress*, p. 269. The EC accounted for 14.5 percent of this trade from the Andean countries, 20.2 percent from the Southern Cone, and 19.0 percent from the Caribbean.

27. *The Economist*, May 1, 1993, p. 55.

28. Susan M. Collins and Dani Rodrik, *Eastern Europe and the Soviet Union in the World Economy* (Washington, D.C.: Institute of International Economics), pp. 39–40. The authors picked the most "normal" pre–Great Depression year for which they had complete data as their base line. In 1928, 54.8 percent of Czechoslovak imports and 43.9 percent of its exports were with the Community, as compared to 32.4 percent and 25 percent for Hungary and 54.4 percent and 55.9 percent for Poland.

29. András Inotai, "Latin America's Competitive Position vis-à-vis Central and Eastern Europe," p. 22. The paper was prepared for the Seminar on Latin America's Competitive Position in the Enlarged European Market, sponsored by IRELA and the Institute für Iberoamerikanische Kunde, Hamburg, March 24–25, 1993.

30. David Marsh and Lionel Barber, "Morsels from a Groaning Table," *Financial Times* (London), June 7, 1993.

31. Ibid.

32. Excluding food and food products, exports in these areas account for 5.4 percent of total EC employment, but especially affect regions in France, Germany, and southern Italy. *Financial Times*, October 19, 1992.

33. *The Economist*, May 1, 1993, pp. 54–55.

34. Foreign investment in Eastern Europe totaled nearly $30 billion in 1992. See the Simon and Purcell contribution to this volume (Chapter 2).

35. Marsh and Barber, "Morsels from a Groaning Table." Somewhat more successful has been the PHARE program, which the EC set up to help small and medium-sized enterprises gain access to investment credits and loans for Eastern European activities. On this program, see Rosaria Cerrone, "The Economic 'Reform' in Central and Eastern Europe," *The Journal of Regional Policy* (Naples), Vol. 13 (January–March 1993), pp. 103–105.

36. For a very useful review, see Vittorio Corbo, Fabrizio Coricelli, and Jan Bossak, eds., *Reforming Central and East European Economies: Initial Results and Challenges* (Washington, D.C.: World Bank, 1991), especially Chapter 2 (Andrés Solimano, "The Economies of Central and Eastern Europe: An Historical and International Perspective") and Chapter 7 (Stanley Fischer and Alan Gelb, "Issues in the Reform of the Socialist Economies").

37. According to the IMF *Direction of Trade* statistics, 64.2 percent of total Spanish trade in 1991 was with the European Community.

38. The discussion in this paragraph draws on the excellent analysis in op. cit. (Inotai), especially pp. 19–21.

39. IADB, *Economic and Social Progress*, Appendix Table 7, p. 266.

40. Argentina, Brazil, Chile, Colombia, Mexico, and Venezuela.

41. Inotai, "Latin America's Competitive Position," pp. 22–23. The author used the German trade classifications of agricultural, manufactured, and semifinished goods as well as end products.

42. Ibid., p. 48. See Table 9. The actual volume of ABC exports increased by 362 million DM, but this was quite small in comparison to the Visograd 4 countries' exports, which increased by nearly 8 billion DM.

43. The Latin American version involved the use of quotas and tariffs and took place within the broad parameters of a market economy. The East European "socialist" model of industrialization entailed a more complex array of import prohibitions and rationing, operating in a system where the public sector dominated output and the Soviet Union dictated patterns of specialization.

44. Jeffrey Ryser, "Will Latin America Land on Its Feet?" *Global Finance*, November 1992, pp. 85–88. Since 1989, the Chilean government of Patricio Aylwin has approved $13.9 billion in foreign investments. More than $1.4 billion were actually invested in 1992. *Business America*, February 8, 1993, p. 15.

45. Ernest S. McCrary, "It's Testing Time for Latin America's Free Market Will." Cited in *Global Finance*, May 1993, p. 70. The estimates were made by John F. H. Purcell, head of Salomon Brothers' emerging markets research unit.

46. J.M. Lawrence, "Can Pay, Won't Pay," *Euromoney* (London), September 1992, p. 122.

47. Mohamed A. El-Erian, "Restoration of Access to Voluntary Capital Market Financing," *IMF Staff Papers*, Vol. 39, No. 1, 1992, pp. 175–194.

48. Salomon Brothers, *Emerging Markets*, February 12, 1992, p. 2.

49. El-Erian, "Restoration of Access," p. 177.

50. Much of the analysis in this paragraph is drawn from an excellent monograph by Frederick Z. Jaspersen and Juan Carlos Ginarte, "Capital Flows to Latin America 1982–92: Trends and Prospects," a paper prepared for the Economic and Social Development Department of the Inter-American Development Bank, 1993; especially pp. 19–21.

51. IADB, "Capital Flows to Latin America 1982–92," p. 19.

52. This item and a more general evaluation of Latin American stock markets is contained in Alan Robinson, "What goes up . . . ," *Hemisfile* (California), Vol. 3 (November-December 1992), pp. 1–2, 12. See also "Will Latin America Land on Its Feet?" *Global Finance*, November 1992, pp. 85–88.

53. The desire to serve these markets has been one of the motivations behind European investment in Latin America. See *Foreign Direct Investment in Latin America and the Caribbean: An Overview of Flows from Europe, Japan, and the United States, 1979–1990* (Madrid and Paris: Inter-American Development Bank Special Office in Europe and Institute for European–Latin American Relations, 1993), p. 48. The booklet contains much useful information on FDI sources.

54. For a discussion of Latin America's social safety net and of the reform of social security pensions in the region, see the special issue of *Hemisfile*, Vol. 4 (March/April 1993) as well as "Investment Follows Market Reform," Kim Chan, Eric DiMiceli, and Jeffrey Lee, "Comparative Advantages of Capital Investments in the Emerging Markets of Eastern Europe and Latin America," Columbia University School of Business, July 1993.

55. Cited in *Reforming Central and East European Economies: Initial Results and Challenges* (World Bank, 1992), p. 49.

56. Inotai, "Latin America's Competitive Position," p. 28.

57. Ibid.

58. Further information on these investments may be found in Paul J. J. Welfens, "Foreign Investment in the East European Transition," *Management International Review* 32 (1992/93), p. 216.

59. Neil Smith and Douglas Rebne, "Foreign Direct Investment in Poland, the Czech and Slovak Republics and Hungary: The Centrality of the Joint Venture Entry Mode," *The Mid-Atlantic Journal of Business* 28 (December 1992), pp. 189–211, 191.

60. *Euromoney Supplement*, March 1993, p. 134. Moreover, when the Hungarian government presented its first fixed-rate five-year bond in late 1992 (the first to be made available to foreign investors), the latter subscribed to less than 1 percent of the Ft7 billion issue.

61. Paul M. Sacks, "Privatization in the Czech Republic," *Columbia Journal of World Business,* Vol. 28 (Spring 1993), p. 192.

62. *Emerging Markets* (Salomon Brothers), October 30, 1992, p. 5.

63. *McKinsey Quarterly,* no. 1 (1993), p. 21.

64. El-Erian, "Restoration of Access," p. 191.

65. For those interested in a country-by-country summary of foreign investment regulations, see the *Euromoney World Economics Handbook*.

66. Andrew Ewing, Barbara W. Lee, and Roger Leeds, "Accelerating Privatization in Ex-Socialist Economies," *Columbia Journal of World Business,* Vol. 28 (Spring 1993), pp. 159–67.

67. El-Erian, "Restoration of Access," p. 194.

# 6

# The Trilateral Relationship: Latin America, Europe, and the United States

## *Riordan Roett*

The potential for the slow but steady decline of the hegemonic presence of the United States in Latin America and the Caribbean and the emergence of a renewed role for Europe in the hemisphere has been noted for some time.[1] Washington has nonetheless retained and, particularly during the 1980s, asserted its leadership position in Central America and the Caribbean. To the degree that Washington showed a relative lack of interest in South America over the last few decades, however, the spread of pluralism—albeit erratic—fueled speculation about a renewed role for Europe in the region. With the end of the Cold War and the collapse of international communism, this potential may now be realized: The United States no longer has an overriding concern with hemispheric security, and the renewed commitment by Latin America to expanding trade and investment ties between the region and the international system will provide opportunities for other states to assume a greater role in the hemisphere.

Although many observers believed that the time had come to redefine the U.S.–Latin American–European relationship, the 1980s saw limited progress toward this end. But symbolic steps have been taken that, in time, may well be seen as an important turning point in the trilateral relationship. In the 1990s, the slow erosion of U.S. hegemony in Central America and the Caribbean will continue, although Washington's long-held view of the Caribbean as a U.S. "lake" is not likely to change overnight. Furthermore, given their limited economic development, population pressures, and low resource endowments the countries of Central America and the Caribbean will likely remain unstable, prompting the United States to retain a residual security interest in both subregions.

The potential for greater diversity and pluralism in South America is real. Historical linkages between South America and Europe are older and stronger than those between Central America and the Caribbean and

Europe. Capital flows and trade opportunities provide strong incentives for both European and South American countries to pursue even closer ties. And the complexities of the emerging new world order will require Washington to become far less exclusive with respect to the involvement of nonhemispheric states with the larger countries of South America.

## HISTORICAL TIES

Prior to 1914, particularly in South America, the European–Latin American ties were extensive. As Stanley Hilton has observed, from 1880 to 1945, European countries were the major suppliers of capital, armaments, and technology to Latin America.[2] European military missions played an essential role in modernizing the region's armed forces, and many Latin American officers were trained in Europe, particularly in Germany and France. Latin America drew its ideological and cultural models from Europe. The elites in the region looked to France particularly. The importance, Hilton argued, of Latin America to Europe before World War I can be measured in the intense intra-European rivalries to exercise influence there.

Beginning with the promulgation of the Monroe Doctrine (1823), the United States tried throughout the nineteenth century to counter this European influence. But even as Latin America became independent of Europe politically, it remained dependent on Europe economically, culturally, and commercially. U.S. initiatives, such as Secretary of State James G. Blaine's failed attempts to create a Pan-American movement in the 1880s, led to increased trade and commercial ties between the United States and the countries of the region, especially the Caribbean and Central America, where the European powers ceded ground earlier than in the rest of Latin America. By the turn of the century, there was a sense among the Europeans that a standoff with Washington in those areas would be a losing battle and costly in other areas of interaction. The taking of the Philippines and Cuba by the United States in the War of 1898 heralded the emergence of a self-assured and confident United States, as did the actions of President Theodore Roosevelt, who made it clear that he considered control of the Caribbean to be a critical component of his national defense policies. From the European perspective, it was more reasonable to recognize the emergence of a new power on the world's stage and to try to integrate it into the existing structure of world power.

Godfrey Hodgson captured the evangelical mood of the United States toward its "backyard" during this period in describing the appropriation of the land for the Panama Canal:

Roosevelt justified this practice with a theory called the "Roosevelt corollary to the Monroe Doctrine." The argument went like this: Under the Monroe Doctrine, European powers were to be excluded from the Western Hemisphere. Unfortunately, Central and South American governments were only too likely to behave in such ways that European powers had money claims against them. The Europeans could vindicate these claims only by seizing territory. But only the United States was allowed to seize territory in the Western Hemisphere.[3]

Hodgson pointed to the irony in U.S. policy at the end of the nineteenth and early twentieth centuries. The Monroe Doctrine prevented Europe from taking an active role in the Western Hemisphere, even when Latin American countries took actions that impinged on the interests of European companies or governments. To preclude the European powers from pressing their claims as a result of such misconduct, the United States would assume a tutelary role in Latin America, administering, reorganizing, and educating the small countries to act responsibly. In so doing, the argument went, U.S. interests would be served through the maintenance of regional stability and there would be no excuse for European meddling.

The United States took advantage of Europe's preoccupation with events at home during World War I to seek to replace the European economic and commercial presence in Latin America. But the Germans and the British, in particular, returned with a vengeance after Versailles. The interwar years were ones of intense rivalry among Washington, Berlin, and London for markets and investment opportunities in the region. Although Britain and Germany were able to recover some of the ground they had lost, it was clear that they now faced a new and powerful contender in the United States, one able and willing to challenge Europe for dominance in the region.

During World War II, Latin America gained added significance for both the United States and Europe. Aside from the obvious importance of the Panama Canal, the region's raw materials, foodstuffs, and minerals were critical to the conduct of the war. Brazil lay on the convoy routes of the Allies, and the Brazilian northeast was a critical jumping-off place for ferrying materiel to the North African and Middle Eastern fronts. Early in the conflict, there was concern in Washington that the Axis powers might attempt to claim the remaining European colonies in the Caribbean, as Germany vanquished one after the other of the major continental powers. Utilizing the framework of the emerging Inter-American System, which would be formalized after the end of the war, Washington convinced the Latin American states to support a "no-transfer" doctrine precluding the transfer of U.S. territory to the Axis, even in the event the colonial power lost its sovereignty. The Caribbean played a relatively minor role in the overall conflict and remained very much under U.S. control.

## THE U.S. ERA IN LATIN AMERICA

With the collapse of the Axis powers in 1945, the United States emerged as the leader of the Free World. With the onset of the Cold War, the Western Hemisphere took on added importance in U.S. security policy. Washington gave very high priority to securing membership for Latin American countries in the United Nations because it envisioned the General Assembly as an important forum for promoting U.S. interests. The votes of the twenty-odd Latin states would be critical to the United States.

During the late 1940s, the United States constructed the Inter-American Security System, with the Rio Treaty as its linchpin and the Organization of American States (OAS) as a convenient umbrella organization under which social, economic, and political issues would be effectively dealt with to the satisfaction of the United States. Washington made it clear to the countries of the region that hemispheric security was to be a vital component of its overall security planning for the postwar era. But it also made it clear that there would be no Marshall Plan for Latin America. Indeed, at the 1947 Rio Conference, as Gordon Connell-Smith recounted, Washington indicated that it believed it had to choose between Europe and Latin America:

> Secretary of State Marshall, addressing the conference as head of the United States delegation, endeavored to show both the greater plight of Europe and that the latter's rehabilitation was vital to the economy of the Western Hemisphere. Moreover, he asserted that long-term economic development in Latin America required a type of collaboration in which a much greater role falls to private citizens and groups than is the case in a program designed to aid European countries to recover from the destruction of war.[4]

Private-sector development would substitute for government assistance. Responding to this signal, U.S. investors and multinationals became the principal engines of growth in Latin America in the ensuing decades.

In 1954, it also became crystal clear that Washington would define the security interests of the hemisphere from its own perspective without consideration for other actors—Latin or non-Latin. With the Central Intelligence Agency's covert involvement in the overthrow of the Jacobo Arbenz regime in Guatemala, the OAS was used for diplomatic endorsement of U.S. policy goals. The Europeans were in no position to protest and, in general, Cold War governments in Western Europe either sympathized with, or chose to overlook, the use of U.S. force in the region. The strategic concept that the United States had attempted to establish in the nineteenth century with the Monroe Doctrine, which the Europeans had chosen to overlook for over a century, had become a reality in the early 1950s.

Military ties between the United States and Latin America expanded rapidly. The training of officers, the standardization of weaponry, and the coordination of tactics and strategy in the Americas became essential elements of the U.S. design to protect the Panama Canal and preclude foreign encroachment anywhere in the region. During this period, it was unclear whether U.S. security policy supported military regimes because they were seen to be more stable than civilian governments or because the armed forces were central to containing communism. At times, one position appeared dominant; in other instances, both were applicable. "This military alliance," Augusto Varas observes, "was refined through bilateral Military Assistance Programs (MAPs) signed by all Latin American governments and the United States between 1951 and 1958. By participating in the Inter-American military system, the Latin American armed forces to some extent defined their nations' defense interests in terms of the security system of the United States."[5] The strong anticommunist position taken by the military regimes that came to power in many countries after 1945 further solidified ties with the United States. It was relatively easy to justify military aid for those in the hemisphere who professed to share Washington's aversion to totalitarian ideologies.

With the overthrow of the Fulgencio Batista regime in Cuba in 1959 and the establishment of the Castro dictatorship, the European view of U.S.–Latin American relations began to change. Fidel Castro's successful consolidation of power gave the Soviet Union a toehold in the Western Hemisphere. The U.S. response to this turn of events led to the Bay of Pigs debacle in 1961 and the missile crisis of October 1962. It was apparent to Europe that any effort by the Soviets, or their Cuban surrogates, to extend their revolutionary doctrine in the region would be met with stiff resistance from Washington. The historical preoccupation of the United States with any foreign presence on its doorstep could, in the context of the superpower confrontation, have dangerous implications for everyone in the West.

This strategic assessment was accompanied by the first signs of a resurgence of interest in Europe in trade and investment in the largest countries of the region—Brazil, Mexico, and Argentina. By 1958, the revitalized economies of Western Europe began to explore the possibility of reestablishing their commercial and trade ties with the countries of Latin America and the Caribbean. At the same time, transnational actors began to pay increasing attention to Latin America: The Social Democratic and Christian Democratic movements began to work with their Latin American counterparts; the Roman Catholic Church and European political party foundations went to work at the grass roots and began to build ties with unions and university students in Latin America.

## THE RETURN OF EUROPE
## TO THE WESTERN HEMISPHERE

### Testing the Waters

Latin America tried to establish a dialogue with Europe in the 1960s. The Comisión Especial de Coordinación Latinoamerica (CECLA), was created in 1963 as a vehicle for direct communications with the European Economic Community (EEC). CECLA produced the "Carta de Buenos Aires" in 1970, which called for economic and political discussions with Brussels. The first "Latin American Year" designated by the EEC was 1971, and a "mechanism for dialogue" was created, which provided for at least one yearly meeting between Latin American ambassadors and their counterparts in Brussels. Within a short time, however, the European–Latin American dialogue was subsumed by the EEC's overall Third World framework, which did not differentiate between degrees of development in the developing world. As the European Community (EC) established its foreign policy framework for dealing with nonindustrialized countries, it also took a single approach. The Lomé Convention, concluded in 1975, which granted trade preferences with the EC, excluded Latin America, save for former European colonies in the Caribbean. This decision probably reinforced the view from Brussels that underdeveloped Latin America did not merit separate policies.

Throughout this period, Latin America was itself preoccupied with ongoing efforts to find appropriate mechanisms for regional and subregional integration. These efforts produced the Central American Common Market in 1951; the Latin American Free Trade Association in 1960 (and its successor, the Latin American Integration Association in 1980); the Caribbean Free Trade Association in 1965 (and its successor, the Caribbean Community and Common Market in 1973); the Andean Pact in 1969; the Latin American Economic System in 1975; and the Eastern Caribbean Common Market in 1981. Each of these organizations made some contribution to the economic growth of the region, but none had anywhere near the authority of the EEC. The Latin states often appeared more interested in protecting their domestic industries than in dropping trade barriers. Political leadership was weak. Historical suspicions made it difficult to forge a common vision. And none was able to draw more than passing interest from Brussels, which was intently fixated on its internal European development and, ultimately, on the expansion of the EEC itself.

For these reasons, among others, it was difficult for Europe and Latin America to establish a common framework within which restored or new ties could be forged. It was widely assumed that the United States would continue to play the role of the regional hegemony. U.S. investment and commercial activity in Latin America had surpassed Europe's in the 1950s. Immigration from Europe, which had been a major factor in Europe's relationship with Latin America in the nineteenth and early twentieth centuries, meant far less by the 1970s: U.S. culture was a growing force, and English had become the preferred second language for most educated Latin Americans, especially those in the industrial/investment community.

The most important issue with regard to European–Latin American relations, however, was the rise of the bureaucratic-authoritarian state in the major countries in the region. Beginning in 1964 with the overthrow of President João Goulart of Brazil, democracy disappeared in Argentina, Uruguay, Peru, Bolivia, and Chile, and in the Central American states as well. It would not reappear again until the 1980s.

It became clear to the Europeans that Washington was not only favorably disposed toward the overthrow of regimes that were thought to be leaning toward communism—in Guatemala, Cuba, and the Dominican Republic—but that it looked with favor on bureaucratic-authoritarian regimes because of their forthright condemnation of the Soviet bloc. A tolerance for authoritarianism appeared to inform U.S. foreign policy. The individual European states and the European Community, therefore, took increasingly hands-off political and diplomatic positions with regard to these regimes in Latin America, although this did not result in the curtailment of economic and commercial ties. It has been argued that the Europeans' postwar experiences had left them with little tolerance for right-wing regimes. And the incorporation of communist and socialist parties in their political processes after 1945 gave them the practical experience needed to deal with democratic left-of-center parties and movements in Latin America. The United States tended to equate left-of-center with "communist" after the end of World War II.[6] Mutual U.S.-European security concerns in any case continued to be given highest priority in both the United States and Europe; events in Washington's backyard were of less importance to a Europe protected by the U.S. nuclear shield. This reality was formalized with the creation of the North Atlantic Treaty Organization (NATO) in 1949.

The events of April 1982 confirmed the primacy of the relations between the United States and Europe in postwar diplomacy. After a brief hesitation, because of U.N. Ambassador Jeane Kirkpatrick's enthusiastic support of Argentina, the Reagan administration strongly endorsed the British government's position on the Falkland/Malvinas conflict. The European Community firmly endorsed the British response to Argentina's invasion of the disputed islands, supported the United States and Great Britain at the United Nations, and endorsed the use of sanctions against the government of General Leopoldo Galtieri in Buenos Aires. The pressure brought to bear by the United States and the Community led to the rapid disintegration of the military regime in Argentina and to free elections in 1983, which restored civilian government and brought Raul Alfonsín to power. But European efforts to return to the region were put on hold because the Latin Americans felt betrayed by their putative new partner.

Europe's "return" to Latin America up to this point had been hesitant and unstructured. Although some efforts had been made toward strengthening the ties between the two regions, the European Community remained primarily concerned about its own development and, in the foreign policy arena, East-West issues dominated the agenda.

## Taking the Plunge

With the inauguration of President Ronald Reagan in January 1981, the United States became embroiled in a near-decade-long military conflict in Central America. The 1980s also saw the U.S. invasion of Grenada, an intensification of the guerrilla insurgencies in Colombia and Peru, the apogee of the power of the violent Colombian drug cartels, and the bloody invasion of Panama and the ouster of General Manuel Noriega. This was also the decade in which civilian government returned to the region. By the early 1990s, all of the countries in the hemisphere, with the exception of Haiti and Cuba, would be formally democratic. But the road was long and tortuous. It was this road on which Europe chose to travel and to become increasingly involved in the region once again.

From the perspective of the conservative Republicans and "neoconservative" Democrats who came to Washington in early 1981, the dominoes in the hemisphere had begun to fall in 1979 with the collapse of Anastasio Somoza in Nicaragua in July, the installation of the New Jewel Movement in Grenada, and the overthrow of the military dictatorship in El Salvador in October. The global situation further deteriorated that year with the seizure of the U.S. embassy in Teheran in November and the invasion of Afghanistan by the Soviet Union in December.

As President Reagan's first secretary of state, Alexander Haig, later recalled, the new administration believed that "grave though its plight might be, El Salvador was not merely a local problem. It was also a regional problem that threatened the stability of all of Central America, including the Panama Canal and Mexico and Guatemala with their vast oil reserves. And it was a global issue because it represented the interjection of the war of national liberation into the Western Hemisphere." Furthermore, "there could not be the slightest doubt that Cuba was at once the source of supply and the catechist of the Salvadoran insurgency. Cuba, in turn, could not act on the scale of the rebellion in El Salvador without the approval and the material support of the U.S.S.R."[7]

It soon became evident to the European Community that the Reagan administration meant to act. Haig's later analysis went to the source of

Europe's concern—that events in Latin America could lead to a hostile confrontation with the Soviet Union, with potentially deadly repercussions for Europe. The Europeans feared a nuclear exchange between the Soviets and the U.S. forces stationed in Europe, and this fear made them less willing than they might otherwise have been to understand Washington's deep concern over changes in the Soviet-U.S. global balance of power, were the revolutionary movements in Central America to be successful. The primary reason, then, for a resurgence of interest by Europe in the region was the fear that the superpower competition for influence in Latin America would escalate into a major conflict. There was also a general commitment on the part of the EC to democracy and development in the Third World—although there are those who will argue that its commitment was selective because it developed a higher profile in Latin America than in Asia and Africa. European nongovernmental organizations (NGOs) also played a role. Their agendas, which emphasized social justice and human rights, complemented the agendas of the parties on the left and in the center of the political spectrum, and at least caught the attention of the parties on the right. Finally, many Latin American political leaders were anxious for the Europeans to act as mediators, as a buffer between their countries and Washington, and as a constraint on U.S. military action in Central America and the Caribbean.

The decade of war in Central America also coincided with a growing transnationalization of the European political parties, particularly the Socialist and Social Democratic parties, which had become increasingly active in the 1970s in support of the transition to democracy in Spain and Portugal. The European parties had provided campaign funding, leadership training, and media coverage, among other things. "Emboldened by this experience and eager to extend their links elsewhere in the world," noted Eusebio Mujal-León, "the principal European political families turned their attention to Latin (and Central) America during the 1970s, transporting to the region not only their vast array of networks but also a political style that emphasized transnational and regional cooperation." The European Socialist movement took the lead: "The 'intellectual architects' of this involvement considered the region an arena where European socialism could both reassert its historic identity as an anticapitalist force and make a positive contribution to the democratization of the region. At the same time, through their criticism of and competition with the United States, these parties could also affirm their nationalist credentials."[8]

The involvement of the European parties went through three phases. During the first (1978–1981), they were highly supportive of revolutionary change in Central America, which they saw as both desirable and feasible. The Germans, French, and Spaniards led the charge, and Socialist party leaders from those countries were actively involved in party-to-party negotiations with their counterparts in Latin America. The second phase

(1982–1986) was one of growing disenchantment with the Sandinistas in Nicaragua as well as with the Farabundo Martí Front for National Liberation (FMLN) in El Salvador. Atrocities were clearly being committed by both the governments in power and the insurrectionary forces in each case. This situation resulted in a shift in emphasis toward a search for negotiated settlements. The third phase (1986–1989), saw renewed activism and strong support for a diplomatic solution: The European Socialists now wanted to become the "honest brokers" of the region. The emergence of regional peace initiatives within Latin America itself—beginning with the formation of the Contadora Group in January 1983—offered them the opportunity to do so.[9] (The original Contadora members—Colombia, Mexico, Panama, and Venezuela—were joined in July 1985 by a "Support Group" comprising Argentina, Brazil, Peru, and Uruguay.)

The Socialists and the Social Democrats were not the only ones in Europe dismayed by conditions in Latin America. "Throughout Western Europe," noted Wolf Grabendorff in 1984, "the regional approach to the Central American crisis has definitely taken priority over the global approach. The general view in Western Europe is that internal socioeconomic and political conditions must be improved before any stabilization of the region will become feasible. A return to the old order in Nicaragua and El Salvador or a continuation of it in Guatemala and Honduras is viewed as neither possible nor desirable."[10]

This generalized concern in Europe was institutionalized in a historic conference of ministers that took place in San José, Costa Rica, in September 1984. It was the first time that the European Community had met formally with the countries of the region. A second conference followed in Luxembourg in November 1985. As a result of this meeting, the EC and the countries of Central America and Panama signed the Economic Cooperation Agreement and the Final Act concerning the political dialogue between the two regions as well as political and economic communiqués. The Final Act provided for an annual meeting of ministers from the EC, the countries of Central America and Panama, and the members of the Contadora Group. This was the first time that the EC had instituted a regular political dialogue with Third World countries.

The political communiqué, signed by the twenty-one ministers, supported the Contadora Group and the Contadora Agreement. The twelve members of the European Community stated that, if asked to do so, they would be willing to diplomatically endorse and seek to facilitate the implementation of the terms of the agreement for peace and cooperation and help with evaluation, control, and verification procedures. In so doing, the EC made clear its sharp differences with the Reagan administration— which opposed the Contadora process—over Central American policy. In their final communiqué, the foreign ministers agreed to "back up efforts to put an end to violence and instability in the region, particularly the efforts of the States of Central America in the context of the Contadora Group's diplomatic initiative, which had been supported from the outset by the countries of the European Community." It was their objective to "achieve on the basis of the proposals arising from the Contadora process a negotiated global, political solution for the region originating in the region itself and funded on the principles of independence, non-intervention, self-determination, and the inviolability of frontiers."[11]

This position, which emphasized the internal causes of violence in Central America, contrasted sharply with the findings of the report of the National Bipartisan Commission on Central America, often referred to as the Kissinger report, after the commission's chairman, Henry A. Kissinger. Although the report, published in 1984, also called for negotiations to end the conflicts in Central America, it emphasized the external, rather than the internal, causes of violence in the region. Soviet objectives, beginning with Cuba in the early 1960s, the report argued, had been to end the unchallenged U.S. preeminence within the hemisphere and possibly to see other "Cubas" established, to divert U.S. attention from other parts of the world that were of greater importance to Moscow; to complicate U.S. relations with its Western European allies; and to burnish the Soviet Union's image as a revolutionary state.[12]

The election of George Bush in November 1988 set the stage for a shift in Washington's Central American policy. The new president and his secretary of state, James Baker, were determined to end the polarization that had existed between the Democratic-controlled Congress and the Reagan White House. The 1980s had been marked by bitter debates over the legality and political viability of U.S. support for the contras—the U.S.-financed opposition to the Sandinistas in Nicaragua—and over economic aid to El Salvador. A second issue was whether or not the elections held in El Salvador had been fairly organized, given the violence and polarization in the political process. Bush and Baker negotiated a deal with the Democratic leadership, agreeing to curb financing for the contras in exchange for congressional support for free elections in El Salvador and the continuation of U.S. aid to that country. Both the White House and Congress also agreed to support democratic elections in Nicaragua.

President Bush launched the Enterprise for the Americas Initiative in 1990. It was received enthusiastically in Latin America and served as an important indication to Washington of how welcome U.S. initiatives on trade, debt reduction, and development would be in the new, reformist-minded Latin America. The Brady Plan for debt restructuring played a significant role in allowing for the renegotiation and restructuring of Latin America's outstanding debt with the private commercial banks. The December 1989 invasion of Panama raised concerns that the Bush administration was reverting to the policies of its predecessor, but such worries disappeared quickly as Panama's new civilian government, led by Guillermo Endara, settled in—although it failed to capitalize on the opportunity for economic and social reform.

These initiatives should be viewed against the backdrop of the end of the Cold War. The collapse of communism, the destruction of the Berlin Wall, the breakup of the Soviet Union, and related developments served as a catalyst to the Bush administration to begin to review U.S. policies worldwide. In Latin America, the victory of the democratic forces in Nicaragua's presidential elections and the end of Soviet aid to Cuba allowed Washington greater freedom in reassessing U.S. security interests.

The change in U.S. policy toward Latin America occurred as an important process of multilateral diplomacy was being institutionalized there. Meeting in Acapulco, Mexico, in November 1987, the heads of state of the Member Countries of the Permanent Mechanism for Consultation and Concerted Political Action (the Contadora Group and Its Support Group) officially became the Group of Eight, or the Rio Group. Meeting annually, the Rio Group has become a useful forum for the discussion of economic development and transnational policy issues in the region. Over the last three years, a number of positive diplomatic initiatives have built on the Contadora process, the Arias peace plan, and the work of the Rio Group. In December 1990, the foreign ministers of the European Community and their counterparts from the Rio Group signed the Declaration of Rome, signaling their aim to develop regularized political contacts and greater cooperation on trade, economic development, and science and technology issues, and to create mechanisms to deal with the problems of drug trafficking and terrorism.

In July 1991, the first Ibero-American summit was held in Guadalajara, Mexico, bringing together twenty-three heads of state, including those of Spain and Portugal. The summit, which reflected Spain's and Portugal's desire to upgrade their diplomatic and political ties with their former colonies, provided an opportunity for the Latin American states to broaden their international contacts while reinforcing their cultural and historical ties with Iberia. (Fidel Castro was a prominent presence at the summit; the United States was not invited.) In their closing declaration, the participants reaffirmed their commitment to international law and promised to promote human rights and eradicate misery by the end of the century. They also proposed the establishment of a common front in the drug war and the creation of a fund for indigenous peoples to protect them from the inroads of uncontrolled frontier settlement. Bilateral talks during the summit led to the consolidation of a free trade agreement among Mexico, Venezuela, and Colombia, and a treaty on the nonproliferation of nuclear arms signed by Argentina and Brazil. Spain and Portugal reaffirmed their role as a bridge between Latin America and Europe.

The second Ibero-American summit took place in Madrid, Spain, in July 1992. The leaders of Spain, Portugal, and seventeen Latin American countries used the occasion to confirm intergovernmental commercial accords. (Fidel Castro was once again present but, given the growing political isolation of his country and the rapid deterioration of its economy, he cut a far less powerful figure than he had the year before.) The summit process is now becoming routinized and is an important element in the return of Europe to Latin America. The third summit, held in Brazil in July 1993, emphasized economic development and social justice. "An Agenda for Development," with an emphasis on social development, was drafted for presentation to the United Nations. The 1994 meeting convened in Cartagena, Colombia. The principal themes were economic integration and trade expansion.

This time around, the return of Europe to Latin America and the Caribbean has been less hesitant and more structured. From the late 1970s and early 1980s, when the focus was on the escalating civil wars in Central America, through the lost decade of debt, to the beginnings of diplomatic and political conversations and summits, the linkages between Latin America and Europe have been strengthened. Indeed, one can argue that it is at the level of political and diplomatic support that the most progress has been made. To take one example, although German–Latin American political relations have not been strong at the governmental level, close political links between Latin American and German nongovernmental bodies expanded rapidly during this period. Recent German government initiatives in Latin America suggest that Germany is making new efforts to bring its official political relations in line with the broad nature of its relations with the region in general. Economic investment has grown steadily. And there are strong transnational links between German political parties, trade unions, and churches and their respective counterparts in Latin America.[13] The same can be said of the efforts of such organizations in France, Belgium, the Netherlands, Sweden, and other members of the European Community, which have also played a significant role in the growth of educational institutions, labor unions, social organizations, and political groups in Latin America. Although they have worked separately, the results of their efforts have been complementary and, at the societal level, widely welcomed and applauded.

There is little doubt that the flowering of these links in the last fifteen years has redefined the European–Latin American relationship. And it is fairly clear that—in the last few years at least—Washington considers these development to be benign and to present little challenge to the overall security and foreign policy concerns of the United States. But what about official development assistance (ODA), trade opportunities, and capital flows? Is Europe's record as positive and optimistic? If we are to have a full picture of the emerging triangular relationship in the 1990s, we must also examine these issues.

## THE UNITED STATES, LATIN AMERICA, AND EUROPE IN THE 1990s

### Economic Relations

Although Latin America's share of European trade has declined during the last decade (it accounts for less than 2 percent of Europe's exports and only 2 percent of its imports), in terms of intensity of trade flows, Europe ranks second behind the United States. Europe buys 23 percent of Latin America's exports and provides about the same percentage of its imports. In comparison, Latin America's trade with the United States accounts for 41 percent of exports and almost 45 percent of its imports.[14]

The United States will undoubtedly continue to play a dominant role in the region's foreign trade for some time to come, given the trade dynamics of the European Union. In the area of foreign direct investment, however, there is hope for greater diversification. Europe is second to the United States in total investment stock for most of the countries of the region. In Brazil, Argentina, Paraguay, and Uruguay, Europe's investment stock is greater than that of the United States. In terms of investment flows to the region, Europe surpasses the United States in Brazil and is a close second in Argentina and Ecuador. In terms of new investments, however, U.S. flows were twice that of Europe's with the exception of Brazil, where Europe invests more than the United States. In terms of total accumulated foreign investment stocks in Latin America, the United States is the primary investor in Mexico and Central America, and Europe is the major investor in MERCOSUR, the Southern Cone common market. From 1985 to 1990, the share of European investment rose in Brazil, Ecuador, Mexico, Peru, Uruguay, Venezuela, El Salvador, Guatemala, and Panama. The overall U.S. position, although it remains significant, declined over that five-year period; U.S. stocks increased only in Argentina, Chile, and Colombia, among the larger countries.

Continued European interest in South America was confirmed at a European Union summit meeting in Essen, Germany, on December 9–10, 1994. A decision was taken to begin negotiations on a free trade zone with MERCOSUR. Negotiations between the EU and Mexico, to enhance economic relations, are scheduled for 1995.

In banking and finance, there is a strong historical tradition of European interest in Latin America, although the United States took the lead in this area after 1945. During the period leading up to the debt decade of the 1980s, European commercial banks returned to the region, and by mid-decade

European banks held about a third of commercial bank claims, compared to the 40 percent held by U.S. and Canadian banks. By 1987, as the smaller U.S. banks abandoned their positions, European bank claims actually surpassed those of U.S. banks. By 1990, European banks held 40 percent of Latin debt, and U.S. banks, which, under the Brady Plan had sold off much of their Latin American debt, held only 21 percent.

As a result of changes in the lending patterns of individual European countries, Europe as a whole is now on its way toward becoming the largest lender to Latin America, with Brazil the largest borrower. Euromarket borrowings—the issuance of bonds in the European capital markets—are of critical significance in Latin American finance. The Latin American Eurobond market continued its rapid development in 1992, with US $8.4 billion in Eurobonds issued, compared with US $5.7 billion in 1991. Issue volume amounts were more widely distributed by country than the year before, with the Brazilian and Argentine markets doubling in size. The year was also notable for the first Eurobond issue from Uruguay. The investor profile also changed in 1992. Whereas retail investors were the main players in the market previously, institutional investors became the primary buyers of Latin American Eurobonds in 1992, reflecting the growing sophistication of the market.[15]

Europe is also making a strong showing in the area of official development assistance. In 1990/91, 16.2 percent of total U.S. ODA was directed to Latin America, compared to 11.6 percent of European ODA. In dollar terms, however, Europe surpassed the United States—$2.7 billion, compared to $1.5 billion—and European assistance to Latin America is increasing more rapidly than U.S. assistance. The U.S. public has shown little tolerance for foreign aid, and Congress has reacted accordingly. The Europeans view development assistance as an important component of their foreign policy, supporting their overall development objectives and "softening" the region for future investment and trade opportunities.

The Inter-American Development Bank (IADB) reports that although foreign direct investment (FDI) flows from Europe dropped in the 1980s, following a global pattern, they showed less volatility than FDI flows from the United States or Japan. Although from 1979 to 1982, European FDI flows were well below those of the United States, between 1983 and 1988, they far exceeded those of the United States. European direct investment in Latin America started to lag again from 1989 onwards. The acceleration of U.S. direct investment after 1989 can be explained in large part by U.S. investors acting on the favorable expectations generated by the NAFTA with Mexico.[16]

As this brief overview reveals, a more varied and complex set of economic interrelationships exist between Europe and Latin America than is usually asserted. The United States is still Latin America's dominant trading partner. Trade is of critical importance for Latin America because it is through trade that it earns the foreign exchange required to finance current and future purchases abroad and investments at home. Unless Europe changes its current policies, the U.S. leadership role will remain unchallenged. As the IADB report notes, "some of the highest tariffs imposed by the EC are in products for which the Latin American economies have the greatest comparative advantage. Tariffs on textiles, clothing and footwear are more than twice the average EC tariff."[17] Furthermore, the controversial trade preferences provided to the ACP countries (Asia, Africa, and the Pacific) under the EC's Lomé Convention, discriminate against other countries of the region that compete in the same markets. Such is the case with the proposed import regime for bananas, which has raised protests from non-ACP banana growers.[18] In the other areas we have examined—developmental aid, foreign direct investment, and banking and finance—Europe holds it own when compared to the United States.

## Transnational Linkages

Relations between nongovernmental organizations form an increasingly important area of interaction between Europe and Latin America. We have already noted the links between German and Latin American transnational actors—between political parties, trade unions, and churches—and their attempts to strengthen Latin American civil society under the regime of dictatorships in the region. Such links have also developed over the past few decades between transnational actors and their counterparts in Latin America. There is now a rich and widely developed network of these links. Pluralistic and overwhelmingly ideological, these interactions have been supportive of democracy, civil and human rights, and civilian control of government as well as of education, labor training, sustainable development, agriculture, and social involvement.

These activities have generally been complementary to U.S. interests in the region whenever it has been the policy of the United States to support democratic regimes. During the 1980s, the European transnational—and governmental—presence in Central America was resented by the Reagan administration, which believed that such European efforts were undercutting its attempts to address a critical foreign policy and security challenge in the region. The Bush administration, given the end of the Cold War, was much more benign toward the European transnationals. On the whole, U.S. labor confederations, political parties, and churches (with the exception of the Pentecostal churches) are less engaged than their European counterparts. They tend to support the status quo and to reflect current U.S. policy in the region. This situation is not surprising in the light of the divergent nature of U.S. and Latin American nongovernmental organizations. Although Socialist and Christian Democratic Parties of Europe and Latin America find significant common ground, they have little in common with the major U.S. parties. U.S. labor organizations share few of the values, social goals, or institutional linkages that the major labor confederations in Europe and their counterparts in Latin America do. The political party foundations of Germany are deeply engaged in the political process in Latin America; the Ford, Tinker, or Rockefeller Foundations cannot work in the same way, no matter how serious their development programs.

European transnational involvement in Latin America, in an era of civilian governments, is much less apt to generate conflict that it did during the days of dictatorship. This moderation, combined with the end of superpower confrontation in the region, may well open avenues of cooperation that will further strengthen the mutual interest of Latin America, Europe, and the United States in the consolidation of strong and participatory democratic Latin American societies less vulnerable to military intervention and more committed to social equity and justice.

## *Joint Ventures in Public Policy*

A number of new issues have appeared on the global agenda in the last few years in which the roles of the three partners in the trilateral relationship have yet to be determined. Environmental problems and drug trafficking are two of the most important.

The European Union gives high priority to the environmental issue and, according to a report of the Institute for European–Latin American Relations, "despite Latin America's traditionally low ranking on the EC's hierarchy of preferences with external partners, Europe's ecological concern has prompted the European Commission's recommendation that the countries of Latin America should become favored partners in the Community's bilateral cooperation schemes."[19]

This position was reinforced by the Rome Declaration of December 20, 1990, between the representatives of the EC and the Rio Group, which reaffirmed the primacy of the environment as a major area of biregional cooperation. Both sides stated their determination to reinforce the biregional relationship by promoting economic development through environmentally sound and sustainable management as it refers both to human and natural resources [and by] protecting the environment through appropriate domestic measures and adequate regional and international cooperation.[20] At subsequent EC–Rio Group meetings, in April 1991 and May 1992, both regions reaffirmed their commitment to this issue. Nonetheless, this may become a contentious issue between the European Community and Latin America. Many Latin American exports, and some services, will be negatively affected by tighter EU environmental regulations. Of particular concern to Latin America will be EU demand for low-octane oil products and upgraded automotive fuels because much of Latin America still processes high-octane fuels that are great polluters; packaging regulations for semiprocessed and manufactured goods that emphasize recoverability and recycling; and more stringent norms on noise and fume emissions for airlines operating in European airspace.

There is clearly room for cooperation—as well as conflict and competition—between Latin America and the United States and Europe in the area of the environment. U.S. vice-president Al Gore's long-standing interest in environmental issues may lead to greater coordination in defining ecological issues and developing appropriate policies. Whether the initiative for such cooperation will come from Europe or the United States remains to be seen.

On the issue of drug trafficking, the Clinton administration will replace the Bush administration's Andean Drug Strategy with a plan of its own, although its details are not yet known. This is another area that may well lend itself to a joint approach. The EU got a late start on this problem, but with the creation of a ministerial-level coordinating body, the European Committee for the Fight Against Drugs, the mechanism for developing a joint approach now exists. At its July 1990 summit in Dublin, the EC decided to establish a central European antidrug agency, along with a training program for special antidrug agents from transit and producer countries. The Program for the Fight Against Drugs was approved in December 1990. And a European Commission directive regarding the laundering of drug profits came into force on January 1, 1992.

The European Union and the states of Latin America have worked together to try to find effective means to control the production and export of drugs, without notable success. Washington, with its emphasis on stemming the flow of illegal drugs through interdiction rather than on decreasing demand, has not fared any better. The European Union has endorsed Colombia's drug control efforts and has granted trade preferences to Bolivia, Colombia, Ecuador, and Peru for their exports in order to encourage farmers to produce substitute crops. A tremendous amount more needs to be done, of course. The Clinton administration offers an important opportunity for collaboration, since President Clinton has indicated that a new approach to dealing with the drug challenge is needed.

## *The Trilateral Relationship After the Cold War*

The antagonisms between Europe and the United States over policy differences in Central America and the Caribbean were a major source of tension in the 1980s. With the exception of disagreement over Cuba, these antagonisms generally disappeared with the election of George Bush in 1988 and the evolution of democratic institutions in Central America. Europe and the United States have taken similar stances with regard to the return of democracy to the region and have supported a similar position with regard, for example, to the extraconstitutional decisions of President Alberto Fujimori in Peru.

The pattern of the emerging trilateral relationship remains indistinct. There is good will and support for the consolidation of market reforms and civilian governments, but this alone is insufficient if Latin America is to continue to progress along the paths of modernization and democratization. A relatively liberal trade regime is necessary if Latin America is to earn the foreign exchange required to service its debt, import whatever it needs for economic development, and invest in social-equity programs at home. The European Union's regulatory structure and the vagaries of the U.S. economy are impediments to establishing such a regime.

Europe and the United States together do not provide direct economic assistance to Latin America in amounts sufficient to determine whether economic reform efforts will fail or succeed. ODA is helpful at the margins and will probably continue at about today's levels. Bank lending, investment flows, and the Euromarkets are dynamic and unpredictable areas of interaction in which the United States and Europe play complementary roles in Latin America. The United States will retain its leadership role in these areas in Mexico and Central America for the foreseeable future. European investment and financial activity in this region will grow slowly. In the Southern Cone, however, where European influence has historically been stronger, European activity will accelerate in the coming years. Longstanding cultural and historical ties give Europe a natural advantage there, and economic complementarities between Europe and the countries of the Southern Cone have led to a clear interest on the part of European investors in becoming involved in the privatization of state companies and in undertaking other profitable ventures.

The activities of transnational organizations will continue to have a positive impact on civil society in Latin America. Varied and usually uncoordinated, such efforts, while important, will probably not drive public policy. Interactions between organizations on both sides of the Atlantic strengthen the European–Latin American linkage, but in a fairly amorphous way. U.S. transnationals are unlikely to sharply increase their activity in Latin America and will therefore continue to have relatively little impact there.

## CONCLUSIONS

The trilateral relationship continues to evolve. In the absence of the Cold War and critical U.S. security concerns in the hemisphere, there is more room at the margin for European involvement in Latin America and the Caribbean. But to the degree that Europe, understandably, remains Eurocentric and is sensitive to U.S. economic and security interests in the

Americas, there will be no overt plan by the European Union to challenge the United States in the region. Slow but steady increases in European investment, financial operations, and bank lending not only do not threaten U.S. interests but are welcomed, given the mutual interest in Europe and the United States in seeing Latin America develop economically. Transnational activity is now, in the post–Cold War era, viewed as benign. Latin American trade will continue to be dominated by the United States, with Europe playing a subordinate role. To the degree that trilateral approaches to the environment and drug trafficking can be developed, the trilateral relationship will be strengthened.

The Europeans and the Latins will continue to be concerned about the U.S. response to such events as the fall of Castro in Cuba, a crisis surrounding the Panama Canal, a surge of immigration from Haiti or Cuba, and the continuing flow of drugs. To the degree that the Clinton administration seeks a broader forum in which to discuss these and other issues, it will find a receptive response in both Latin America and in Europe. Our expectations should not be unrealistically high, but the groundwork has been done: The short- to medium-term possibilities for pluralism in Latin America and slow but steady increases in trilateral cooperation are better now than at any time since 1945.

As the Cold War fades and the international system seeks a new agenda of development issues, the possibilities for cooperation among the three partners will expand. The impressive and rapid economic growth of the Latin American economies since the late 1980s will make them more resilient players at the international level. Opportunities for trade and investment among the three partners should expand over time. Building on the strong historical and cultural ties of the past, the Latins and Europeans appear to be searching for a new relationship. The United States should welcome this linkage as a means of addressing fundamental Latin American development issues. The United States will remain the dominant political actor of the three for some time to come. Washington would therefore do well to view the opening between Latin America and Europe as an important opportunity for U.S. leadership in collaboration with old friends and allies in the new global context.

## NOTES

1. See Wolf Grabendorff, "Reevaluating the Atlantic Triangle: An Overview," in Wolf Grabendorff and Riordan Roett, eds., *Latin America, Western Europe and the U.S.: Reevaluating the Atlantic Triangle* (New York: Praeger Publishers, 1985), p. xiv.
2. Stanley Hilton, "Latin America and Western Europe, 1880–1945: The Political Dimension," in Grabendorff and Roett, eds., *Latin America, Western Europe and the U.S.*, pp. 3–5.

3. Godfrey Hodgson, *The Colonel: The Life and Wars of Henry Stimson, 1867–1950* (New York: Alfred A. Knopf, 1990), pp. 91–92.

4. Gordon Connell-Smith, *The Inter-American System* (London: Oxford University Press, 1966), pp. 151–152.

5. Augusto Varas, ed., *Hemispheric Security and U.S. Policy in Latin America* (Boulder, Colo.: Westview Press, 1989), p. 48.

6. Laurence Whitehead, "International Aspects of Democratization," in Philippe C. Schmitter, Laurence Whitehead, and Guillermo O'Donnell, eds., *Transitions from Authoritarian Rule: Comparative Perspectives* (Baltimore: Johns Hopkins University Press, 1986), pp. 41–42.

7. Alexander Haig, *Caveat: Realism, Reagan, and Foreign Policy* (New York: Macmillan, 1984), p. 118.

8. Eusebio M. Mujal-León, *European Socialism and the Conflict in Central America* (New York: Praeger Publishers, 1989), pp. 94–95.

9. On January 8 and 9, 1983, the foreign ministers of Mexico, Colombia, Venezuela, and Panama met on the Panamanian island of Contadora. The official purpose of the meeting was to discuss the dangers to regional peace and security posed by the Central American crisis. The four countries were thereafter referred to as the "Contadora Group." The four presidents met in Cancún, Mexico, in July 1983 and issued the "Declaration of Cancún," which formalized the basic concerns of the Contadora Group. The criteria stated in the Cancún Declaration served as the basis for subsequent Contadora documents, the first of which, the "Document of Objectives," was presented to the Central American governments in September 1983. In December 1983, a second document, titled "Norms for the Execution of Commitments Assumed in the Document of Objectives," was issued. In June 1984, Contadora presented the Central American foreign ministries with a draft of the "Act of Peace and Cooperation for Central America." That document is generally known as the Contadora Agreement.

10. Wolf Grabendorff, "West European Perceptions of the Crisis in Central America," in Wolf Grabendorff, Heinrich-W. Krumwiede, and Jorg Todt, eds., *Political Change in Central America: Internal and External Dimensions* (Boulder, Colo.: Westview Press, 1984), p. 287.

11. "Joint Political Communiqué of the Luxembourg Ministerial Conference on Political Dialogue and Economic Cooperation Between the Countries of the European Community, Spain and Portugal and the Countries of Central America and of Contadora," November 11–12, 1985, p. 5.

12. *Report of the National Bipartisan Commission on Central America*, January 1984, p. 122. Mimeograph.

13. See Chapter 3 in this book.

14. The economic data in this discussion are derived from Chapter 1 in this book.

15. *The First Annual Latin Bonds Supplement*, a supplement in *Latin Finance* (January/February 1993), p. 28.

16. Caroline Beetz and Willy Van Ryckeghem, "Trade and Investment Flows Between Europe and Latin America and the Caribbean," Background Paper, Annual meeting, Inter-American Development Bank: Seminar on Latin America's Competitive Position in the Enlarged European Market, Hamburg, Germany, March 24–25, 1993, p. 3.

17. Ibid., p. 19.

18. Ibid., p. 20. See also, James Brooke, "A Forbidden Fruit in Europe: Latin Bananas Face Hurdles," *New York Times*, April 5, 1993, p. 1.

19. "Latin America, Europe and the Environment: The Greening of Biregional Relations," Institute for European–Latin American Relations (Madrid) Dossier no. 42, January 1993, p. 32.

20. Ibid., p. 34.

# Acronyms
# and Abbreviations

| | |
|---|---|
| ABC | Argentina, Brazil, Chile |
| ACP | African, Caribbean, Pacific |
| ADLAF | German Association for Research into Latin America |
| ALADI | Asociación Latinoamericana de Integración |
| ANFAVEA | Associação Nacional dos Fabricantes de Veículos Automotores |
| APEC | Asia-Pacific Economic Cooperation Forum |
| BMZ | German Federal Ministry for Economic Cooperation and Development |
| CACM | Central American Common Market |
| Caricom | Caribbean Community and Common Market |
| CDU | Christian Democratic Union (Germany) |
| CECLA | Comisión Especial de Coordinación Latinoamericana |
| CEPAL | Comisión Económica para América Latina y el Caribe |
| CET | common external tariff |
| CMEA | Council for Mutual Economic Assistance |
| CORDIPLAN | Coordinación de Planificación de la Presidencia de la República (Venezuela) |
| CPM | cost per thousand advertising impressions |
| CSU | Christian Social Union (Germany) |
| DEG | German Investment and Development Association |
| DM | deutsche marks |
| EBRD | European Bank for Reconstruction and Development |
| EC | European Community |
| EC-12 | European Community (12 members) |
| ECIIP | Economic International Investment Partners |
| ECLA | Economic Commission for Latin America and the Caribbean |
| ECSC | European Coal and Steel Community |
| ECU | European Currency Unit |
| EEA | European Economic Area |
| EEC | European Economic Community |
| EFTA | European Free Trade Association |
| EIB | European Investment Bank |
| EMU | Economic and Monetary Union |

195

| | |
|---|---|
| EPC | European Political Cooperation |
| ERM | exchange rate mechanism |
| FDI | foreign direct investment |
| FDP | Liberal Party (Germany) |
| FMLN | Farabundo Martí Front for National Liberation (El Salvador) |
| GATT | General Agreement on Tariffs and Trade |
| GDA | German development assistance |
| GDP | gross domestic product |
| GDR | German Democratic Republic |
| GM | General Motors |
| GNP | gross national product |
| GSP | Generalized System of Preferences |
| GTZ | Association for Technical Cooperation |
| IMF | International Monetary Fund |
| IRELA | Institute for European–Latin American Relations |
| KFW | German Credit Association for Reconstruction |
| LA | Latin America |
| LAC | Latin America and the Caribbean |
| LDC | less developed country |
| MERCOSUR | Mercado Común del Sur (or Southern Cone Common Market) |
| NAFTA | North American Free Trade Agreement |
| NATO | North Atlantic Treaty Organization |
| NGO | nongovernmental organization |
| NIC | newly industrializing country |
| OAS | Organization of American States |
| ODA | official development assistance |
| OECD | Organization for Economic Cooperation and Development |
| RPK | revenue passenger kilometer |
| SECOFI | Secretaría de Comercio y Fomento Industrial (Mexico) |
| SEM | Single European Market |
| SPD | Social Democratic Party (Germany) |
| STET | Societá Finanziaria Telefónica |
| VW | Volkswagen |
| YPF | Yacimientos Petrolíficos Fiscales |

# Selected Bibliography

Bataller M., Francisco, "La Transformación Política y Económica de América Latina y la Contribución de la Comunidad Europea a la Democratización y a la Protección de los Derechos Humanos en la Región," in Alberto Herrero, ed., *Los Derechos Humanos en Latinoamérica: Una Perspectiva de Cinco Siglos*, Cortes de Castilla y León, Valladolid 1992.

Beetz, Caroline and Willy Van Rycheghem, "Background Paper," Seminar on Latin America's Competitive Position in the Enlarged European Market, Hamburg, Germany, March 24–25, 1993.

Bradford, Colin I., ed., *Strategic Options for Latin America in the 1990s*. OECD, Paris 1992.

CEPAL, *Inversión Extranjera Directa en América Latina y el Caribe 1970–90*, Volumen I: Panorama Regional, Santiago, Chile, September 14, 1992.

Corbo, Vittorio, Fabrizio Coricelli, and Jan Bossak, eds., *Reforming Central and East European Economies: Initial Results and Challenges*, Washington, DC: World Bank, 1991.

*Latin America at a Glance*, Economist Intelligence Unit, New York, NY, 1994.

*Solving Latin American Business Problems*, Research Report, Economist Intelligence Unit, New York, 1994.

Enderlyn, Allyn and Oliver Dziggel, *Cracking Latin America*. Probus, Chicago, IL, 1994.

*Foreign Direct Investment in Latin America and the Caribbean: An Overview of Flows from Europe, Japan, and the United States, 1979–1990*, Madrid and Paris: Inter-American Development Bank Special Office in Europe and Institute for European–Latin American Relations, (IRELA), 1993.

Grabendorff, Wolf and Riordan Roett, eds., *Latin America, Western Europe and the U.S.: Reevaluating the Atlantic Triangle* (New York: Praeger Publishers, 1985).

Hufbauer, Gary Clyde, and Jeffrey J. Schott, *Western Hemisphere Economic Integration*, Washington, DC: Institute for International Economics, July 1994.

Institute for European–Latin American Relations (IRELA), *Latin America and Europe: Towards the Year 2000*, Madrid, 1992.

Institute for European–Latin American Relations (IRELA), *Prospects for the Processes of Sub-regional Integration in Central and South America*, Madrid, 1992.

International Monetary Fund, *Direction of Trade Statistics Yearbook*, Washington, DC, 1988 and 1992.

*Latin Finance*, "The Ibero-American Community: A Latin Finance Supplement," October 1992.

Ohmae, Kenichi, "The Rise of the Region State," *Foreign Affairs*, Spring 1993, pp. 78–87.

Pohl, Gerhard and Piritta Sorsa, *European Economic Integration and Trade with the Developing World*, World Bank, 1992.

Smith, Peter H., ed., *The Challenge of Integration: Europe and the Americas*, The North-South Center, University of Miami, Miami, FL, 1993.

Tovias, Alfred, *Foreign Economic Relations of the European Community: The Impact of Spain and Portugal*, Lynne Rienner Publishers, Boulder & London, 1990.

Viñas, Angel, "Spanish Policy Toward Latin America: From Rhetoric to Partnership," Iberian Studies Institute, University of Miami, May 1992.

Weintraub, Sidney, ed., *Free Trade in the Western Hemisphere* (The Annals of the American Academy of Political and Social Science, Vol. 526, March 1993).

# Study Group Sessions
# and Participants

Gonzalo de Las Heras, Group Chairman
Susan Kaufman Purcell, Director
Linda S. Pakula, Rapporteur

*First Meeting*—January 19, 1993: "The Economic Relationship Between Europe and Latin America"
Commentator:
> A. Blake Friscia, Adjunct Professor of Economics, New York University

Discussants:
> Weine Karlsson, Director, Institute of Latin American Studies, University of Stockholm
> Angel Viñas, Head of Delegation, Delegation of European Communities to the United Nations

*Second Meeting*—February 17, 1993: "The Impact of Regional Integration on European and Latin American Economic Relations"
Commentators:
> Susan Kaufman Purcell, Vice President, Americas Society
> Françoise Simon, Adjunct Professor, Columbia University Graduate School of Business

Discussants:
> Francisco Bataller M., Principal Adminstrator, Directorate General—External Relations, Commission of the European Communities, Brussels
> Luis Rubio, Director, Centro de Investigación para el Desarrollo (CIDAC), Mexico City

*Third Meeting*—March 17, 1993: "Case Studies of European and Latin American Relations"
Commentators:
> Wolf Grabendorff, Director, Instituto de Relaciones Europeo-Latinoamericanas (IRELA), Madrid
> Eusebio Mujal-León, Professor of Government, Georgetown University, Washington, D.C.

Edward Schumacher, Director, The Spanish Institute, New York

*Fourth Meeting*—April 21, 1993: "The Trilateral Relationship: Latin America, Europe and the United States"
Commentator:
  Riordan Roett, Director, Latin American Studies Program, The Paul H. Nitze School of Advanced International Studies (SAIS), Johns Hopkins University,Washington, D.C.
Discussants:
  H. E. Rubens Ricúpero, Ambassador of Brazil to the United States
  Alan Riding, Paris Bureau Chief, *The New York Times*

### Study Group Participants

| | |
|---|---|
| Eduardo Barbera | Cordoba Trade Center |
| Stephanie Bell-Rose | The Andrew W. Mellon Foundation |
| Stephen Blank | Americas Society |
| Claudio Campuzano | *Noticias del Mundo* |
| Carlos Fligler | Delta Capital Corporation |
| Nina Gardner | Societá Finanziaria Telefónica |
| Marcia Grant | Institute of International Education |
| Alfredo Gutierrez | J.P. Morgan and Company |
| Roberta Lajous | Partido Revolucionario Institucional, Mexico |
| George Landau | Americas Society |
| Martha T. Muse | The Tinker Foundation |
| Arnaldo Musich | Techint Inc. |
| Patrick Paradiso | Deutsche Bank Government Securities Inc. |
| Ponchitta Pierce | Independent TV Producer and Writer |
| Ray Raymond | British Information Service |
| Nohra Rey de Marulanda | Inter-American Development Bank |
| Arnold Schaab | Pryor, Cashman, Sherman & Flynn |
| L. Ronald Scheman | Heller, Rosenblatt & Scheman |
| Marilyn Skiles | J.P. Morgan and Company |
| John Stevenson | Sullivan & Cromwell |
| Alan Stoga | Kissinger Associates |
| John Tessier | IBM Latin America |
| Richard Weinert | Leslie Weinert & Co. Inc. |

# The Contributors

*A. Blake Friscia*, at the time of his death in June 1993, was adjunct professor of economics at New York University Graduate School. He served as vice president and international economist at the Chase Manhattan Bank from 1966 to 1990. At the Chase Manhattan Bank, Dr. Friscia was director of the Western Hemisphere Economics Section responsible for Latin America, Canada, and the Caribbean. He was the author of *The Lost Decade? Debt and Latin American Development*.

*Wolf Grabendorff* is the founding director of the Institute for European–Latin American Relations in Madrid, a position he has held since 1985. Dr. Grabendorff specializes in Latin American international relations. In 1990, he was awarded the University of Augsburg's Prize for Spanish and Latin American Studies. His publications include *Lateinamerika, Kontinent in der Krise* (1973); *The Central American Crisis and Western Europe: Perceptions and Reactions* (1982); and *Latin America, Western Europe and the United States: Reevaluating the Atlantic Triangle* (coeditor).

*Eusebio Mujal-León* is associate professor of government at Georgetown University, where he has also served as director of undergraduate and graduate Studies. Dr. Mujal-León was a fellow at the Woodrow Wilson International Center for Scholars in Washington, D.C., 1989–1990. He has been chairman of the Iberian Peninsula Course at the School of Area Studies of the Foreign Service Institute at the U.S. Department of State since 1981, and in 1990, he was awarded the Order of Isabela la Reina Católica in the name of King Juan Carlos I. Dr. Mujal-León has published extensively on European and Latin American affairs. Among his books are *Communism and Political Change in Spain* and *European Socialism and the Conflict in Central America*. He is currently at work on *Looking Beyond the Pyrenees: Spanish Foreign Policy in the Post-Franco Era*.

*Susan Kaufman Purcell* is vice president of the Americas Society in New York City. From 1981 to 1988 she was a senior fellow and director of the Latin American Project at the Council on Foreign Relations. She also served on the Policy Planning Staff of the U.S. Department of State (1980–1981). Prior to that, she taught at the University of California, Los Angeles. Dr. Purcell's publications include *Japan and Latin America in the New Global Order* (coeditor and coauthor); *Latin America: U.S. Policy After the Cold War* (coauthor); and *Mexico in Transition* (editor and coauthor).

*Riordan Roett* is director of the Latin American Studies Program at the Paul H. Nitze School of Advanced International Studies at Johns Hopkins University in Washington, D.C. Dr. Roett also serves as director of International Relations, Emerging Markets, at the Chase Manhattan Bank, where he was director of International Relations, Western Hemisphere, from 1983 to 1991. He has spoken and written extensively on Latin America. Dr. Roett's publications include *Mexico's External Relations in the 1990s; Latin America, Western Hemisphere and the U.S.: Reevaluating the Atlantic Triangle* (coeditor); and *Brazil: Politics in a Patrimonial Society.*

*Edward Schumacher* is currently a writer, consultant, and international development adviser for the *Wall Street Journal.* He served as director of the Spanish Institute from 1991 to 1993. Mr. Schumacher has also been an adviser to the Principe de Asturias Foundation in Spain since 1990. From 1979 until 1987, Mr. Schumacher served as the *New York Times* bureau chief in Madrid and Buenos Aires and as New York City economic development reporter. He has also written for the *Philadelphia Inquirer* and the *Washington Post,* and his articles have appeared in *Foreign Affairs.*

*Françoise L. Simon* is professor of marketing and international business at the Columbia University Graduate School of Business and heads Simon Associates, an international strategy consultancy. From 1986 to 1991, she was a director of Arthur D. Little and previously a principal at Ernst & Young. She has served as vice president and director of the American Marketing Association and is a member of the International Council of the American Management Association. She is a consultant to many Fortune 500 companies and to the United Nations and has published extensively on international strategy in books and journals, including the *Columbia Journal of World Business* and the *Revue Française du Marketing.*

# Index

# About the Book and the Editors

The creation of a single European Market parallels an impressive economic opening and movement toward regional and subregional economic integration in Latin America. At the same time, the end of the Cold War has allowed the United States to redirect its relations with Latin America away from traditional security issues and toward an emphasis on strengthening its economic ties within the Western Hemisphere.

*Europe and Latin America in the World Economy* examines the impact of economic integration in Europe and Latin America on both the relationship between the two regions and the trilateral relationship among Europe, Latin America, and the United States. Based on the work of a high-level study group held at the Americas Society, the book addresses important economic, political, and foreign policy issues and suggests ways of reinforcing the three economic actors' shared interests.

*Susan Kaufmann Purcell* is vice president of the Americas Society in New York City and from 1981 to 1988 was a senior fellow and director of the Latin American Project at the Council on Foreign Relations. Dr. Purcell's publications include *Japan and Latin America in the New Global Order* (coeditor and coauthor); *Latin America: U.S. Policy After the Cold War* (coauthor); and *Mexico in Transition* (editor and coauthor).

*Françoise Simon* is professor of marketing and international business at the Columbia University Graduate School of Business and heads Simon Associates, an international strategy consultancy. She is a consultant to many Fortune 500 companies and to the United Nations and has published extensively on international strategy in books and journals, including the *Columbia Journal of World Business* and the *Revue Française du Marketing.*